Detailing Fundamentals for Interior Design

Fundamentals:

Detailing Fundamentals for Interior Design

Ronald M. Veitch

© 1994, Ronald M. Veitch

All rights reserved. Except as noted, no part of this publication may be reproduced or transmitted in any form or by any means— graphic, electronic, or mechanical —without the prior written permission of the publisher. Any request to photocopy any part of this book, other than pages where permission to reproduce is stated, shall be directed in writing to the Canadian Reprography Collective, 379 Adelaide St. W., Ste. M1, Toronto, ON, Canada M5V 1S5.

Printed in Canada

95 96 97 98 99 5 4 3 2 1

Canadian Cataloguing in Publication Data

Veitch, Ronald M. (Ronald Miles), 1931–

   Detailing fundamentals for interior design

   Includes bibliographical references.
   ISBN 1-895411-57-2

1. Interior architecture. 2. Interior decoration. I. Title.

NA2850.V44 1994   729   C94-920049-2

Illustrations: Jess Dixon
Book and Cover Design: Pat Stanton

Peguis Publishers Ltd.
318 McDermot Avenue
Winnipeg, Manitoba
Canada R3A 0A2

Dedication

to Dudley Melville, formerly chief draftsman of Moody Moore and Partners, Architects and Consulting Engineers. "Mel" was a draftsman of the old school who taught me to appreciate the necessity and intricacy, yet simplicity, of details and the satisfaction of devising a well-founded solution to the joining of materials;

and to Boyd Loendorf, FASID, for giving me the final push to produce the book.

Contents

page ix	**Preface**
x	**Acknowledgments**
1	**Introduction**
3	**1. Basic Joints**
23	**2. Wood**
45	**3. Case Goods/Cabinetry**
87	**4. Connections: Floors/Walls/Ceilings**
117	**5. Wood as a Wall Finish**
145	**6. Doors, Door Frames, and Glazing**
169	**7. Glass, Plastics, and Metals**
195	**8. Fixed Seating**
211	**Conclusion**
213	**Bibliography**

Preface

My intention in writing this book was not to show that I know everything there is to know about detailing, for I do not. Nor is it to include every imaginable detail, for that is impossible. The purpose of *Fundamentals* is to initiate you, the reader, into the wonders and mysteries of interior detailing. Once the unfamiliar has been learned it can be satisfying indeed to create objects and spaces out of various materials and things.

I would like you to discover the joy of detailing. There is pleasure to be found in many aspects of life's professions: the accountant finds it in the beauty of numbers and the stories they reveal; the chef in working out the combination of ingredients and methods to provide an epicurean delight; the interior designer in bringing together disparate pieces to create an aesthetic and functional solution to a problem in the built environment.

Design is involved in the creation of anything, whether it be a budget, a menu, an object, or a space. In the details of the creation lies the effectiveness of the solution. While it is possible to initiate a concept without knowing exactly how it will work, to carry a concept to fruition you must be able to work out the details. Furthermore, it is necessary to describe the details in terms and illustrations that the builder will understand so that you can be sure of getting what you want.

There are many ways to devise a detail. I hope that the details shown here will be taken as exemplar and generic, that you will use them as information, or perhaps inspiration. Allow them to spark your own creativity into passionate action; pick up your preferred tool—be it pencil, pen, or computer—summon your courage, go forth, and create exquisite details that will confound the uninitiated and please the aesthetic sensibilities of the beholder.

Acknowledgments Just as a design project is a result of teamwork, so is this book. I wish to express my thanks to Westnofa of Canada for providing drawings of their chairs for our use; to A & K Millwork for a tour of their manufacturing plant and discussion of detail; to Lonn Trickett, Parcor Ltd., for applying his keen eye in vetting the cabinetry detailing; to Sally Manning for deciphering and typing my original hand-written manuscript; to Bill Stanton, industrial designer, for his invaluable information on plastics and fiberglass; to Jess Dixon for his fine hand in drawing; to Pat Stanton, graphic designer, for her superb talents in creating the design of this book; and to Mary Dixon, publisher and editor, for taking the time to apply her inimitable skills to editing my often complicated text. Without the assistance and cooperation of all of these people this book would not exist.

Introduction

he starting point of a design is the drafting board.
Whole books have been published on the topic of how to do freehand sketching and technical drawing. I assume that you have been exposed to such training and merely offer the following as reminders.

Drafting
☐ Use a sharp pencil—no fuzzy lines.
☐ Do not use thin-lead repeater pencils.
☐ Line weight variations are a must.

Sheet Layout
☐ Have a proper border and title block/notes column.
☐ Locate drawings in a logical sequence and pattern.
☐ Make an orderly arrangement of drawings; sheet will have eye appeal and be easier to read.
☐ Select appropriate scales for plans, elevations, sections, details.

☐ Dimension clearly and appropriately; leave nothing to guesswork. Use gross dimensions on plans and elevations, finer ones on sections and details.

☐ Note all materials neatly by each detail or if repetitive, place in the notes column.

☐ Keep leader lines straight, if possible. Do not cross other leader lines.

Details

☐ Use the appropriate scale so that details are readable and notable.

☐ Bear in mind that line weight variation and pouché are important for readability.

☐ Use a simple universal coding system to identify the detail, to locate it, and to reference it to related drawing sheets.

Basic Joints

CHAPTER 1 2 3 4 5 6

**etailing began as joinery**—systems craftsmen developed to hold solid pieces of wood together so that useful objects could be constructed. A quick study of these joints will help you to develop an understanding of the underlying principles of detailing. A joinery detail should be:

      Suited to the properties of the material
      Structurally sound
      Suited to the task required of it
      Able to be constructed
      Appropriate to and part of the design
      In proportion to the task required and the scale
       of the object.

If the detail fulfils these criteria it is likely to be aesthetically pleasing as well.

In classic joinery wood joints were designed to fit wood pieces together with no recourse to fasteners such as nails or screws. Cut and craftsmanship were important, and various natural source glues were used as adhesives.

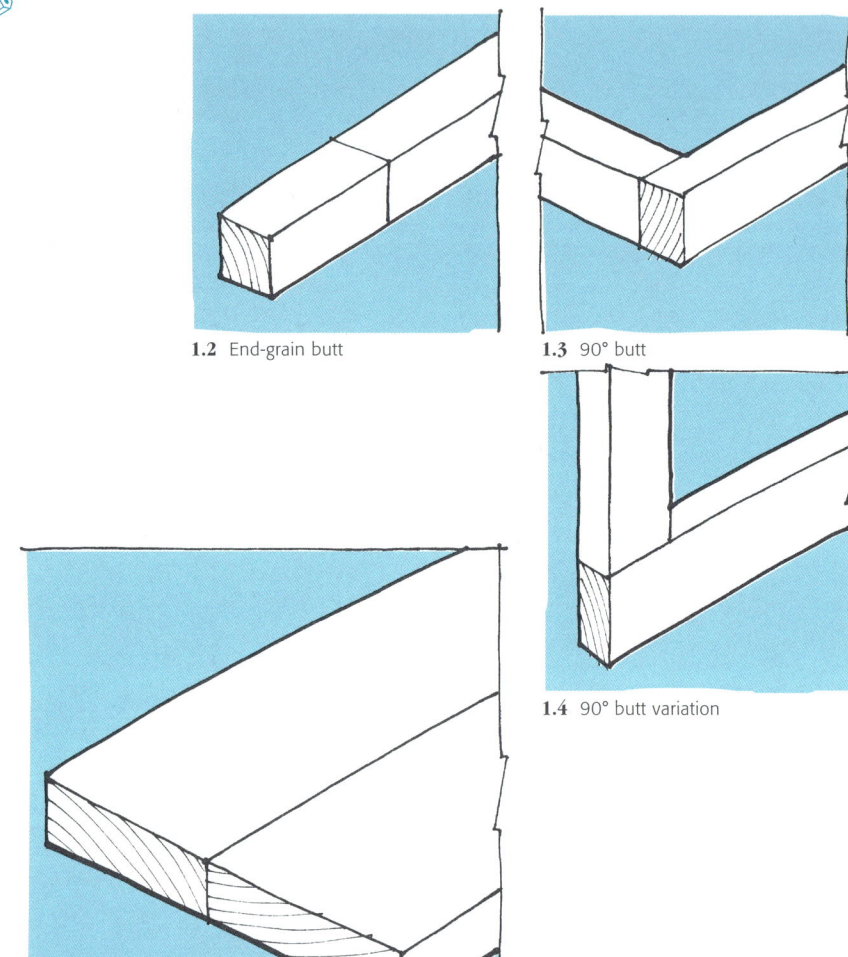

1.2 End-grain butt

1.3 90° butt

1.4 90° butt variation

1.1 Basic butt joint

The butt joint has no strength other than that supplied by the glue used to hold it together. However, with the use of epoxy adhesives it is possible to give considerable strength to it. The **rabbet** joint is a simple answer to the question "How do we get more gluing surface in this joint?"

The **scarf** joint and the **miter** with all of its adaptations are other variations of the basic butt joint, each with its own particular uses and attributes.

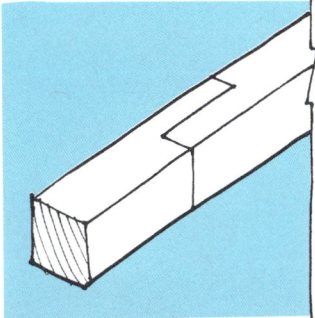
1.6 End-grain rabbet

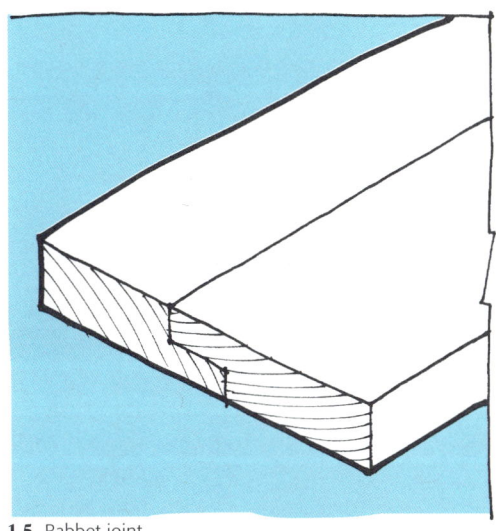
1.5 Rabbet joint

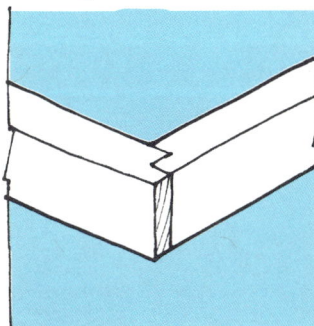
1.7 90° rabbet

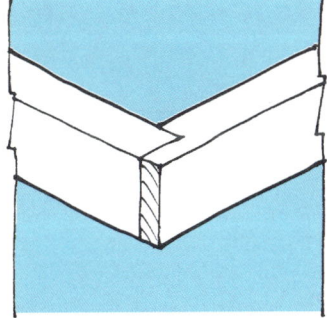
1.8 Half rabbet

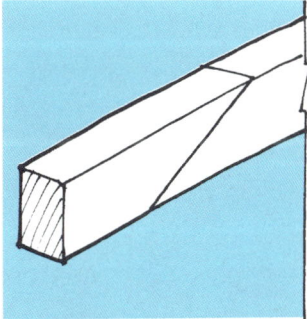
1.9 Scarf joint

A scarf joint is a sloped butt joint and is rarely used other than in hidden framing. Occasionally it can be found where the appearance of an extra long length of wood is required in a species of wood available only in short pieces.

1.10 Basic miter

The miter is simply a butt joint at a 45° angle. It has the same attributes of strength and holding power as a butt joint, however it gives the appearance of a seamless joint since the join point occurs on a change of plane. The variants of the miter joint have the same attributes of strength and holding power as the joints on which they are based.

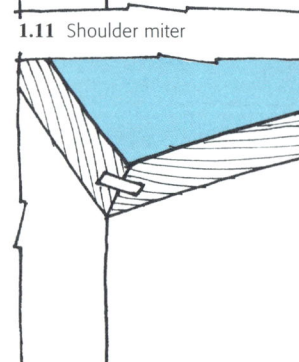

1.11 Shoulder miter

1.12 Locking miter

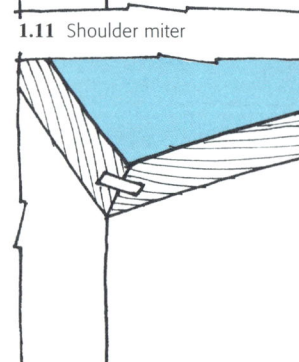

1.13 Miter and spline

1.14 Miter and dowels

1.15 Miter w/mortise and tenon

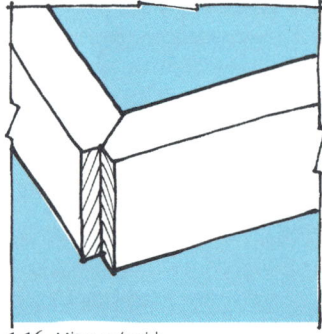

1.16 Miter w/quirk

1.17 Basic dowel joint

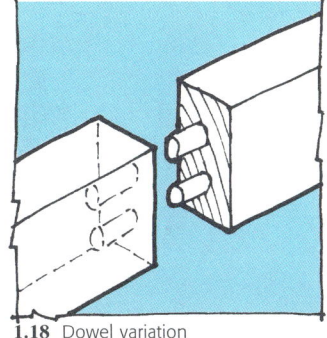
1.18 Dowel variation

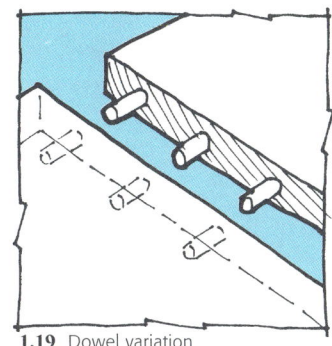
1.19 Dowel variation

The dowel is one of the most useful of the adaptations in the art of joinery. Always used in sets of two or more to resist torque (twisting action), dowels are occasionally used with a "tight fit" and no glue. Use of both a tight fit and an adhesive is recommended due to shrinkage of the wood under drying conditions.

A **spline** is a thin strip of wood which is inserted in routed grooves or channels in each piece of wood to be joined. A spline greatly increases the strength of a joint, not only providing more gluing surface but also holding the two pieces together so they cannot separate.

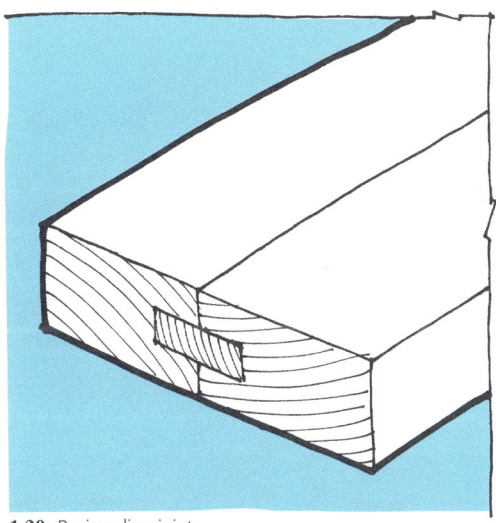
1.20 Basic spline joint

Splines add a lot to the strength of joints—they provide more gluing surface and also hold the pieces together.

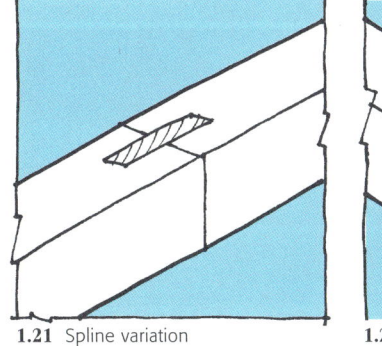
1.21 Spline variation

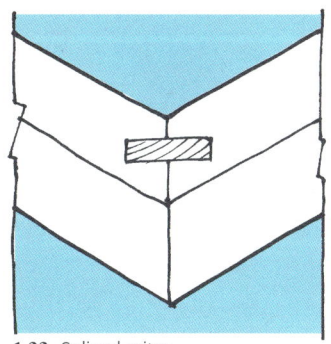
1.22 Splined miter

1.24 Slotted mortise and tenon

1.23 Basic mortise and tenon

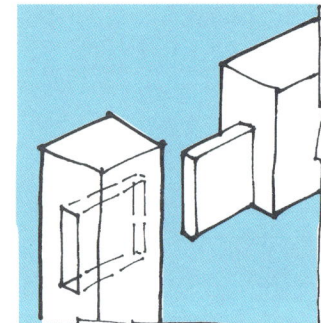
1.25 Through mortise and tenon

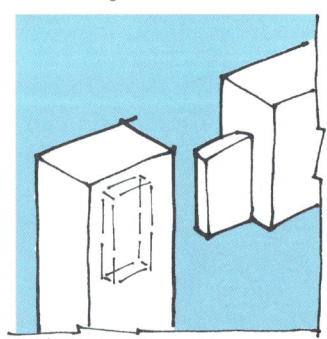
1.26 Blind mortise and tenon

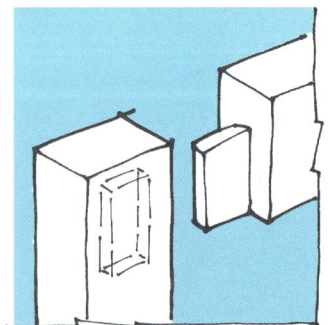
1.27 Stub mortise and tenon

The mortise and tenon is a natural extension of the butt joint, and acts in a similar way to a dowelled joint in that its dimension prevents torque. Each variation has its merits and suitability for the particular species of wood and thickness of section.

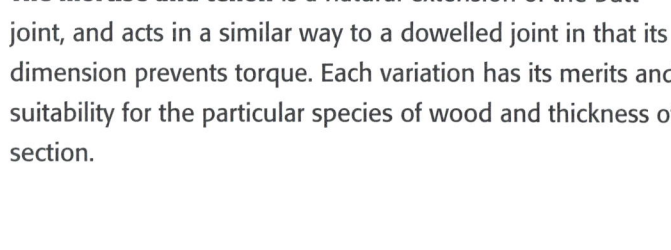

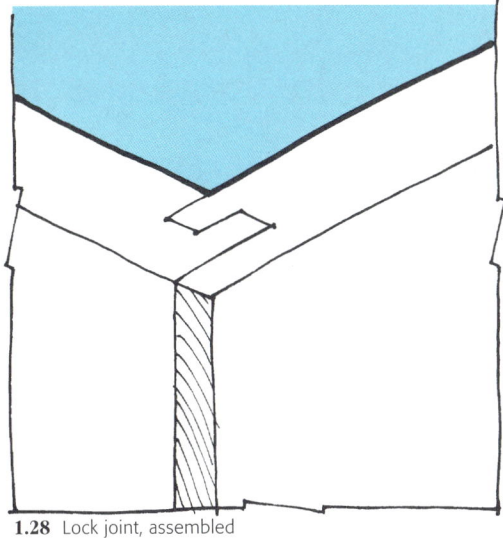

1.28 Lock joint, assembled

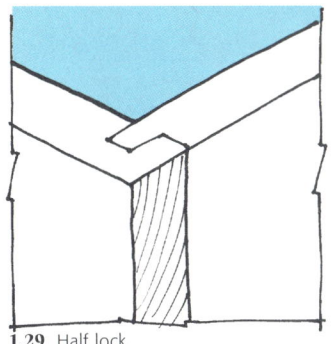

1.29 Half lock

The lock joint provides additional surfaces for gluing and also inserts wood into wood for greater strength. The **lap** joint, shown below, and the **dado, blind dado** and **dovetail dado,** shown on the following pages, are all variations on the lock joint.

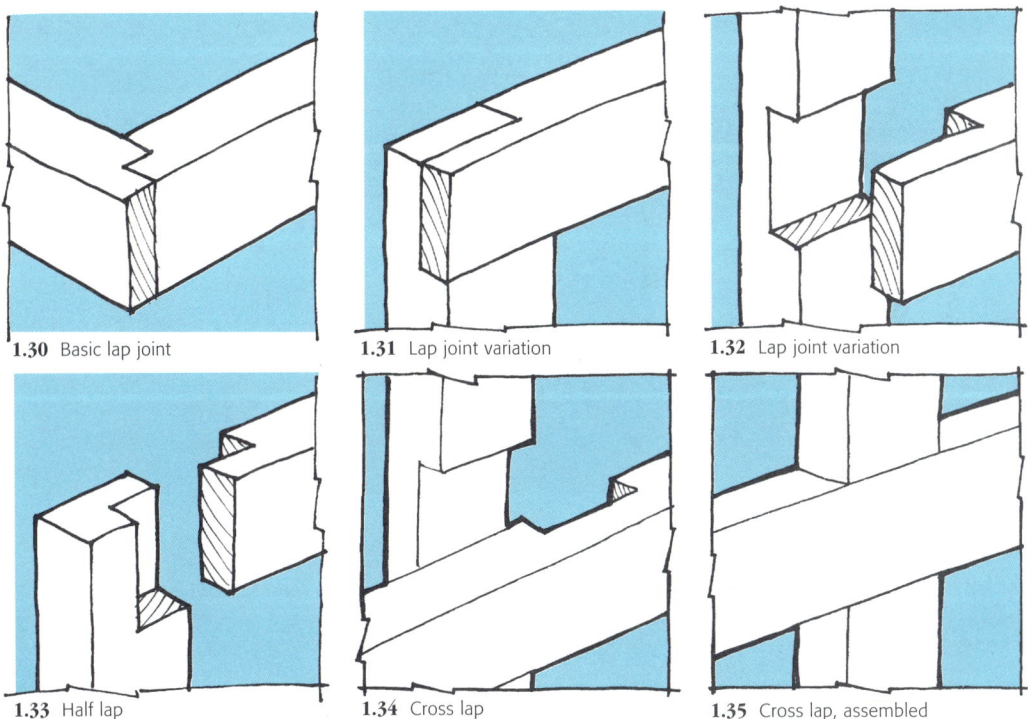

1.30 Basic lap joint **1.31** Lap joint variation **1.32** Lap joint variation

1.33 Half lap **1.34** Cross lap **1.35** Cross lap, assembled

The lap joint is a variation of the lock joint, particularly suited to rail or frame applications in furniture.

A dado joint is a form of lock joint with increased gluing surface.

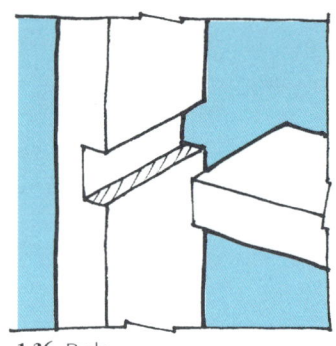
1.36 Dado

1.37 Dado variant, assembled

1.38 Blind dado

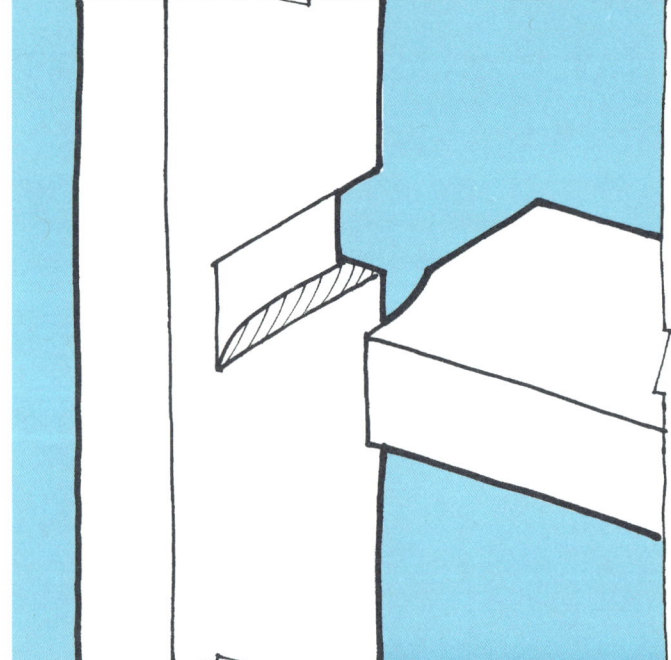
1.39 Stopped dado

The blind and stopped dadoes each combine the strength of a dado joint with the visual simplicity of a butt joint. The advantage of these joints is the uninterrupted appearance of the surface, with no sacrifice in strength.

1.40 Dovetail dado

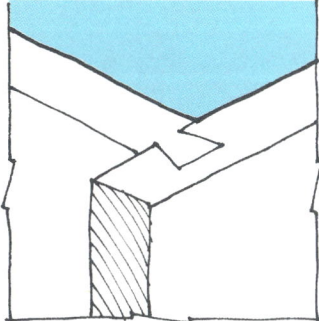

1.41 Dovetail dado, assembled

The dovetail dado increases the strength of the dado because of all the interlocking bonding surfaces. Its use, however, is limited because for assembly it must be slid together from one edge.

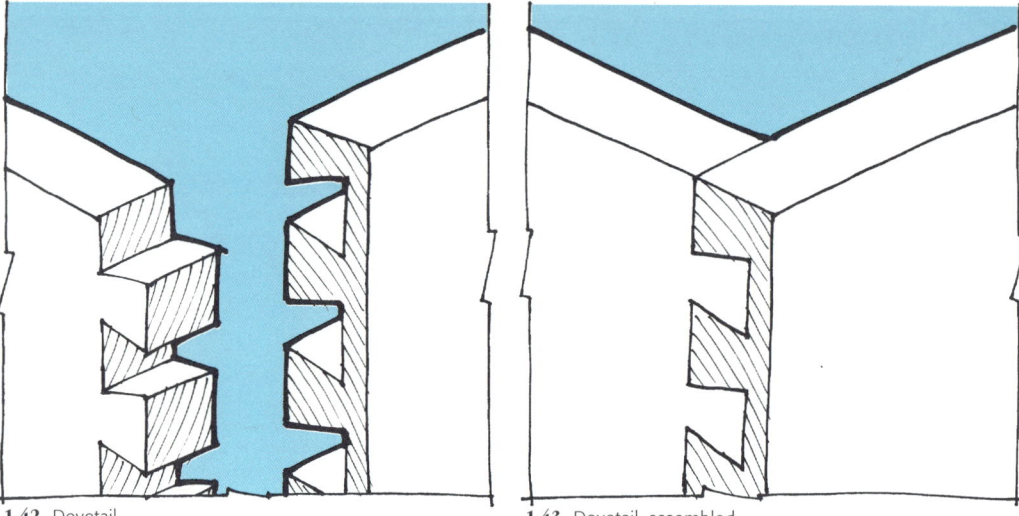

1.42 Dovetail

1.43 Dovetail, assembled

The dovetail is traditionally used for the joining of drawer fronts to drawer sides. The sloped interlocking design provides great strength in a pulling situation.

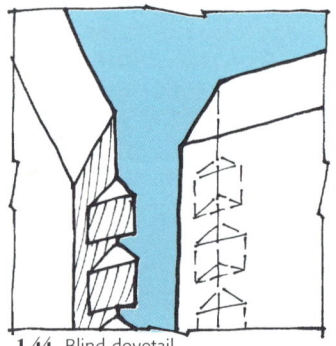

1.44 Blind dovetail

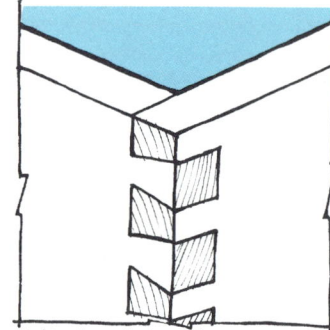

1.45 Through dovetail

1.46 Dovetail rail

1.47 Dovetail rail, assembled

The finger, or comb, joint is a variation of the basic dovetail without the reverse slope form of interlock.

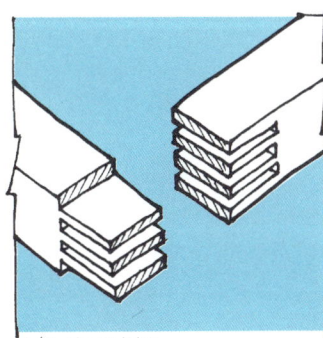
1.48 Finger joint

1.49 Finger joint variant, assembled

Basic Joints

Tongue and groove joinery is commonly used for hardwood floor construction although, along with fillet and batten (where strips of wood cover the joints), it is also used for solid wood panelling.

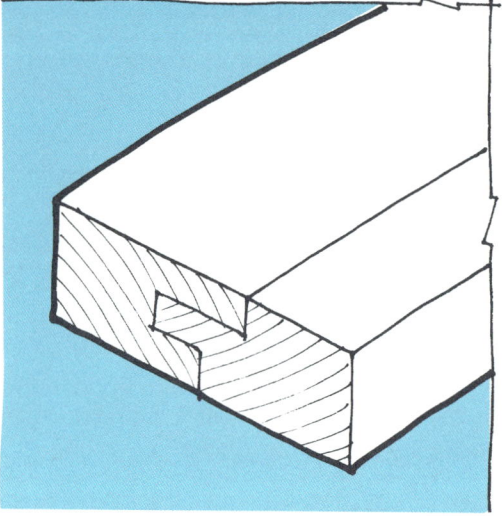
1.52 Offset tongue and groove

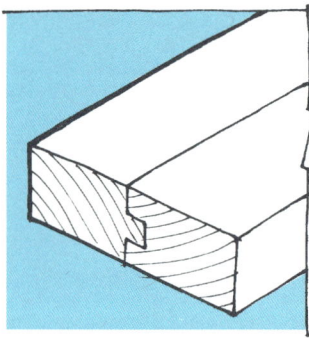
1.50 Tongue and groove

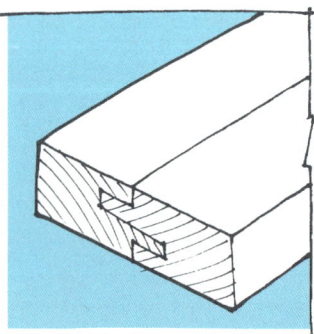
1.51 Multiple tongue and groove

Joint Selection

The selection of a particular joint for a solid wood connection is made on the basis of several factors:

Species of Wood Some woods are very brittle and do not lend themselves to being tooled in certain ways. Others are too soft to be used with some joints.

Grain patterns in some woods provide great strength in two directions, while others may be weak, particularly in cross section.

The cost of certain exotic hardwoods is such that the choice of joint detail may depend on the amount of wood cut away or wasted in making the connection.

Location of Joint Each of the various joints is more appropriate to some applications (such as frame, rail, stretcher, leg, and so on) than to others.

Strength Some joints are stronger than others and are used for the stress points of constructed items.

Aesthetics This criterion must be applied when making all decisions relative to your design. Should the joint detail be visible or invisible? If it is visible, you must consider which detail will be most visually appropriate for the location; for giving an image of strength; for proportion and scale; for grain and color effect; for shape; and for pattern.

Cost The more elaborate the joint, the more expensive it will be to produce. Many details may be used for the corner of a drawer, for example, but it may be worth the additional cost to use a multiple dovetail because it is very strong and/or because it signals to the viewer an expensive and carefully crafted piece.

How do you learn to decide which joint to use in your design?

Study the construction of already built furniture, both historical and contemporary. Two good examples for you to study are shown on the following pages.
Know your wood.

Take your drawings to a cabinetmaker or millworker and seek advice. Placed in the position of being an authority, most will be pleased to share their opinions and expertise.

By developing your knowledge and understanding of the basics, eventually you will be able to concentrate on creating new ways to carry innovative concepts to solution.

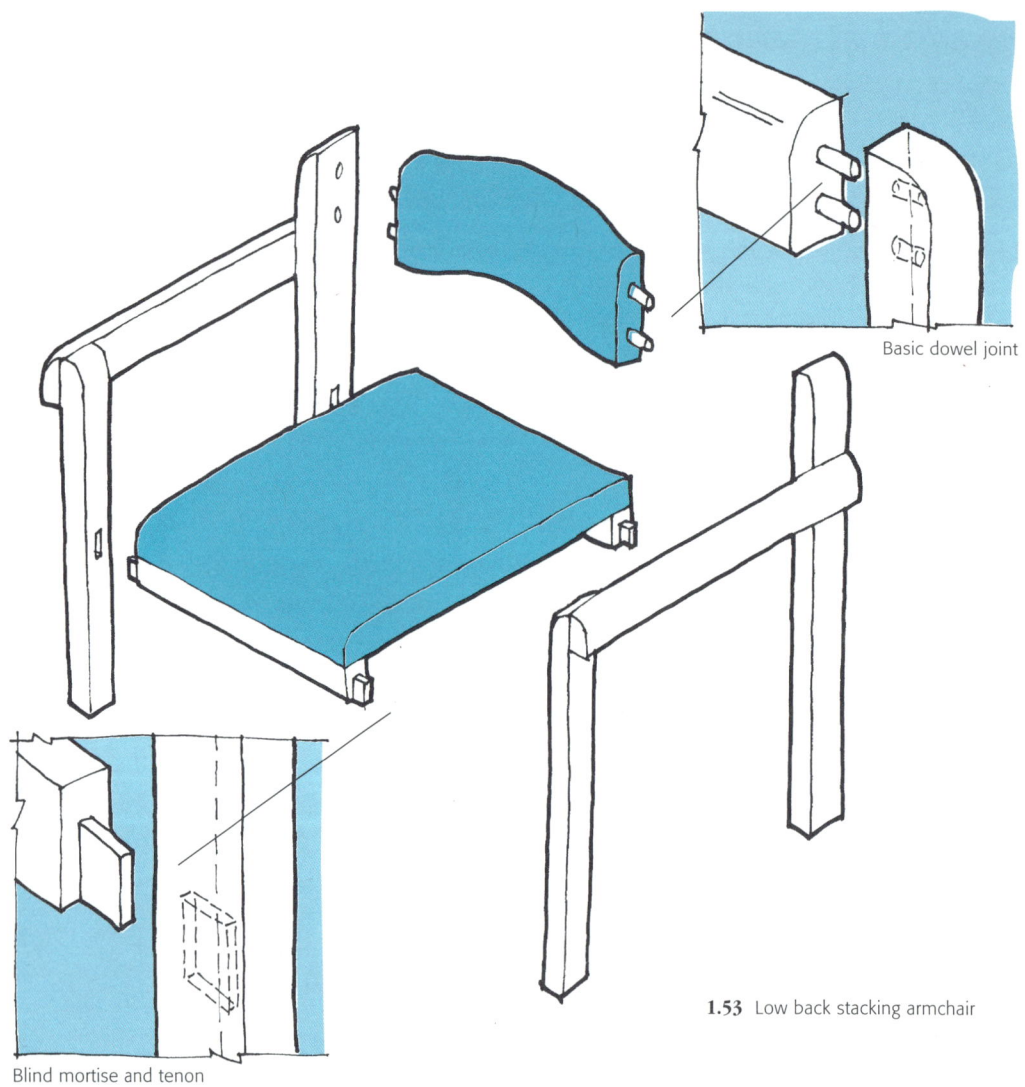

1.53 Low back stacking armchair

Basic dowel joint

Blind mortise and tenon

In these two illustrations, you can see the types of joints selected by one designer/manufacturer as the best for the particular location in each chair.

Low Back Stacking Armchair In 1.53, dowels are used for attaching the chair back to the rear frame. The use of two dowels at each end prevents the back from rotating. The blind type of mortise and tenon joint is used to attach the seat to the frame due to the extra strength needed at that location, and in keeping with the plain aesthetic of the design.

Blind mortise and tenon

Slotted mortise and tenon

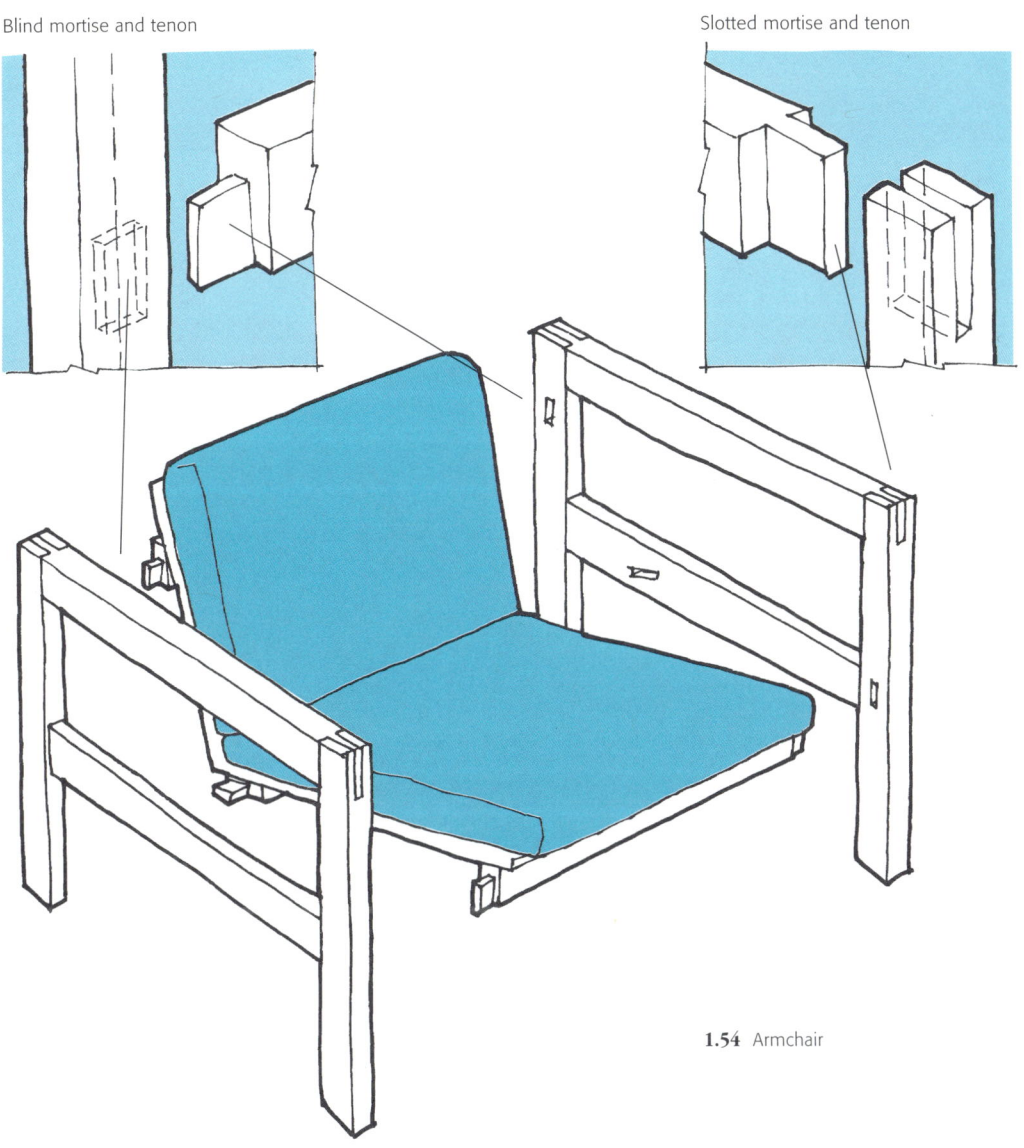

1.54 Armchair

Low Back Armchair A blind mortise and tenon is again used, this time for the heavy-duty support needed for attaching the seat and back stretchers to the frame of the armchair shown in figure 1.54. Likewise it is used for the hidden joints where the crossrails meet the legs. The armrests are joined to the legs with slotted mortise and tenons, chosen for strength and for the visual effect of the detail. Choosing a plain mortise and tenon (see 1.23) or a through mortise and tenon (see 1.25) for the detail would have achieved sufficient strength, but not the desired visual effect.

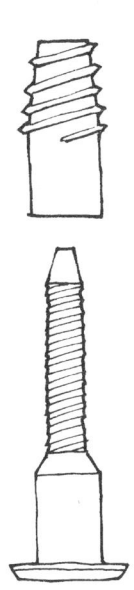
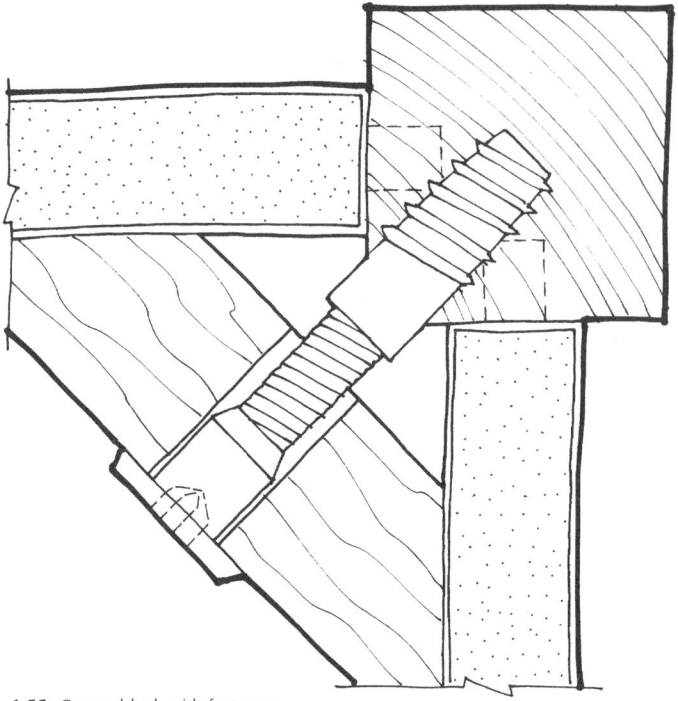

1.55 Corner block with fastener

Replacing Milled Wood Joints with Mechanical Connectors
The advancements in connector hardware design have caused significant changes in the production of solid wood furniture. The examples on these pages indicate some of the various mechanical devices that can be used in place of milled wood joint details.

Frequently, substitution has economic benefits since the purchase and installation costs for the hardware can be less than the cost of labor to produce the detail in wood. Also bear in mind that millwork requires a high-grade wood; mechanical connectors can be used with a broader range of wood grades. However, cost is only one considera-

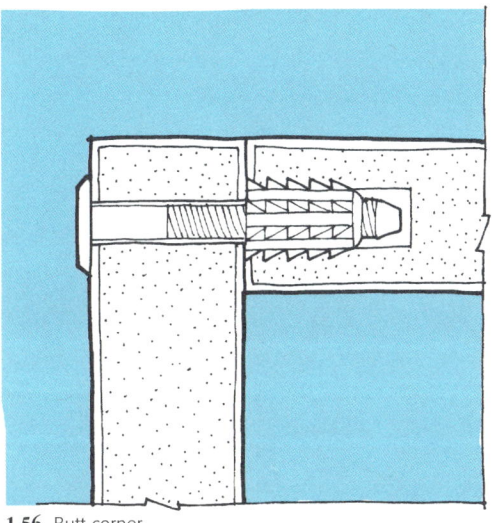
1.56 Butt corner

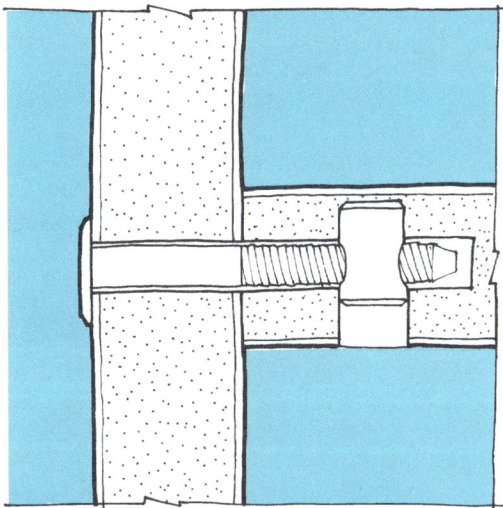
1.57 Butt intersection

These are representative illustrations to demonstrate the variety available in mechanical fasteners for wood furniture. Similar and many other types are available, with many hardware manufacturers servicing the market.

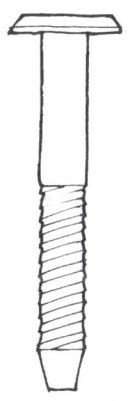

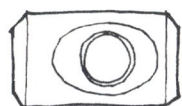

tion, and balancing cost with aesthetics does not mean that the hardware has to be ugly; it simply means that the design will be different. As a designer you must be aware of the differences substitution of mechanical connectors for milled wood joints can make on the visual effect of your design.

As an exercise, design your unit using selected wood joints and design it using mechanical fasteners. Appraise the design effects, and compare the cost totals for labor and components. You will then be prepared to make an informed decision about which methods and design details to use.

Basic Joints

21

Wood

CHAPTER 1 2 3 4 5 6 7 8

T**rees occur in such a variety of environments and in so many different shapes and sizes,** it is not surprising that the wood obtained from trees has an amazing range of properties. Each year of a tree's life, long narrow cells form in the direction of growth, girdling the tree and producing the rings that are visible in cross section when the tree is cut. Spring and summer growth produce soft and hard rings respectively. Medullary rays, which may appear like cracks, run radially from the tree's center and are particularly notable in oak. The long growth cells give the tree its strength and the wood grain its appearance. How the tree is cut, whether into solid lumber or veneers, adds to the huge variety of wood patterns.

Moisture Content and Shrinkage

A living tree is saturated with water; a cut tree must be dried out for woodworking. During the drying process the moisture content of the wood is lowered to about 15% and the wood shrinks. Lumber for exterior use may contain 15% moisture but for cabinetry and millwork it should have only 4%–9% moisture. Since dried wood will reabsorb moisture, the relative humidity of the premises while wood work is under construction, and thereafter, is of concern. Ideally, while the work is underway, job sites should not have more than 55% humidity. If this is not possible the wood may require protection with some type of moisture barrier before or immediately after construction.

After wood units are built they are still subject to some degree of swelling or shrinkage depending on the relative humidity maintained on the site. In geographic locations and interior installations with low relative humidity (usually less than 17%) solid wood may shrink and possibly crack. In such locations, it is recommended that large sections of solid wood should be avoided and details of construction should be designed to decrease or hide unsightly cracking, or prevent it from occurring.

The moisture factor in wood will always have a very great effect on your development of details.

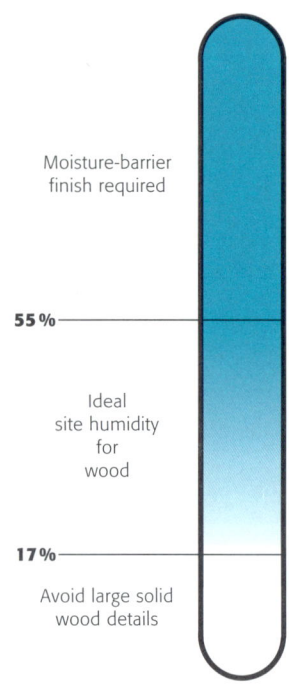

Site Humidity

Grain and Color

The tree's annual rings of spring and summer growth give wood its grain pattern. Differences between the heartwood and sapwood provide color variation. Heartwood is obtained from the inner portion of the tree where cells have filled with deposits; sapwood is from the outer, sap-transporting portion of the tree. Heartwood is usually darker in color than sapwood. In some species of trees this is so pronounced that the woods are marketed separately under different names, for example:

    Select white birch—sapwood of yellow birch tree

    Select red birch—heartwood of yellow birch tree

    Natural birch—both heartwood and sapwood of yellow birch tree.

How the log is cut into pieces of lumber affects the appearance of the grain. The quantity of usable lumber produced, and thereby the cost, also depends upon the cut.

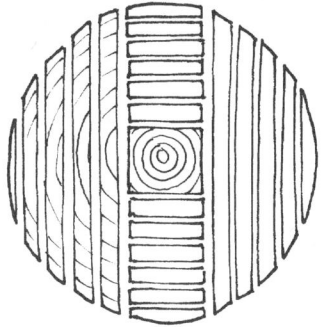 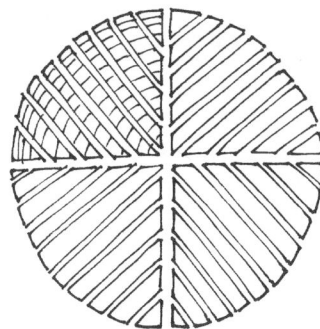

2.1 Plain-sawn lumber   **2.2** Quarter-sawn lumber

Methods of Sawing

Plain (or Flat) Sawn
- 1/2 broad, figured "cathedral grain"
- 1/2 narrow, straight "edge grain"
- widest boards
- least waste
- least expensive

Quarter Sawn
- narrow, straight "edge grain"
- narrow boards
- more waste
- more expensive
- called "ribbon grain" in mahogany

cathedral grain   the grain pattern on the face of a board which resembles the arch and peak of a cathedral ceiling

edge grain   the wood grain that results from logs cut with the annual rings at nearly right angles to the face of the board

flake   a pronounced, thin, flattened mass within the wood grain, a result of the medullary rays

ribbon grain   a fluid, nearly parallel grain pattern running lengthwise through the face of a board

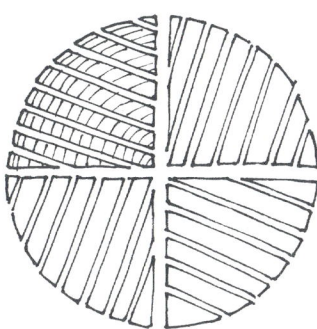

2.3 Rift-sawn lumber

Rift Sawn
–similar to quarter sawn
–narrow, straight "edge grain"
–minimizes the "flake" caused by medullary rays
–usually available only in oak
–more expensive than quarter sawn

Species Living trees—as potential "products"—are classed as hardwoods or softwoods. (Although this classification is useful for harvesting and primary woodworking it has nothing whatever to do with the hardness or softness of wood.) Horticulturally speaking, hardwoods are deciduous trees that shed their leaves seasonally; softwoods are coniferous—their scale-like or needle-like leaves are evergreen.

As a designer, you develop preferences for certain types of wood based on aesthetic appearance, workability, suitability, cost, or a combination of factors. A comparative table of wood species with illustrations and specifications is a valuable tool when considering which wood to use but nothing takes the place of a collection of real wood samples and/or good color reproductions. Examining various woods—observing color, grain pattern, or other visual character, and handling a wood sample—can be a powerful inspiration for your design concepts.

Selection Factors

Appearance
Color Ranges from almost white through yellows, reds, and browns to almost black
Figure Ranges from wildly patterned (figured) to virtually plain
Grain Open or closed pores
Hardness Refers to strength of the wood, resistance to damage, and ability to take a finish
Dimensional Stability Refers to resistance to shrinkage, warpage, twisting
Finishing Requirements Some wood species have relatively open pores and need a **filler** to achieve a smooth touch and appearance. Some species show greater contrast between the hard rings and the soft rings when **stain** is added.

Availability
The availability of sizes is inconsistent from species to species. Check the supply carefully before making your decisions. If matching plywood is required for a project its availability must also be determined beforehand.

Cost
Cost varies widely. It is recommended that you consult local dealers regarding current costs, which vary by species, size, cut, and quantity in both solid wood and plywood.

Size
In dealing with solid wood you must take into account the fact that lumber sizes are stated *nominally:* the size when cut from the log. When planed to smooth surfaces, the dimensions of the boards are smaller. For example, a two-by-two (2″ x 2″) is actually 1 1/2″ x 1 1/2″ (38 mm x 38 mm), a two-by-four (2″ x 4″) is actually 1 1/2″ x 3 1/2″ (38 mm x 88 mm). See the **Lumber and Board Sizes** table on the facing page for true dimensions.

Some expensive hardwoods may be dimensionally cut to order. Check with the distributor regarding the possibility of special sizes and cuts, as well as their availability.

Lumber and Board Sizes
(check with local distributor for sizes available)

nominal size (inches)	actual size (inches)	actual size (millimetres, mm)
1 x 2	3/4 x 1 1/2	19 x 38
1 x 3	3/4 x 2 1/2	19 x 64
1 x 4	3/4 x 3 1/2	19 x 89
1 x 5	3/4 x 4 1/2	19 x 114
1 x 6	3/4 x 5 1/2	19 x 140
1 x 8	3/4 x 7 1/4	19 x 184
1 x 10	3/4 x 9 1/4	19 x 235
1 x 12	3/4 x 11 1/4	19 x 286
1 x 14	3/4 x 13 1/4	19 x 337
1 x 16	3/4 x 15 1/4	19 x 387
2 x 2	1 1/2 x 1 1/2	38 x 38
2 x 3	1 1/2 x 2 1/2	38 x 64
2 x 4	1 1/2 x 3 1/2	38 x 89
2 x 5	1 1/2 x 4 1/2	38 x 114
2 x 6	1 1/2 x 5 1/2	38 x 140
2 x 8	1 1/2 x 7 1/4	38 x 184
2 x 10	1 1/2 x 9 1/4	38 x 235
2 x 12	1 1/2 x 11 1/4	38 x 286
2 x 14	1 1/2 x 13 1/4	38 x 337
2 x 16	1 1/2 x 15 1/4	38 x 387
3 x 4	2 1/2 x 3 1/2	64 x 89
4 x 4	3 1/2 x 3 1/2	89 x 89
4 x 6	3 1/2 x 5 1/2	89 x 140
4 x 8	3 1/2 x 7 1/4	89 x 184
4 x 10	3 1/2 x 9 1/4	89 x 235
4 x 12	3 1/2 x 11 1/4	89 x 286

Plywood

Veneering—covering the surface of a material with a thin layer of a similar or another material—was practiced as far back in time as ancient Egypt. Today, as it applies to wood, veneer is a thin layer of wood (a face veneer) laid over and bonded to layers of less expensive core woods, called plies, or other wood core materials, to produce what we call plywood.

Types of Plywood

Veneer Core All plies are veneer—the middle ply is called the *center;* plies on either side of the center, but beneath the outer plies, are called *cross-bandings.* Outer plies are called *faces* and *backs.* Thickness of plywood varies from 1/8" (3 mm) to 3/4" (19 mm) or more. Plies are in odd numbers, from 3 to 11.

Lumber Core The center ply, called the *core,* is composed of strips of lumber edge-glued into a solid slab. This type of veneer is usually 5-ply, 3/4" (19 mm) thick. Various types of lumber core are available.

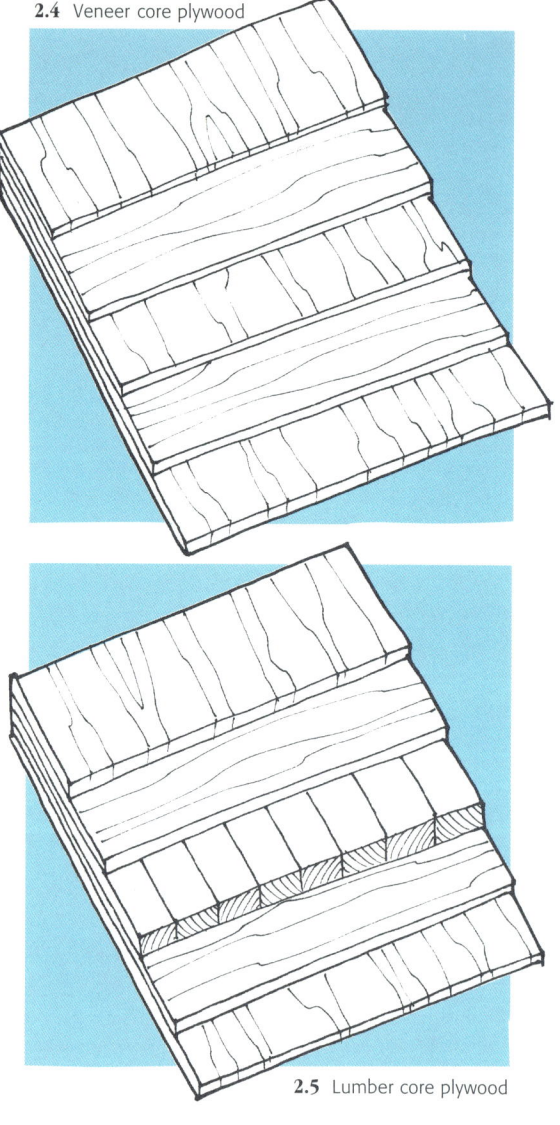

2.4 Veneer core plywood

2.5 Lumber core plywood

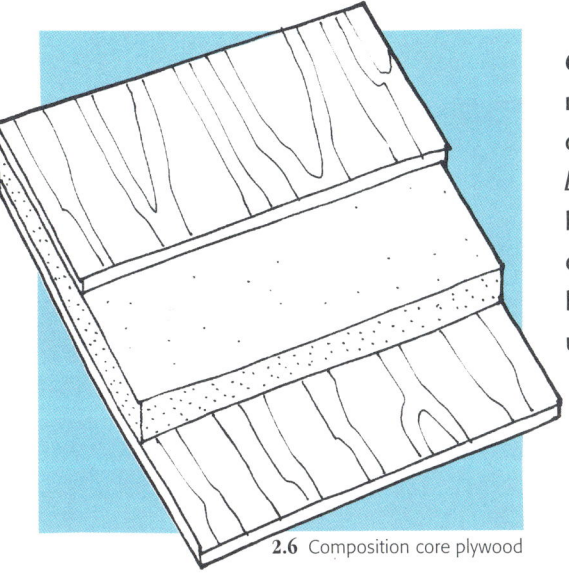

2.6 Composition core plywood

Composition Core Medium density board made from bonded wood particles and called variously *particle board* or *fiberboard* is increasingly being used to replace lumber cores in plywood. Composition cores stand on their own merits with lumber cores in all products where they are used interchangeably.

Selection of Plywood Cores

Core Type	Advantages	Disadvantages
Veneer Core	–superior screw holding	–imperfections in the core plies may show on the face veneer (this is called core telegraphing) –exposed edge is difficult to machine –exposed edge shows core voids and imperfections –most susceptible to warpage
Lumber Core	–easy to machine –exposed edges usually solid –more solid than veneer core	–highest price
Particle Board Core	–stable –no core telegraphing –least expensive core material	–poor edge screw holding –heavy core –exposed edges must be banded
Fiberboard Core (MDF)	–stable –no core telegraphing –superior screw holding to particle board core –uniform density –superior machinability –edges can be shaped and finished with minimum, if any, edge filling	–heavy core –more expensive than particle board core

Types of Veneer

Cutting method is an important factor in producing the various visual effects in veneers. Two samples from the same species, with their veneers cut differently, can have entirely different visual character even though their color values might be similar.

Common Cuts In plywood manufacture there are five principal methods of cutting veneer. The veneer slicer and veneer lathe are the primary equipment employed. The five methods are described here.

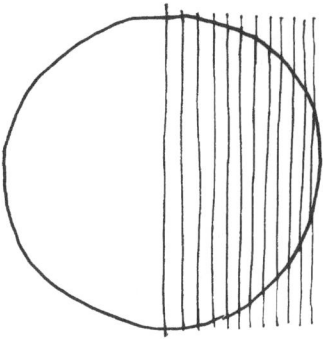

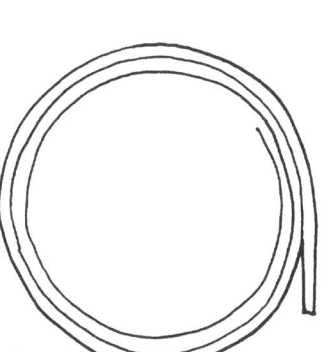

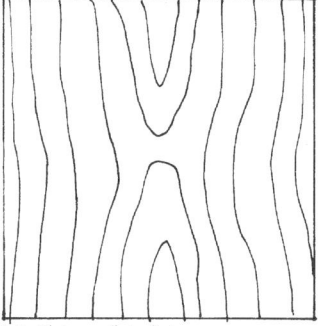

2.8 Plain, or flat, slicing

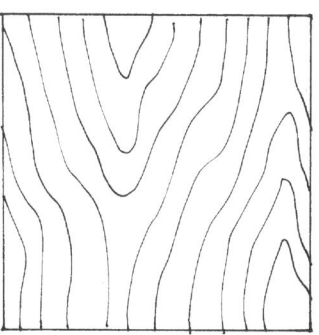

2.7 Rotary cutting

Rotary Cutting The log is mounted centrally in the lathe and turned against a razor-sharp blade, like unwinding a roll of paper. Since this cut follows the log's annual growth rings a bold grain figure is produced. Rotary-cut veneer, being continuous, is exceptionally long, and matching of one cut to another at veneer joints is relatively difficult. Almost all softwood plywood is cut this way. In all hardwoods, lengths are limited to 10'.

Plain Slicing (or Flat Slicing) The log segment, or flitch, in this case a half log, is mounted with the heart side flat against the guide plate of the slicer and the slicing is done parallel to a line through the center of the log. This produces a figure similar to that of plain sawn lumber. The slices, or leaves, in this flitch are of varying widths.

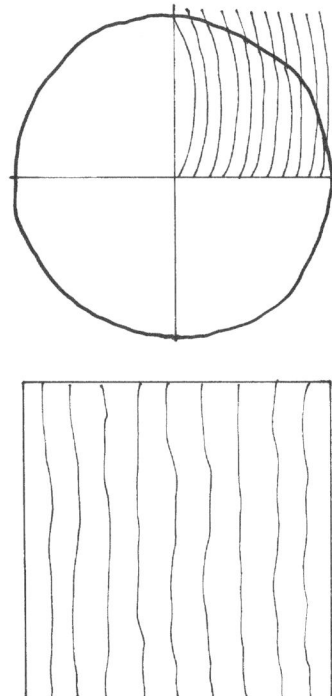

2.11 Rift cutting

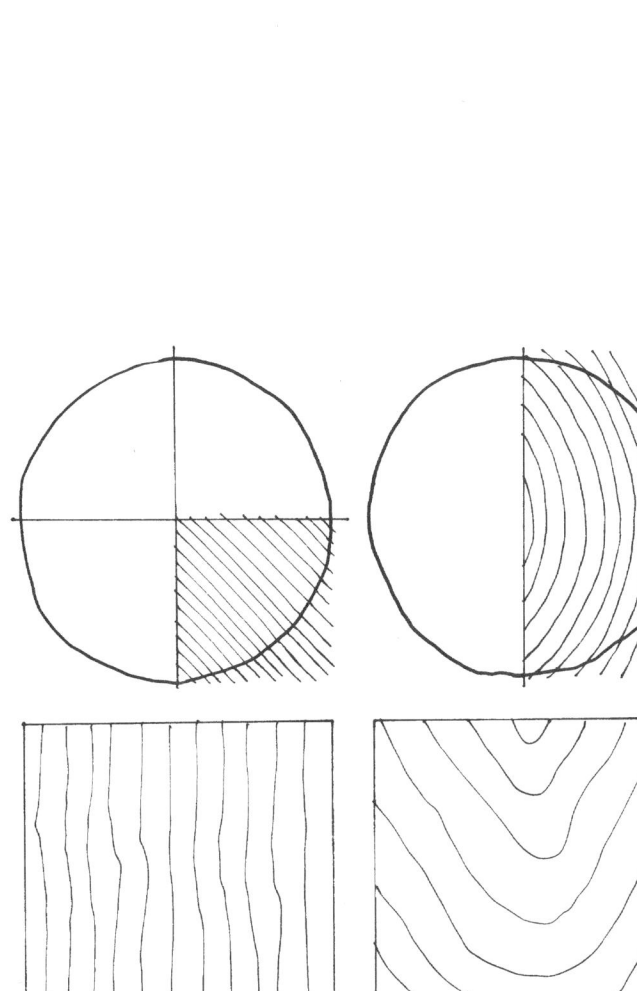

2.9 Quarter slicing

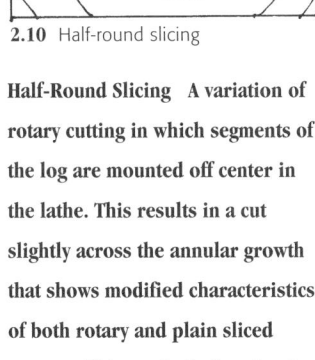

2.10 Half-round slicing

Quarter Slicing A quarter log flitch is mounted on the guide plate so that the growth rings of the log strike the knife at approximately right angles, producing a series of stripes, straight in some woods, varied in others. The leaves in this flitch are of varying widths.

Half-Round Slicing A variation of rotary cutting in which segments of the log are mounted off center in the lathe. This results in a cut slightly across the annular growth that shows modified characteristics of both rotary and plain sliced veneers. This method of cutting is often used on red oak.

Rift Cutting Rift-cut veneer is produced with various species of oak. Oak has medullary ray cells which radiate from the center of the log like the spokes of a wheel. The rift, or comb, effect is obtained by slicing slightly across these medullary rays. This accentuates the vertical grain and minimizes the flake (the mark of the medullary ray).

Combed Grain is a selection from rift-cut material that is distinguished by the tightness and straightness of its grain.

2.12 Stump veneer

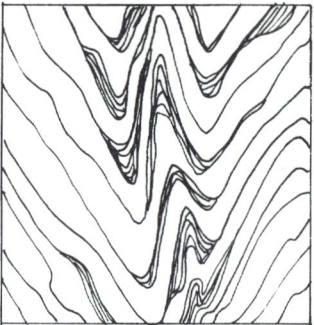

2.14 Crotch veneer

2.13 Burl veneer

Special Cuts A small quantity of veneer may be obtained from specific parts of trees and is used primarily for cabinetry or small sized wall panels.

The **stump,** from the intersection of the roots with the trunk, provides a highly figured and irregularly patterned veneer.

A **burl** is a wart-like growth on the tree trunk, which provides veneer with a greatly distorted pattern. Its use is limited to small surfaces only.

The **crotch** at the junction of the trunk and the larger branches provides small veneers with a feather pattern.

Commonly Used Veneers and Factors Affecting Their Selection

Commonly Used Species	Lengths[1]	Flitch Size[2]	Cost Category[3]
Ash, Plain Sliced White	11'	M	Low
Butternut, Plain Sliced	9'	S	Very High
Cherry, Plain Sliced American	11'	M	Low
Hickory, Plain Sliced	9'	S	Moderate
Mahogany, Plain Sliced African	12'	L	Moderate
Mahogany, Quartered African	12'	L	High
Mahogany, Plain Sliced Honduras	12'	L	Moderate
Mahogany, Quartered Honduras	12'	L	High
Oak, Combed Grain Red	9'	S	Very High
Oak, Combed Grain White	9'	S	Very High
Oak, Plain Sliced English Brown	10'	M	Very High
Oak, Plain Sliced Red	11'	L	Low
Oak, Plain Sliced White	11'	L	Moderate
Oak, Quartered English Brown	10'	M	Very High
Oak, Rift Red	10'	S	Moderate
Oak, Rift White	10'	S	High
Pecan, Plain Sliced	9'	S	Moderate
Teak, Plain Sliced	12'	L	High
Teak, Quartered	10'	M	High
Walnut, Plain Sliced	10'	S	High
Walnut, Quartered	9'	S	Very High

[1] Maximum finished length readily available.
[2] Net footage yield of average flitch: L = Large; M = Medium; S = Small.
[3] Raw veneer costs, weighted for waste or yield characteristics and degree of labor difficulty.

(Architectural Woodwork Quality Standards)

Veneer Matching

Just as different veneer cutting methods can alter grain characteristics, veneer matching can alter the appearance of a given panel or an entire installation. There is a wide choice in the types of matches available in hardwoods. Note that the method of cutting has no bearing in matching.

As a log segment is cut, the leaves of veneer are retained in perfect sequence. The yield of sequential leaves from a single log is known as a *flitch*. A "tapeless splicer" uses glue to join the long edges of the veneer leaves together, in whatever pattern is to be used. The resulting panels formed from a particular flitch are then kept together in sequence.

2.15 Book-match veneer

Matching Veneer Leaves

As a designer, you can achieve certain visual effects on a wood surface depending on how the veneer leaves are arranged. As noted, rotary cut veneers are difficult to match, therefore most matching is done with sliced veneers. The common types of match are:

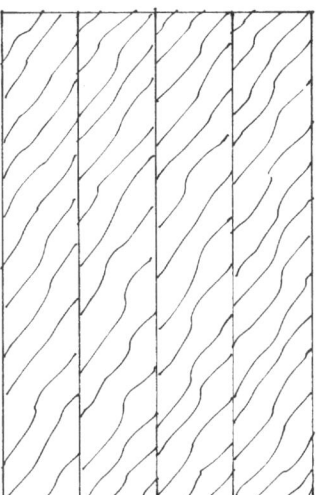

2.16 Slip-match veneer

Book Matching Every other piece of veneer is flipped (turned over front to back), so that adjacent leaves are "opened" as two pages in a book.

Visual effect—The matching veneer joints create a symmetrical pattern. Prominent characteristics will ascend or descend across the match. Book matching yields maximum continuity of grain.

Note that this is the most common match in hardwood veneer. Book matching may be used with plain, quarter, or rift-cut veneers. Because the "tight" and "loose" faces alternate in adjacent leaves, they may refract light differently, resulting in a noticeable color variation in some species or flitches; this can be minimized by specifying appropriate finishing techniques.

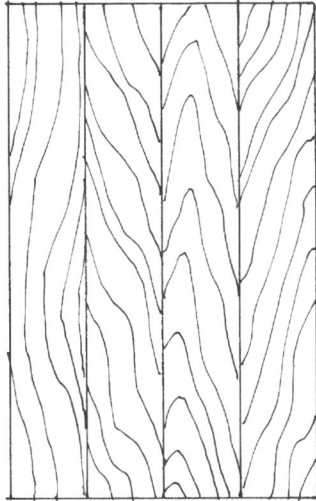
2.17 Random-match veneer

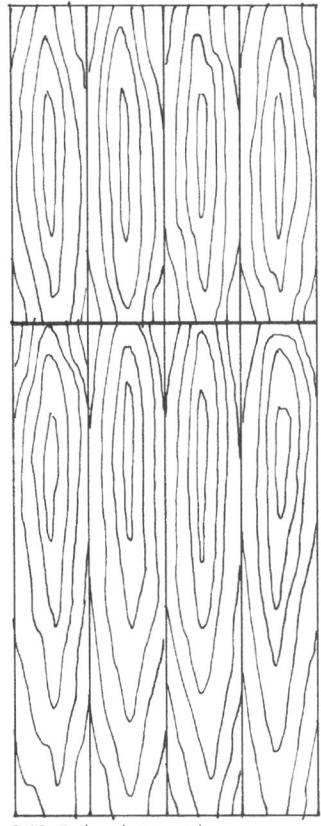
2.18 End- or butt-match veneer

Slip Matching Adjoining leaves are slipped out and spliced in sequence, with all the same-face sides, that is, all tight or all loose faces, being exposed.

> Visual effect—Grain figure repeats but joints do not show grain match.

It is important to note that the lack of joint match may not be noticeable if the grain is straight. Consequently slip matching is most commonly used in quartered and rift-cut oak veneers. (If grain is not exactly vertical, an appearance of slant may occur.) This match produces uniform color because all faces have the same light refraction.

Random Matching Arrangement of the leaves is made by random selection from one or more flitches.

> Visual effect—Casual, "board-like".

Remember that random matching must be specified.

End, or Butt, Matching Leaves are book-matched end to end, as well as side to side.

> Visual effect—End matching yields continuous grain in length as well as width.

Running Match Each panel face is assembled from as many veneer leaves as necessary. Any portion left over from the last leaf may be used as the start of the next panel.

2.19 Running-match panels

Matching Within the Panel Face

Depending on the cut, the individual leaves of veneer in a sliced flitch increase or decrease in width as the slicing progresses. Thus, if a number of panels are manufactured from a particular flitch, the number of veneer leaves per panel face will change as the flitch is used. The manner in which these leaves are "laid-up" within the panel requires book-matching, and various styles of book matching are classified as described on these two pages.

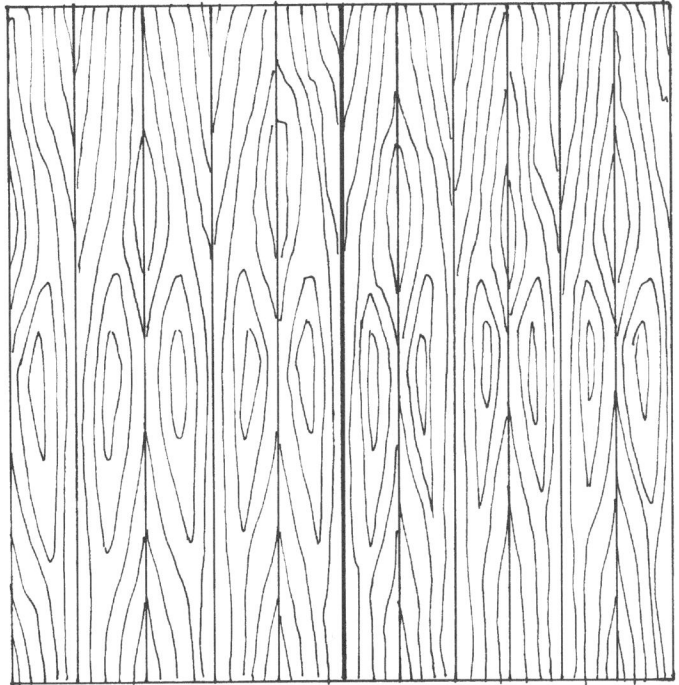

2.20 Balance-match panels

Balance Match Each panel face is assembled from leaves of uniform width. This is generally most aesthetically pleasing for a continuous wall surface.

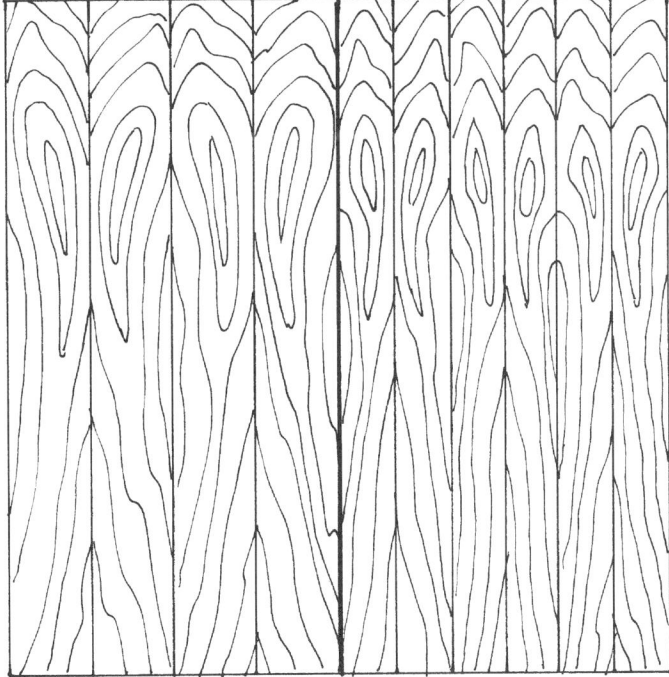

2.21 Center-match panels

Center Match Each panel has an even number of veneer leaves of uniform width. Thus, there is a veneer joint in the center of the panel, producing horizontal symmetry. This is most aesthetically pleasing for individual panels. This match increases waste and consequently cost; it is available on special order.

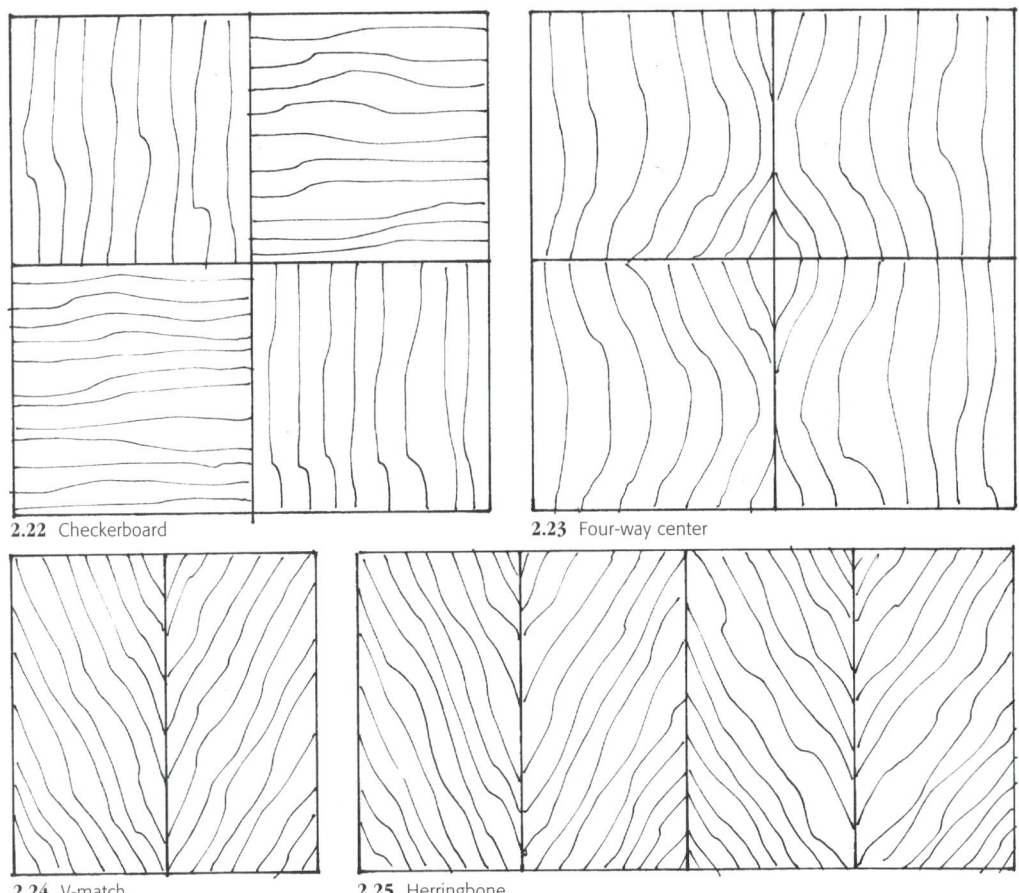

2.22 Checkerboard **2.23** Four-way center

2.24 V-match **2.25** Herringbone

Special Matching

For those special projects when you determine that aesthetic effect is more important that economics, the matches illustrated in figures 2.22—.29 can be custom ordered.

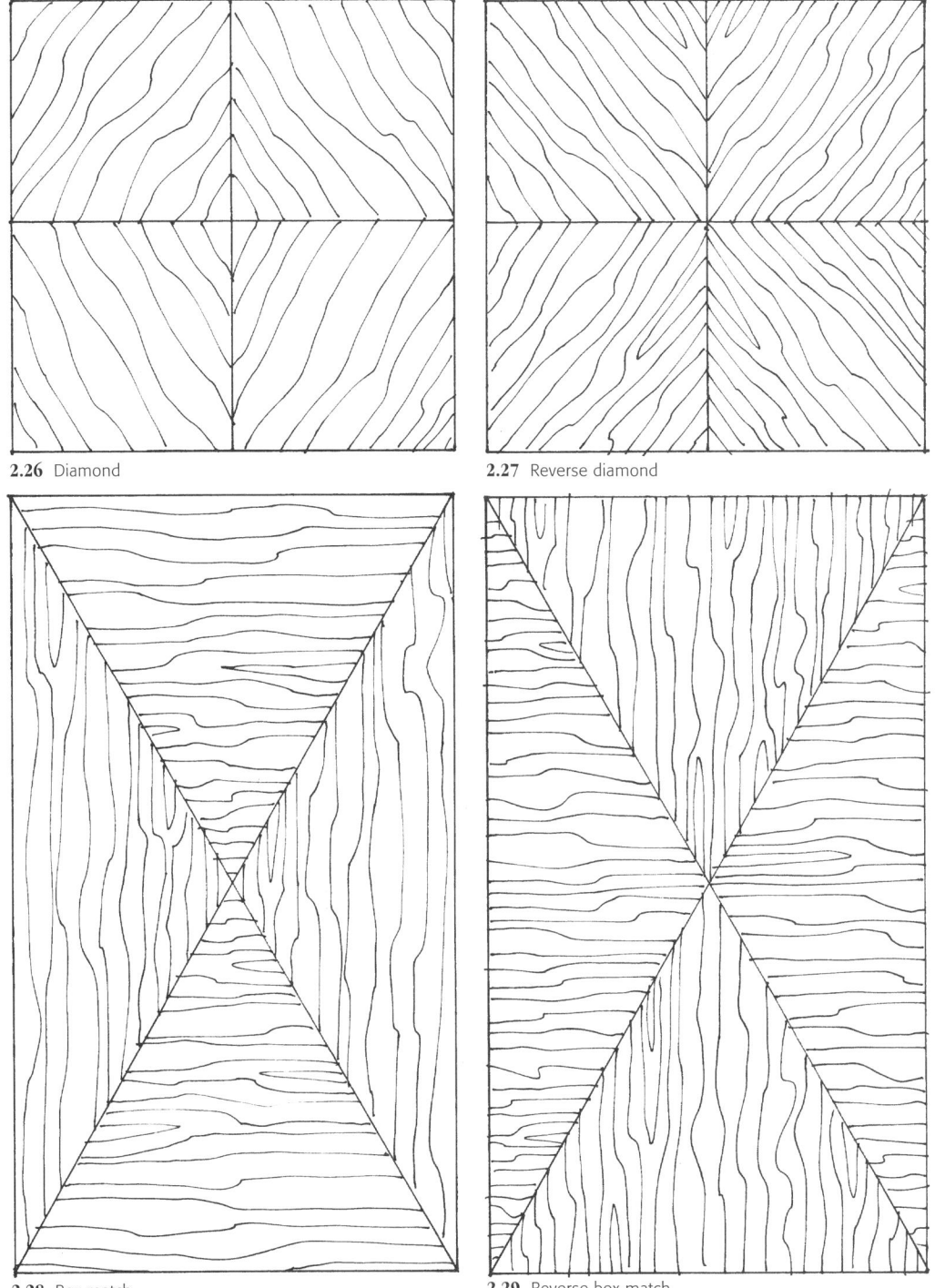

2.26 Diamond

2.27 Reverse diamond

2.28 Box match

2.29 Reverse box match

Advantages and Disadvantages of Plywood

Advantages
Plywood
–permits expensive exotic hardwoods to be used over large surfaces
–is stronger than solid wood
–has much greater dimensional stability than solid wood
–can be bent or machine molded into compound curves
–allows more complete use of logs—less waste
–allows use of unstable parts of a tree, that is, burl, crotch, and stump, for highly decorative veneers

Disadvantages
–Some veneers are cut as thin as 1/85" and therefore require very careful handling, finishing, and usage.
–Exposed edges are generally unacceptable and therefore require a concealing detail.

Case Goods/Cabinetry

CHAPTER 3

ase goods, case work, cabinets, cabinetry, cupboards—all refer to some type of storage unit which may or may not have a work surface on the top. The most basic unit is a kitchen cabinet. If you understand the construction of, and can detail, a kitchen cabinet, you have a good foundation for working out the details of many other types of units.

A kitchen cabinet can vary from being a basic unit to being a complex one. There are three classifications of construction: *economy, custom,* and *premium*. Economy cabinets have the cheapest type of wood, simple construction and details, and are not likely to have a long life. Custom grade is the most common, using good quality wood with sturdy construction techniques. Premium grade cabinets are usually of more expensive materials, and use the best quality of construction with hidden joints and reinforcements.

Compare the elevations shown on the following pages for **cabinetry A** and **cabinetry B**, two versions of what is, essentially, the same cabinetry unit. Cabinetry A has flush overlay doors and drawers, and cabinetry B has an exposed case. The visual effect may be anywhere from slightly to very different but the construction details are considerably different. Both may be acceptable; the higher price of B based on extra labor is only one of many considerations.

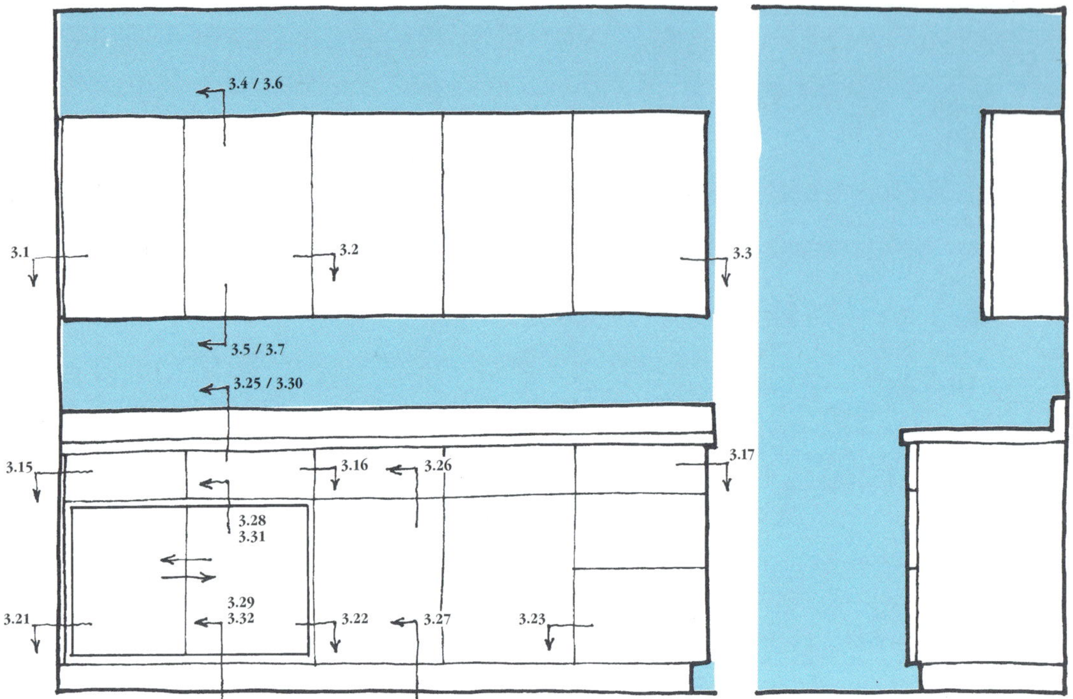

Cabinetry A—Flush overlay cabinetry, elevation

3.1 Case A at wall

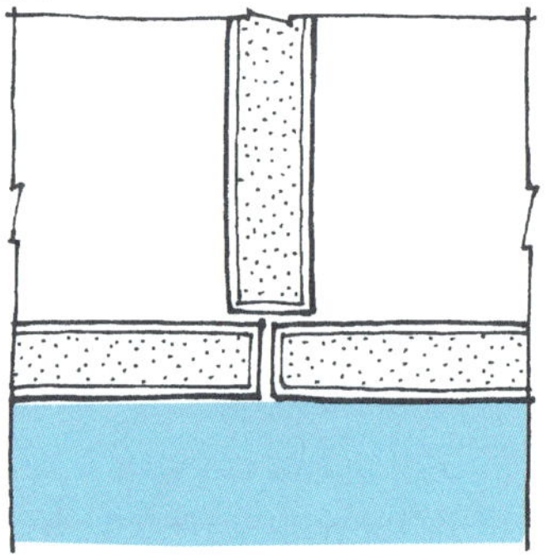

3.2 Case A

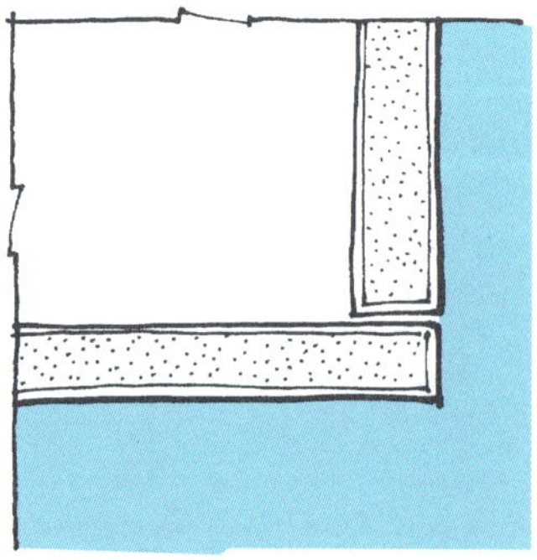

3.3 Case A

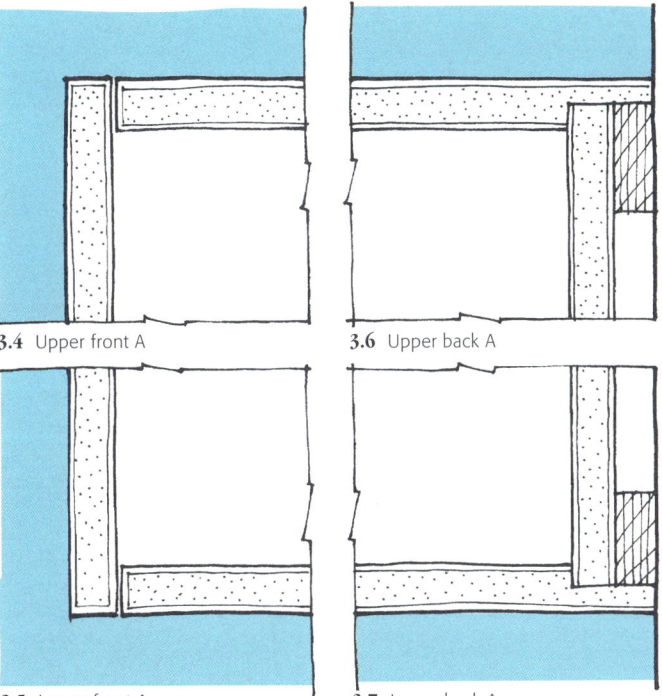

3.4 Upper front A

3.6 Upper back A

3.5 Lower front A

3.7 Lower back A

Details opposite and above show how the doors master the case. With only a hairline crack between the face panels, the surface has a continuous appearance.

Cabinetry A—flush overlay cabinetry—shown on these two pages, is the easiest system to install, and future changes in the facade can readily be accommodated, leaving the basic cabinet intact. Whether their finish is transparent or opaque, the units have a homogeneous, solid mass effect.

In **cabinetry B—exposed case cabinetry—**shown on the following two pages, the case reads separately from the doors and drawers and therefore the unit reads as made up of many parts. Changing the color, finish, or materials of the parts of cabinetry B increases this effect. Cabinetry B is a more expensive design, and more difficult to install if there are imperfections in the built walls. Building movement subsequent to installation could cause maintenance problems. Cabinetry B's facade would be difficult to change without involving the entire cabinet.

Deciding which design you prefer entails many interrelated decisions regarding the detailing of the units. Compare the details of A and B on these and the following pages.

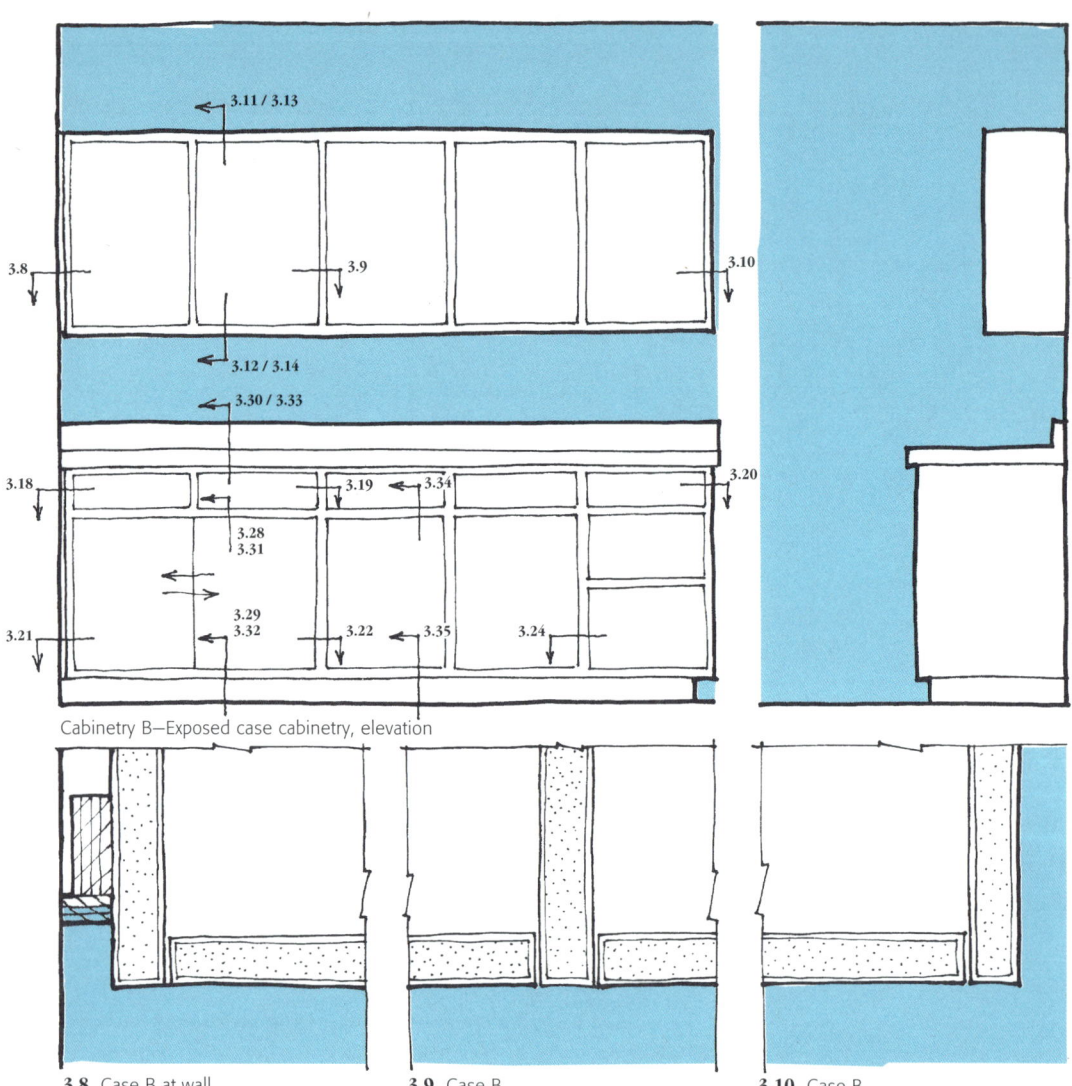

3.8 Case B at wall **3.9** Case B **3.10** Case B

Details above and right allow the case to read through and emphasize the fact that the panels are separate pieces concealing the contents and not a homogeneous mass hanging on a wall.

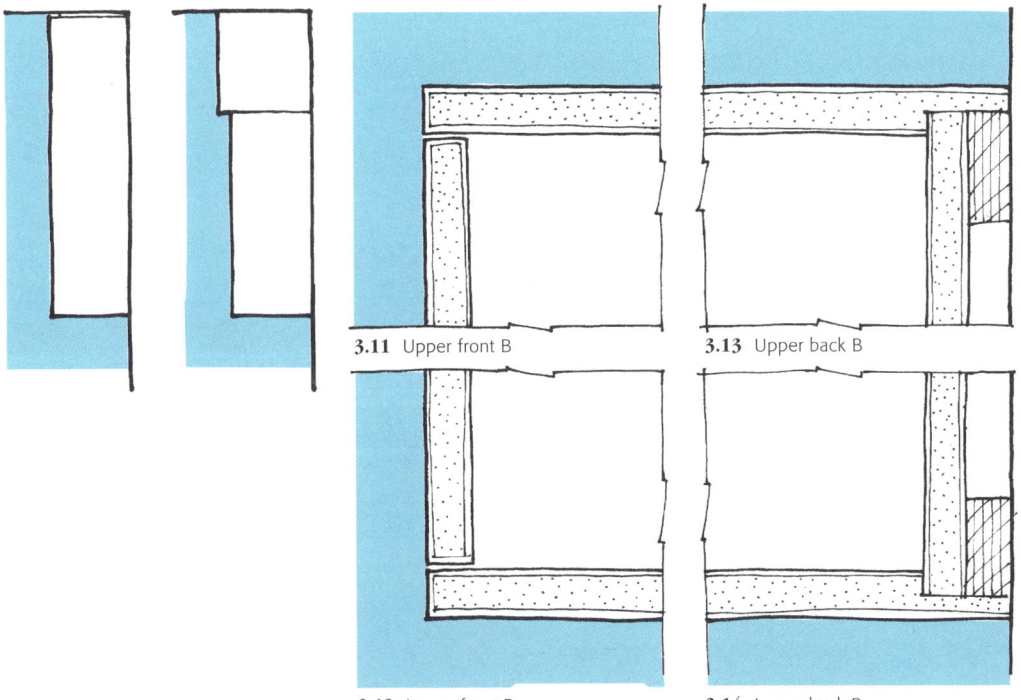

3.11 Upper front B

3.13 Upper back B

3.12 Lower front B

3.14 Lower back B

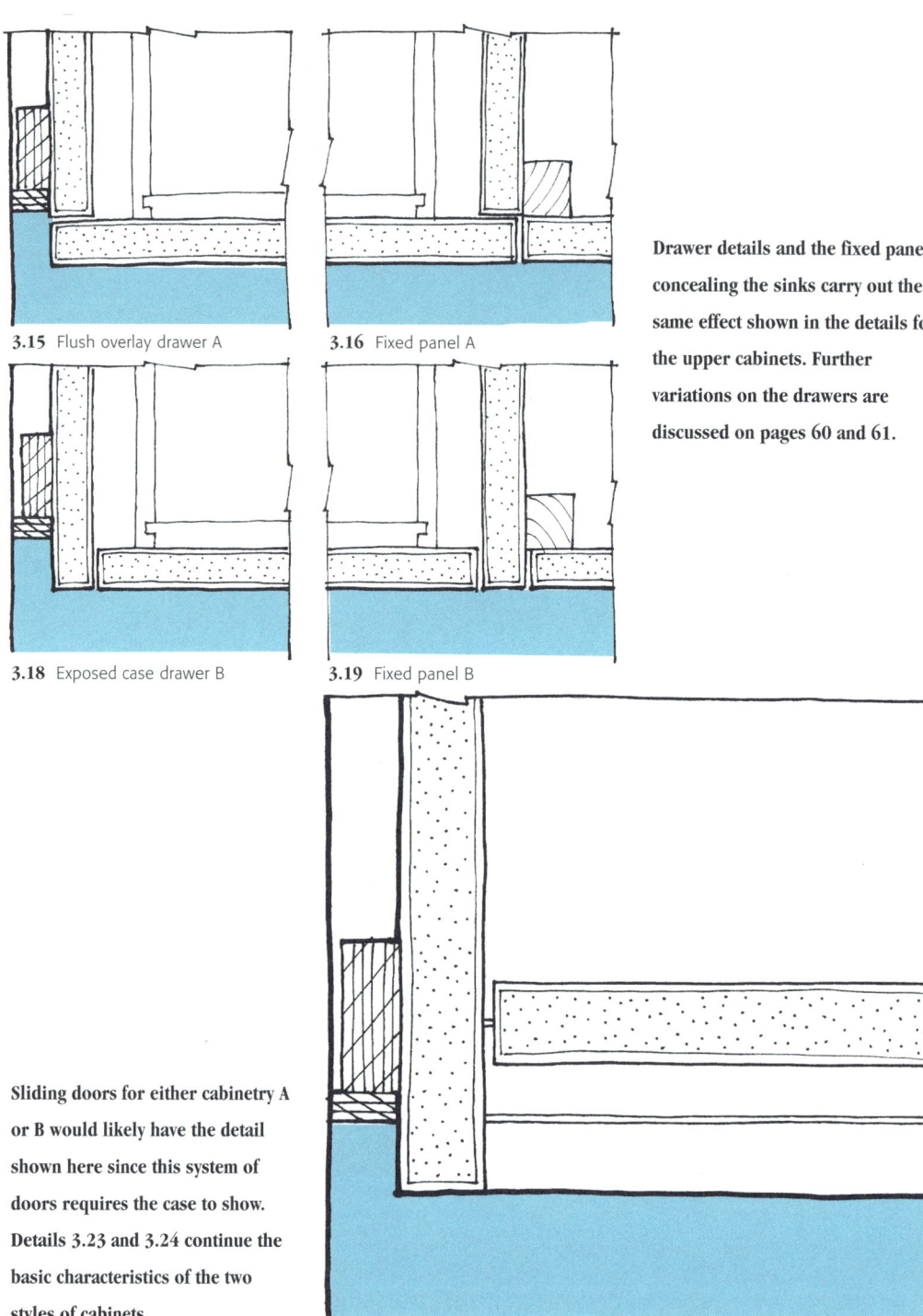

3.15 Flush overlay drawer A

3.16 Fixed panel A

3.18 Exposed case drawer B

3.19 Fixed panel B

3.21 Sliding doors A and B

Drawer details and the fixed panels concealing the sinks carry out the same effect shown in the details for the upper cabinets. Further variations on the drawers are discussed on pages 60 and 61.

Sliding doors for either cabinetry A or B would likely have the detail shown here since this system of doors requires the case to show. Details 3.23 and 3.24 continue the basic characteristics of the two styles of cabinets.

3.17 Drawer A (melamine board)

3.20 Drawer B (melamine board)

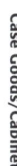

3.22 Sliding doors A and B

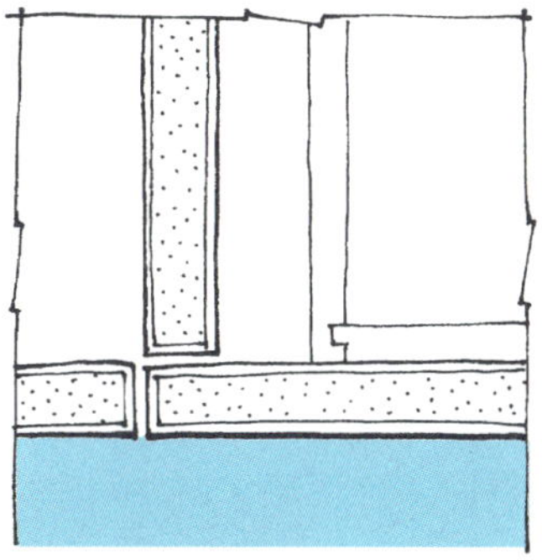

3.23 Drawer A

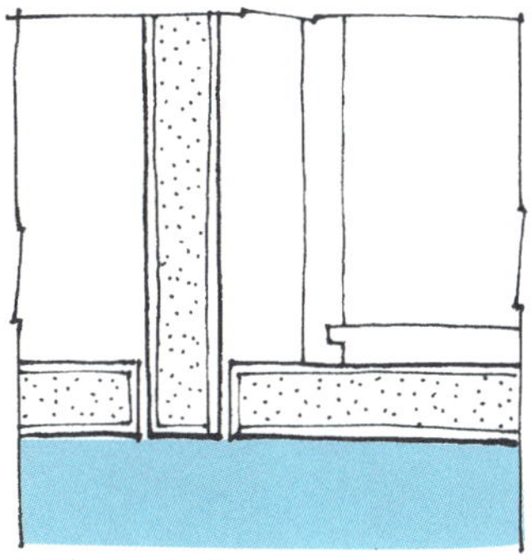

3.24 Drawer B

Case Goods/Cabinetry

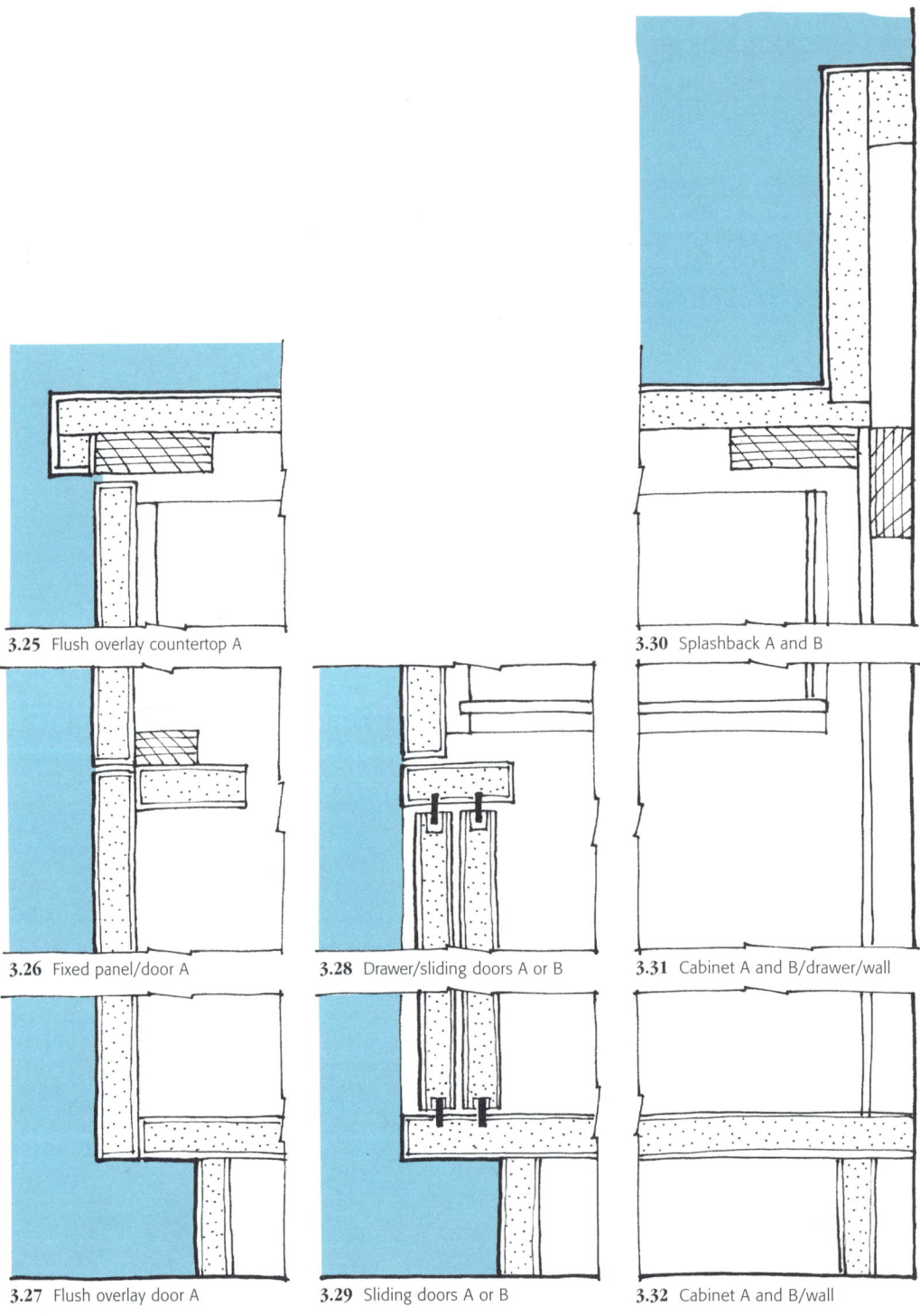

3.25 Flush overlay countertop A

3.30 Splashback A and B

3.26 Fixed panel/door A

3.28 Drawer/sliding doors A or B

3.31 Cabinet A and B/drawer/wall

3.27 Flush overlay door A

3.29 Sliding doors A or B

3.32 Cabinet A and B/wall

A countertop for cabinetry A or B is usually built as a separate piece and installed after the cabinet has been fixed in place. (A variety of edges and splashback/wall connections are detailed on pages 66 through 70.)

Details on these two pages should be examined carefully. Compare the two front-view styles being used, and note the resulting similarities and differences.

Details 3.25, 3.30, and 3.33 show drawer details, which are more fully described on pages 60–61.

The sliding door details in 3.28–.29 are the same for both the flush overlay style and the exposed face style, while 3.26–.27 and 3.34–.35 have retained the differences apparent in the other details of the two styles. (See Sliding Doors, page 75.)

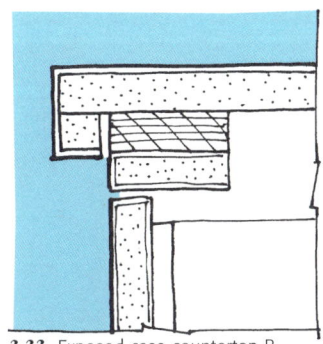

3.33 Exposed case countertop B

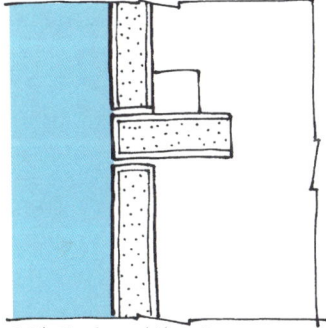

3.34 Fixed panel/door B

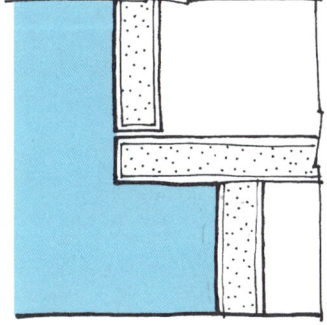

3.35 Exposed case door B

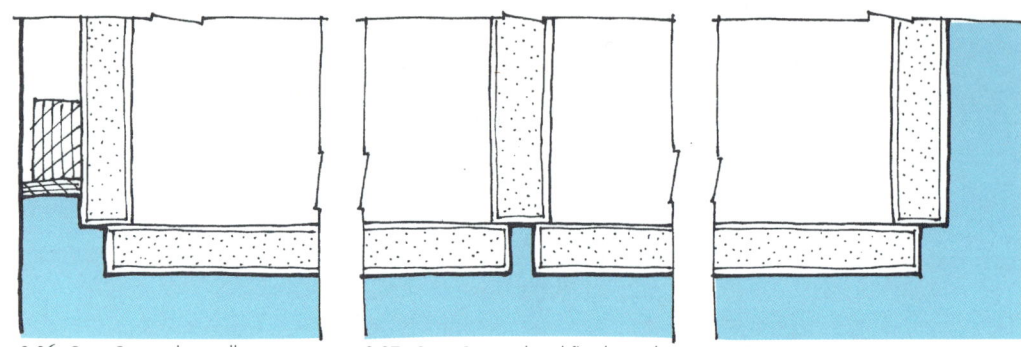

3.36 Case C, reveal at wall   **3.37** Case C, reveal and fixed panel   **3.38** Case C

Cabinetry C, a variation on the flush overlay A style, visually relates to cabinetry B. This is accomplished by leaving a reveal between doors, drawers, and so on, so that the frame is narrowly visible but recessed. Compare details above with 3.1 to 3.3 on page 48.

The other details can be similarly altered and an effect created that is not as homogeneous as cabinetry A but, although similar visually to cabinetry B, has more surface modulation. Further variations can be realized by using the reveal just for either the horizontal or the vertical joints. It is recommended that you try drawing each style in front elevation before fully evaluating the differing visual effects.

Upper Cabinet Choices   Details 3.4–.5 (page 49) and 3.11–.12 (page 51) illustrated the edge details of the upper unit in cabinetry A and B, where open space was left between the cabinet and the ceiling. The 3.40 elevation and detail opposite shows the effect of using the space above for "dead" storage, that is, storage that is too high for everyday convenience but that can be used occasionally with the assistance of a small step-ladder or stool. Elevation 3.41 shows a bulkhead from the ceiling to the top of the upper cabinet.

The importance of these details can best be seen in front elevation. They significantly change the visual appearance of the units.

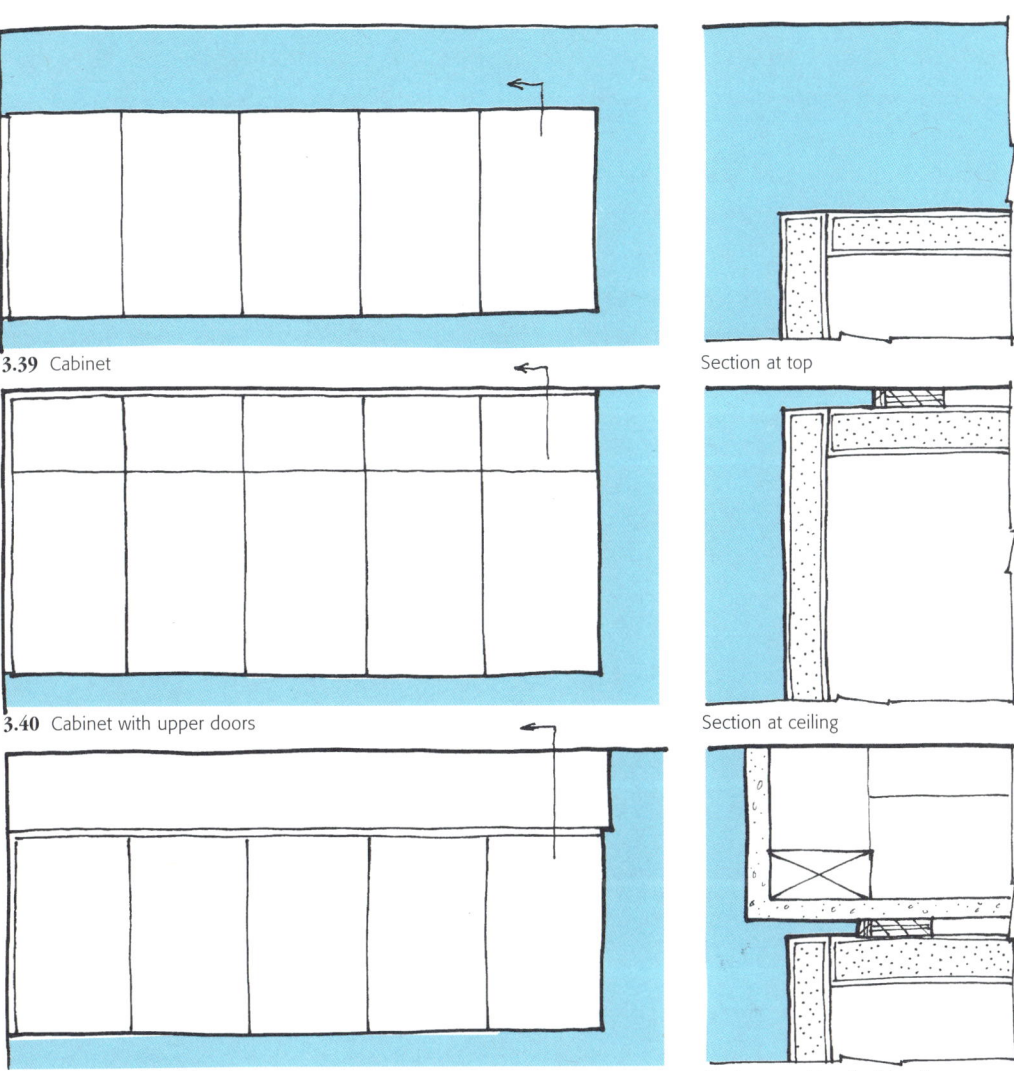

3.39 Cabinet

3.40 Cabinet with upper doors

3.41 Cabinet with bulkhead

Section at top

Section at ceiling

Section at cabinet/bulkhead

Using a reveal detail for either just the horizontal or the vertical joints would create a variation on any of these upper cabinets.

A variation of 3.41 would be to make the front and end faces of the bulkhead flush with the front and end faces of the cabinet, thus altering the appearance once again.

Scribing—fitting a cabinet to an adjacent surface such as a wall or ceiling—is needed since we are dealing with hand-made units and the surfaces to which they are to be secured which, while built to fairly fine tolerances, are not perfect. Waves or bumps in the "flat" surface mean that the straight edge of the cabinet probably will not meet the surface perfectly; an uneven crack will be apparent between them. Designers must accommodate the imperfection by either covering it or cutting something to follow and fill the irregularities.

Details 3.42 and 3.43 show a typical method of scribing. Detail 3.44 shows an added block of wood flush with the face of the cabinet and scribed to the adjacent surface.

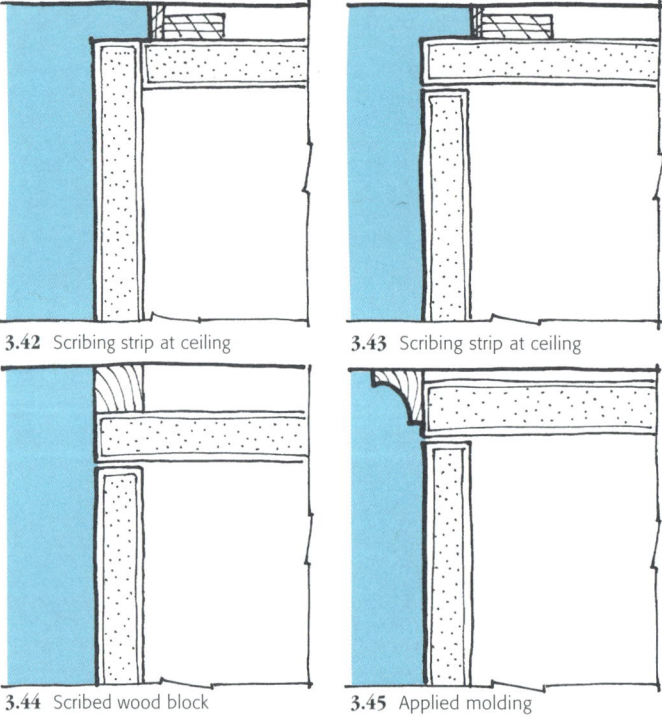

3.42 Scribing strip at ceiling

3.43 Scribing strip at ceiling

3.44 Scribed wood block

3.45 Applied molding

In details 3.42 and 3.43, the scribing strip is sawn and sanded to conform to the adjacent surface so that the line of the cabinet can be perfectly horizontal or vertical.

The disadvantages of using this method are twofold: a crack might form at the junction of the strip and the cabinet edge; the width of the block face from the door edge to the wall could change due to waves in the surface, which would be noticeable.

The easiest and cheapest method of finishing scribing is to cover the space with a molding, as shown in 3.45. While not normally recommended, there may be circumstances where it is acceptable and, depending on the design concept, even desirable. Its most likely use would be where applied moldings are a feature of the design.

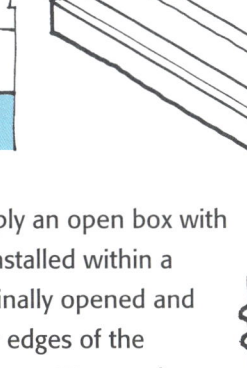

3.46 Center guide

Drawers A drawer is simply an open box with four sides and a bottom. Installed within a cabinet, a drawer was originally opened and closed by sliding the lower edges of the sides along the adjacent frame. Wax used on the contact edges allowed a smoother motion. This method of mounting allowed the drawer to be wiggled from side to side, which caused wear on both the drawer and frame, and frequently caused jamming.

    The bottom center guide, 3.46 above, was an improvement to this system. With a reasonably tight fit, looseness and wear were usually overcome, but if the drawer was unevenly loaded it could still jam. A better method was developed using a guide on the outside of each side panel of the drawer, 3.47. With the use of some wax, this produced a good slide system.

    We now have a variety of manufactured drawer slides such as shown at 3.48, with built-in glides made of steel and nylon, which carry different amounts of load and extend varying lengths out of the cabinet. Center guides are also manufactured out of steel and nylon. Many of these pieces of hardware are cheaper to purchase and install than to make them by hand out of wood.

    The reason for discussing the drawer action before the drawer details is that you must consider the action when deciding on the construction of the drawer itself. Some details cannot be used with some of the sliding systems, or are more difficult to use. Further, since part of the manufactured, or mechanical, slide is attached to the drawer and comes out of the cabinet with it, the drawer face must extend beyond the drawer side to conceal the space taken up by the slide.

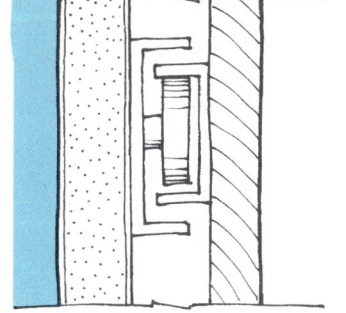

3.47 Side guide

3.48 Manufactured side guide

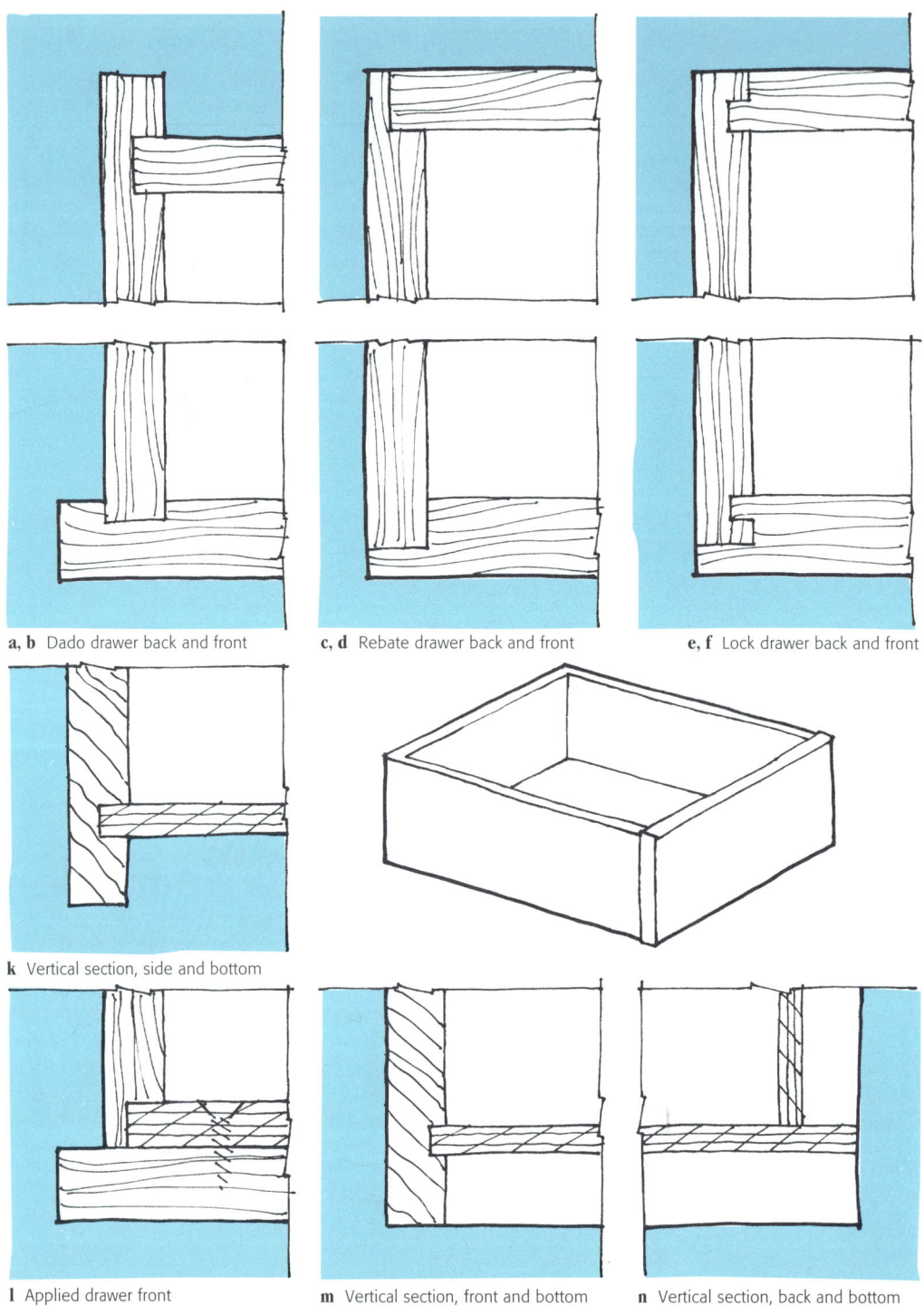

a, b Dado drawer back and front

c, d Rebate drawer back and front

e, f Lock drawer back and front

k Vertical section, side and bottom

l Applied drawer front

m Vertical section, front and bottom

n Vertical section, back and bottom

Case Goods/Cabinetry

60

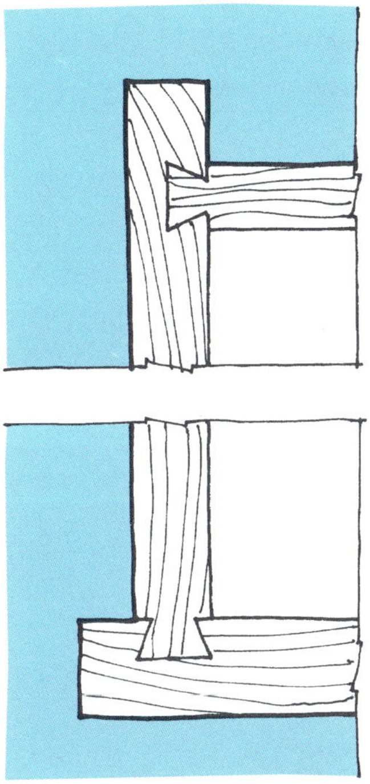

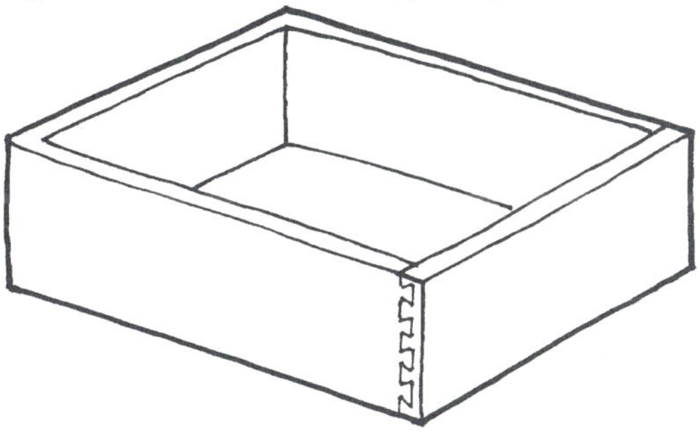

3.49 Drawer Construction Details
Plan views unless noted differently

Details a, b, e, g, h Commonly used.

Detail c Generally used only on economy-grade units.

Detail d Commonly used with melamine construction and a removable front.

Detail f Commonly used with solid wood construction.

Details i, j Used only on expensive premium-grade units.

Details k, m, n Commonly used.

Detail l Applied front may be used with any construction behind.

Detail o Restricted use depending on detail used for back-to-side joint.

Detail p If sides are made of single pieces of solid wood, the top edge is usually rounded as shown here.

Detail q When wood guides are used, a spring drawer-stop will prevent the drawer from being pulled completely out of the unit.

g, h Through dovetail back and front

i, j Multiple dovetail back and front

o Vertical section, var. back, bottom

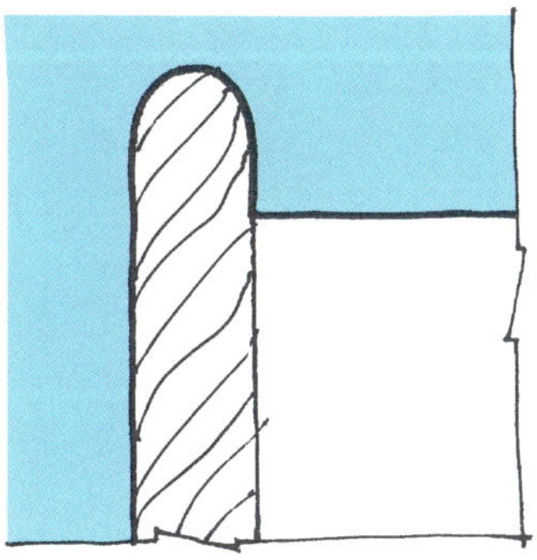

p Rounded top edge, vertical section

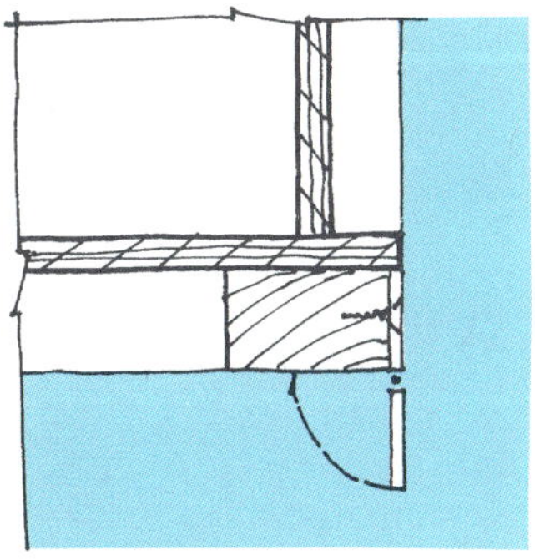

q Spring drawer-stop, vertical section through back and bottom

Case Goods/Cabinetry

61

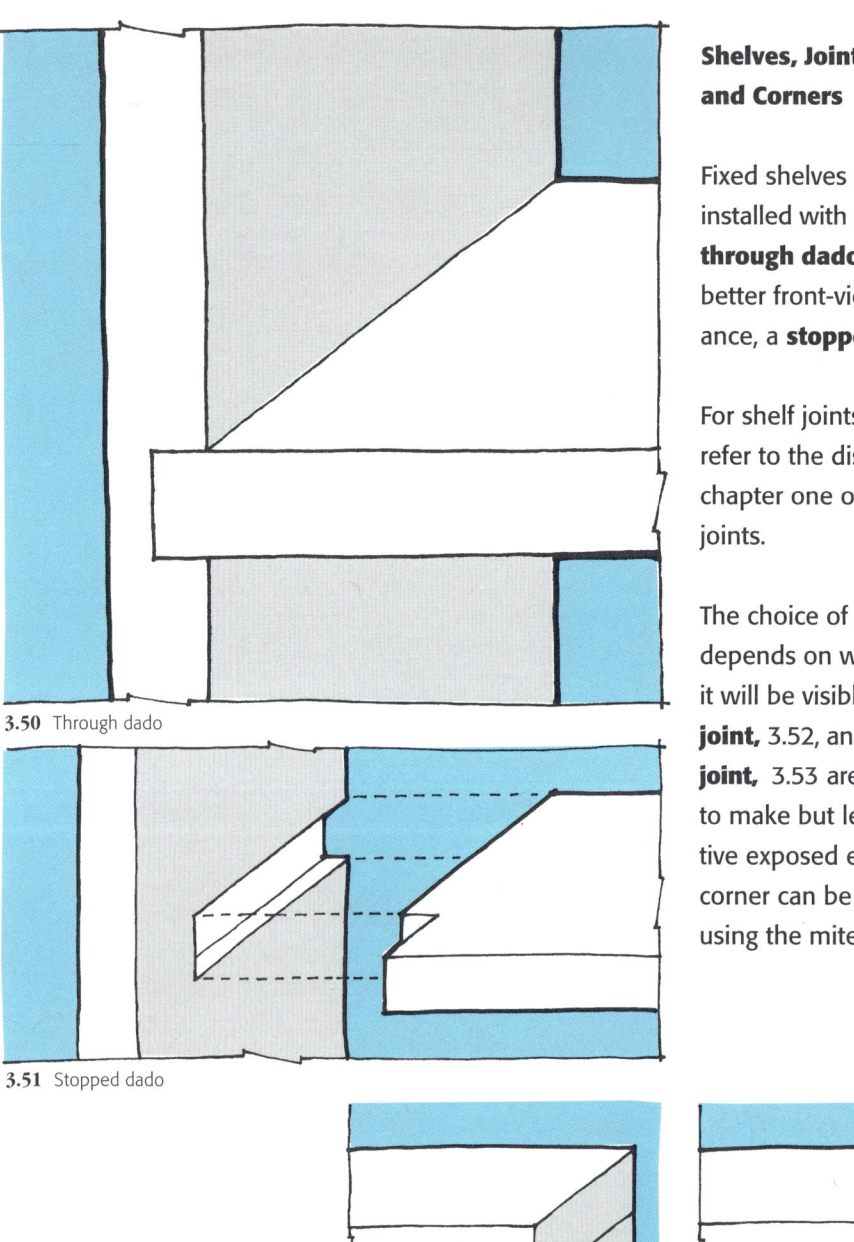

3.50 Through dado

3.51 Stopped dado

3.52 Lock joint

3.53 Rabbet joint

Shelves, Joints, Edges, and Corners

Fixed shelves are usually installed with either a simple **through dado,** 3.50, or for better front-view appearance, a **stopped dado,** 3.51.

For shelf joints and edges, refer to the discussion in chapter one on basic wood joints.

The choice of corner joint depends on whether or not it will be visible. A **lock joint,** 3.52, and a **rabbet joint,** 3.53 are economical to make but leave unattractive exposed ends. A cleaner corner can be constructed using the miter joint.

3.53 Miter

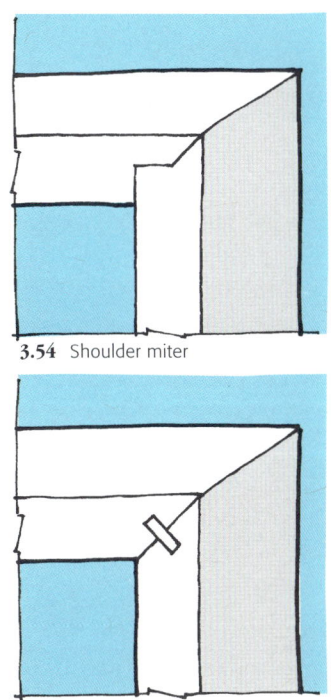

3.54 Shoulder miter

3.55 Splined miter

Three versions of mitered joints are shown above in order of ascending cost and strength. A newer version of the splined miter is one that uses a pre-manufactured, lozenge-shaped spline commonly called a lemon spline or biscuit, approximately 2″ x 3/4″ x 1/8″. Instead of the continuous spline strip, lemon splines are inserted in routed arcs approximately 8″ on center.

3.56 Lemon spline

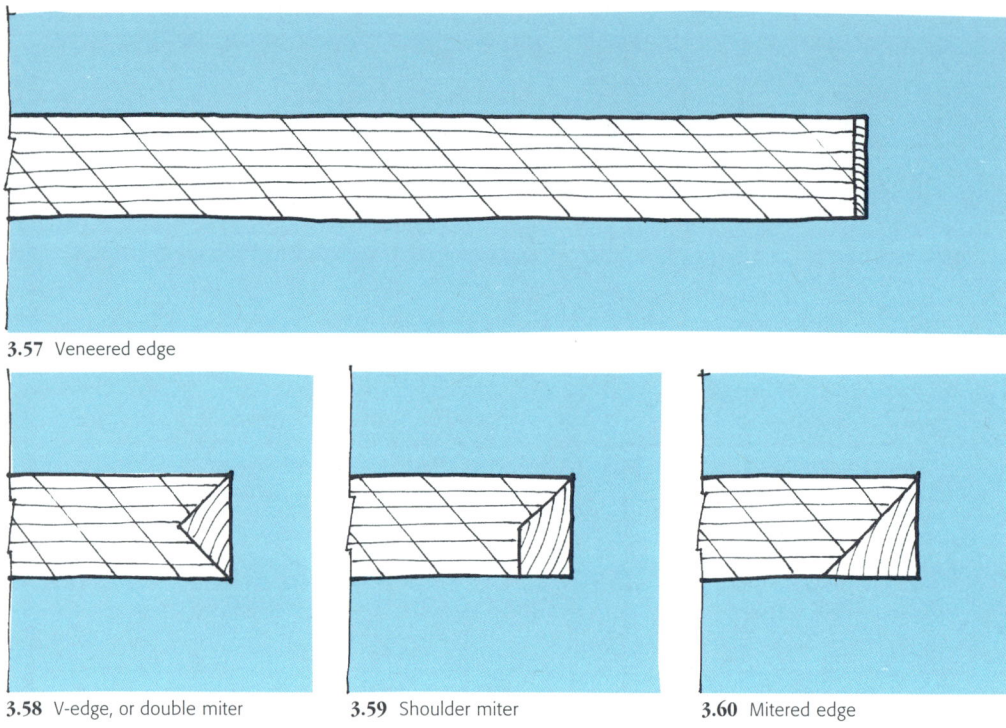

3.57 Veneered edge

3.58 V-edge, or double miter

3.59 Shoulder miter

3.60 Mitered edge

Edges The simplest and most common method of edging plywood is to glue on a piece of veneer that matches the face veneer (3.57). *Veneer tape,* a very thin leaf of veneer with a fiber backing, is produced for this purpose in the most commonly-used wood species. If the tape is not available then a piece of matching veneer is used. Tapes in colored or wood-grained polyester or polyvinyl chloride (PVC) are becoming popular with cabinet-makers using machines to edge panels.

Various versions of solid wood edging are also possible. Your selection of edge treatment will be affected by the cost of the material as well as its location on the unit, its visibility, and whether the finish is to be transparent or opaque. Remember, too, that if the grain pattern of the edge strip and the face veneer run in the same direction, the joint is much less noticeable. With a pattern like rift oak it can be almost invisible.

The V-edge or double miter, 3.58, conceals the joint on both faces, a very expensive method of edging. The shoulder miter, 3.59, conceals the joint on one face, as does the full miter, 3.60. Less expensive but showing the joint on both faces are the plain edge, the tongue-and-groove edge, and the splined edge, 3.61 to 3.63 respectively.

If you want to give the edge a more substantial appearance, these joints can be adapted as shown in 3.64 to 3.66.

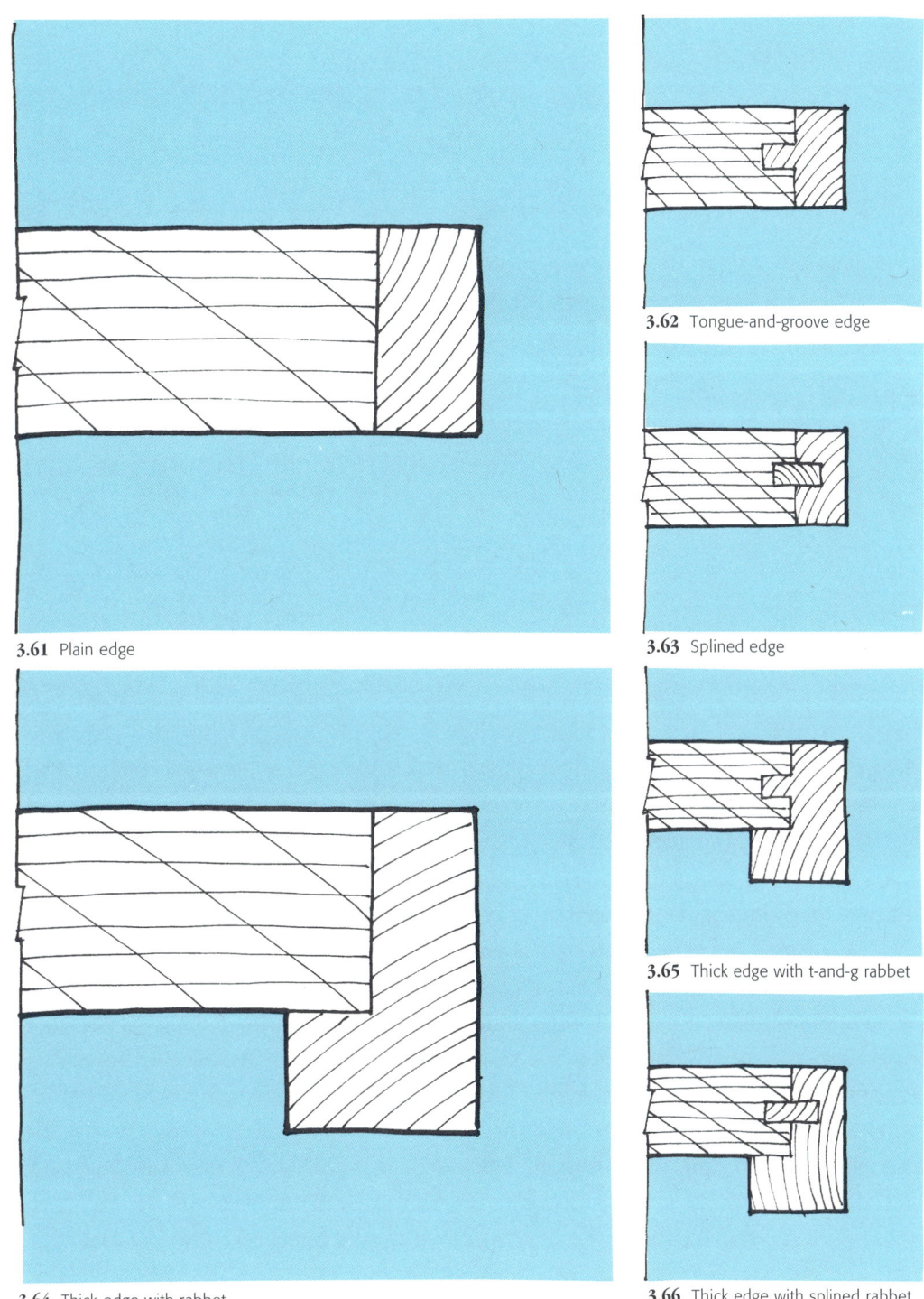

3.61 Plain edge

3.62 Tongue-and-groove edge

3.63 Splined edge

3.64 Thick edge with rabbet

3.65 Thick edge with t-and-g rabbet

3.66 Thick edge with splined rabbet

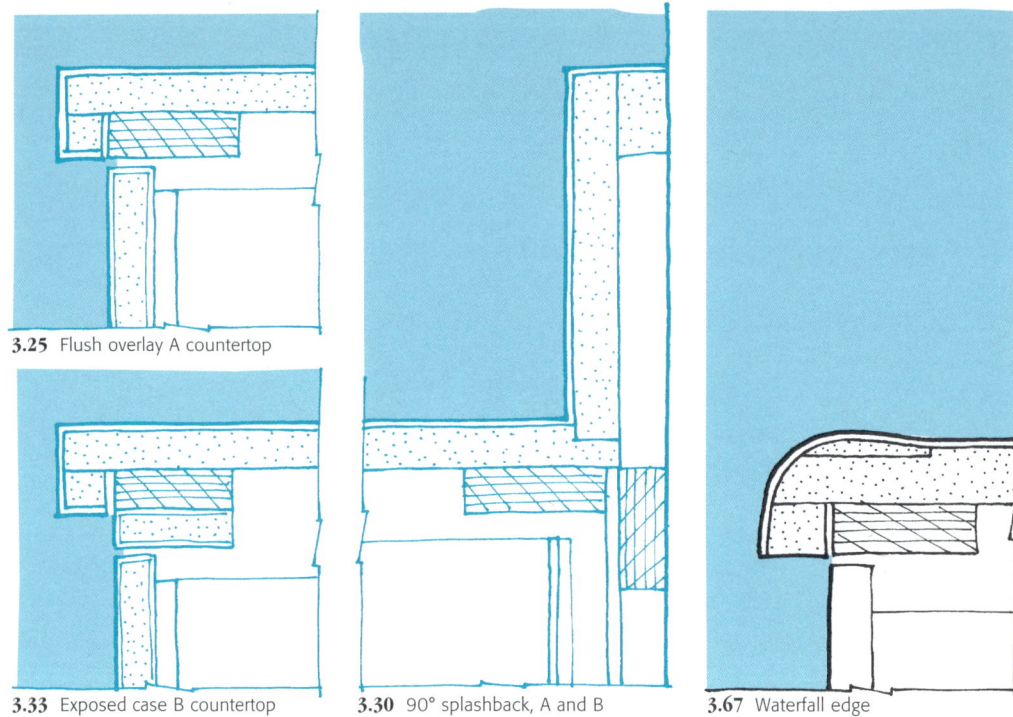

3.25 Flush overlay A countertop

3.33 Exposed case B countertop

3.30 90° splashback, A and B

3.67 Waterfall edge

The basic countertops, A and B shown above in blue, are repeated here for convenience of reference. Typically, a countertop has a front edge with a vertical dimension of approximately 1 1/2". This is made up of the framing member (3/4") plus plywood or particleboard top (3/4"+), plus finish. In these examples the finish indicated is plastic laminate, which is approximately 1/16" thick. Other finishes will also be discussed.

    Plastic laminate has a color sheet under the transparent top layer of melamine plastic and is backed by brown layers of plastic-impregnated kraft paper. When it is joined on an outside corner such as the upper front edge of the counter, the dark layers show, giving a visible dark pencil-line edge to the unit. Chamfering the edge prevents it from having a very sharp, slightly saw-toothed edge. The dark line can be avoided by using the more expensive type of plastic laminate which has solid color throughout all layers. It is important that the top layer of laminate master the front-edge face to protect it from water seepage, and so that movement off the counter edge does not pull the face piece away.

    It is possible to bend post-forming grade plastic laminate to form a "waterfall" edge and return up the splashback, as shown in 3.67 to 3.70.

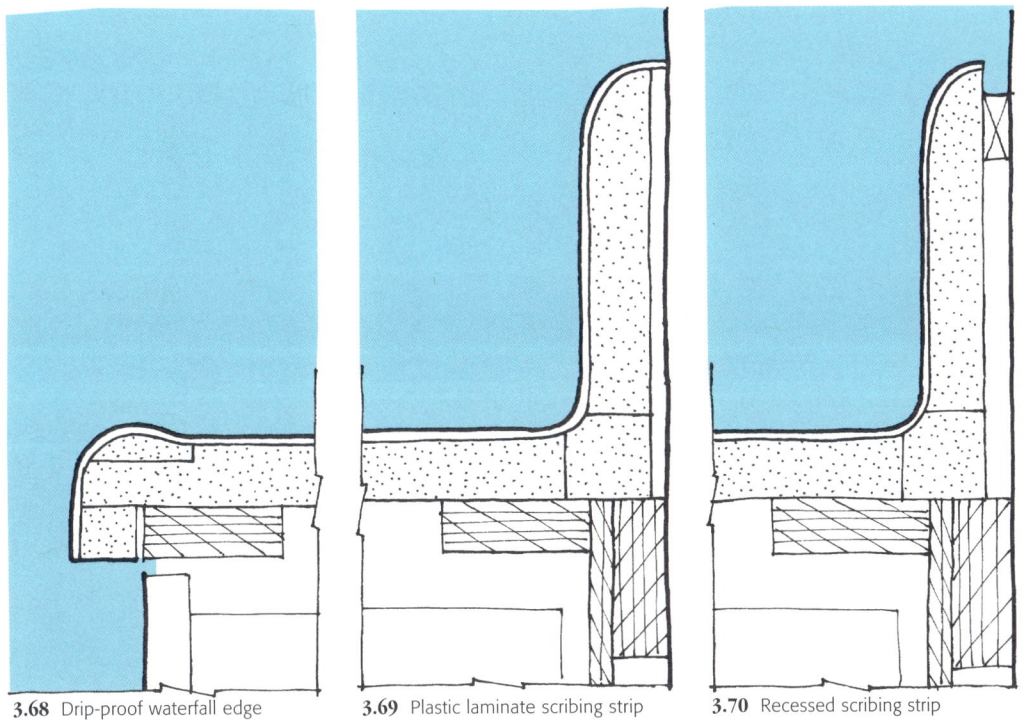

3.68 Drip-proof waterfall edge   **3.69** Plastic laminate scribing strip   **3.70** Recessed scribing strip

Detail 3.69 uses the plastic laminate as a scribing material to fit against imperfections in the wall. Detail 3.70 employs a recessed scribing strip. This is a preferred detail if the wall is particularly uneven so that the top edge does not vary visibly in depth. However, the top of the scribing strip does become a dust-gatherer. You must weigh the pros and cons for the particular situation.

It is possible to use a curved front edge with a 90° back such as 3.30, or a straight front edge with a curved back such as 3.69 or 3.70. The scribing methods can be used with either edge. The splashback can be eliminated if the wall is an easily cleaned material or the tasks performed at the counter do not produce conditions that would damage the walls. A splashback can be carried up to any height desired—even to the underside of the overhead cabinet. Any of these options would affect the visual appearance.

Curved edges work well at the front and rear but, since the plastic laminate cannot be curved in two directions at once, a different detail for the ends of the unit is required.

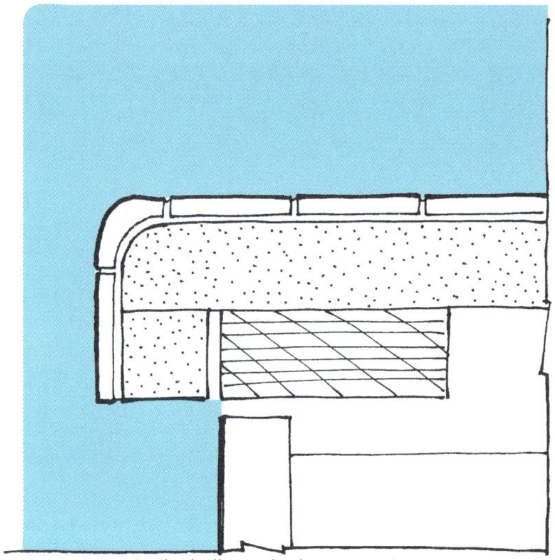

3.71 Ceramic tile, bullnosed edge

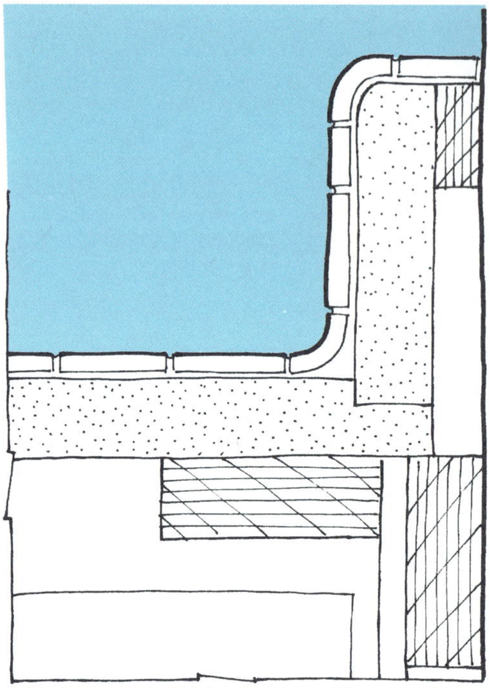

3.72 Counter back with interior and exterior cove units

3.73 Ceramic tile, square edge

3.74 Square corners

Notice that the edge of the tile shows at the edge of the countertop. Verify that the tile you are specifying is colored all the way through or, if glazed, is available with a glazed edge.

Other Countertop Materials Ceramic tile, marble and granite are occasionally used for surfaces. While it is possible to use a traditional metal lath and mortar bed under these products, it is more likely that a thin-set cement, epoxy, or organic adhesive would be used. Thin-set cement might be a layer 3/8" thick, while epoxy or organic adhesives would be

3.75 Stone with chamfered edge

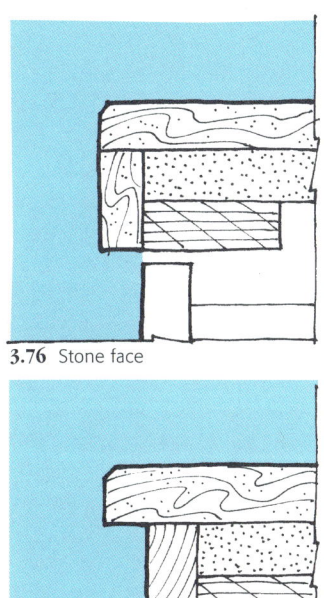

3.76 Stone face

3.77 Wood face

approximately 1/8" thick. Apart from either of these dimensions, other details would be essentially the same.

Details 3.71 and 3.72 show ceramic tile with a bullnosed edge unit at the front, and interior and exterior cove units at the rear on the splashback. If the type of tile that you are using is not available in these profiles, then square corners as shown in 3.73 and 3.74 would be a more likely choice. Note detail 3.74, showing tile mounted vertically, adjacent to the countertop, directly on the wall. A crack could form at the juncture of the countertop tile with the wall-mounted tile; flexible fillers would be used for this situation.

Marble, granite, and slate in thin tiles (1/4") would be applied similarly to 3.73 and 3.74; however, if you choose to use large slabs, the detail would change slightly. In 3.75 the top front edge of the stone has been rounded or chamfered to relieve the sharpness of the edge. The drawer or door front has been brought up to conceal the construction and to diminish the apparent thickness of the top. Other variations can be seen in 3.76 and 3.77.

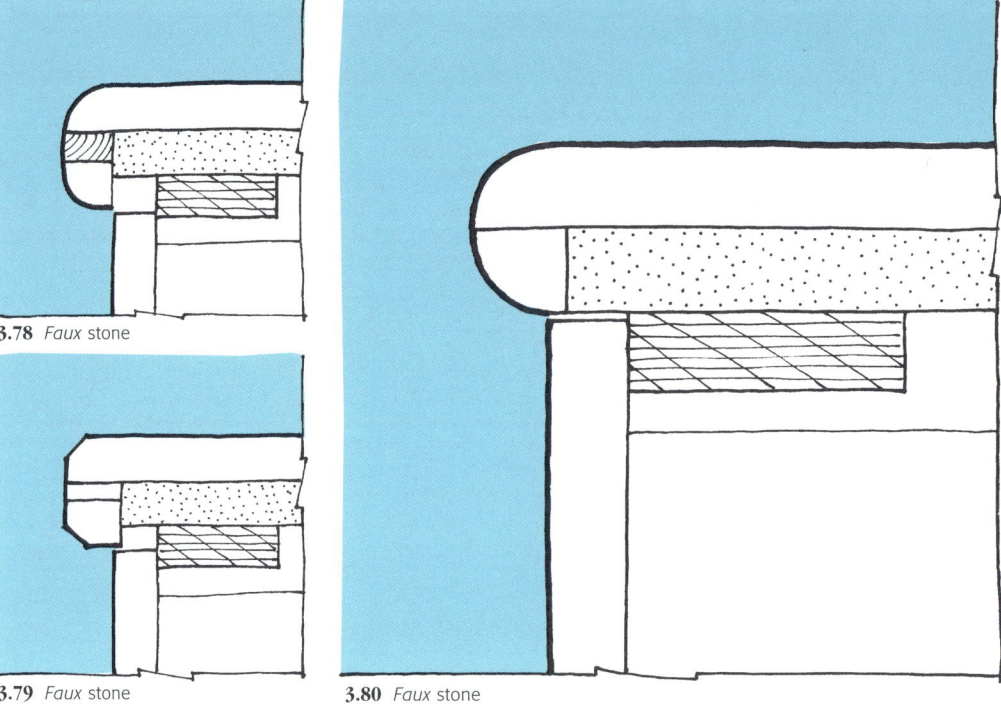

3.78 *Faux* stone

3.79 *Faux* stone

3.80 *Faux* stone

Artificial or *faux* stone, plastic materials marketed under various trade names, are gaining popularity for use as countertop materials. They are available in 1/4″ to 3/4″ thick sheets and can be milled similarly to solid wood. *Faux* stone can be detailed as in 3.76 and 3.77 or in other variations, such as the double-thick ones shown above.

Other variations are possible, of course, with all of these materials. Only your creativity and detailing knowledge are needed to devise the one that suits your concept.

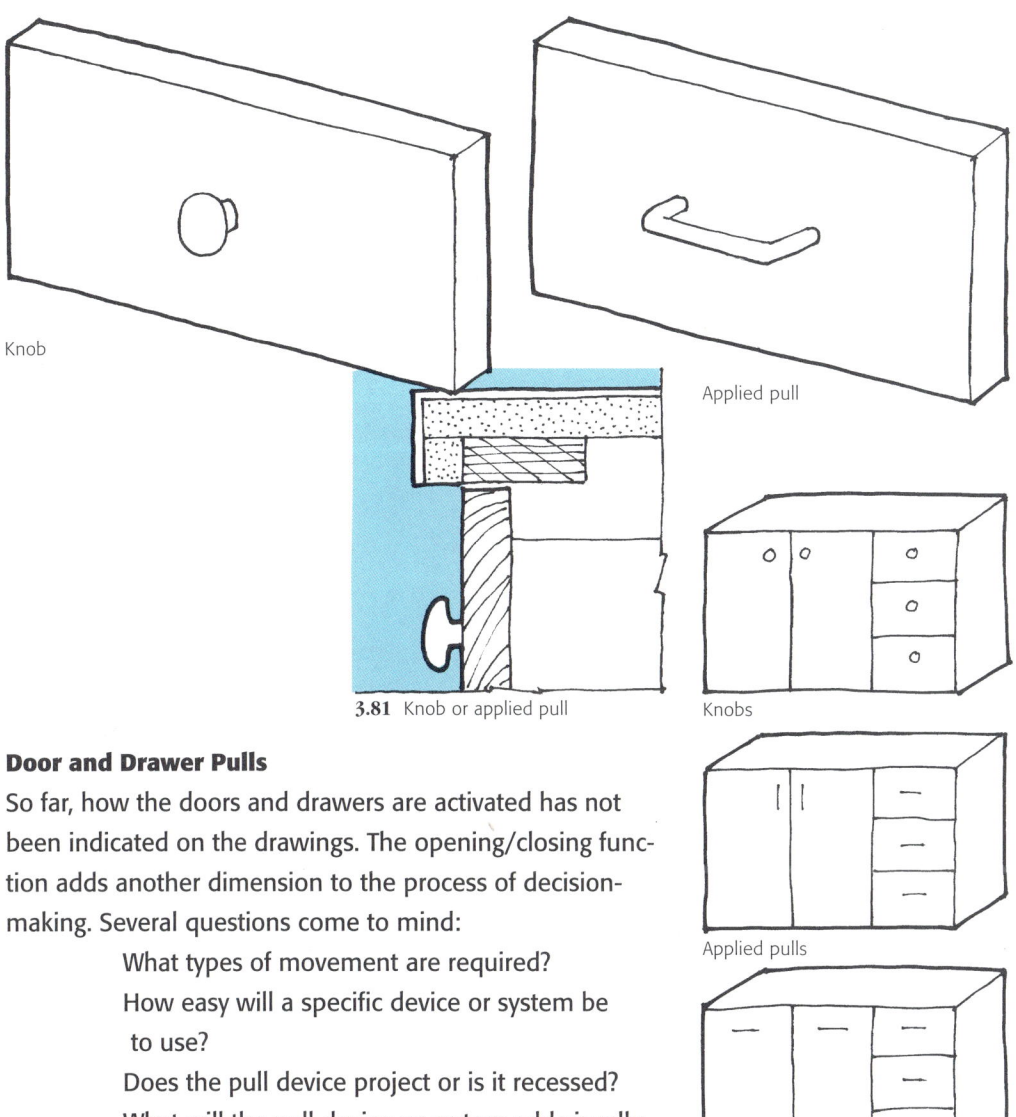

Knob

Applied pull

3.81 Knob or applied pull

Knobs

Applied pulls

Applied pulls, variation

Door and Drawer Pulls

So far, how the doors and drawers are activated has not been indicated on the drawings. The opening/closing function adds another dimension to the process of decision-making. Several questions come to mind:

> What types of movement are required?
> How easy will a specific device or system be to use?
> Does the pull device project or is it recessed?
> What will the pull device or system add visually to the unit?
> How visually prominent do you want it?

The illustrated pulls are fairly generic. There are literally dozens of knobs and applied-type pulls on the market in a fairly wide variety of materials and colors. An important factor in selecting these types is the distance they project from the face of the cabinet. Any pull can be used on a

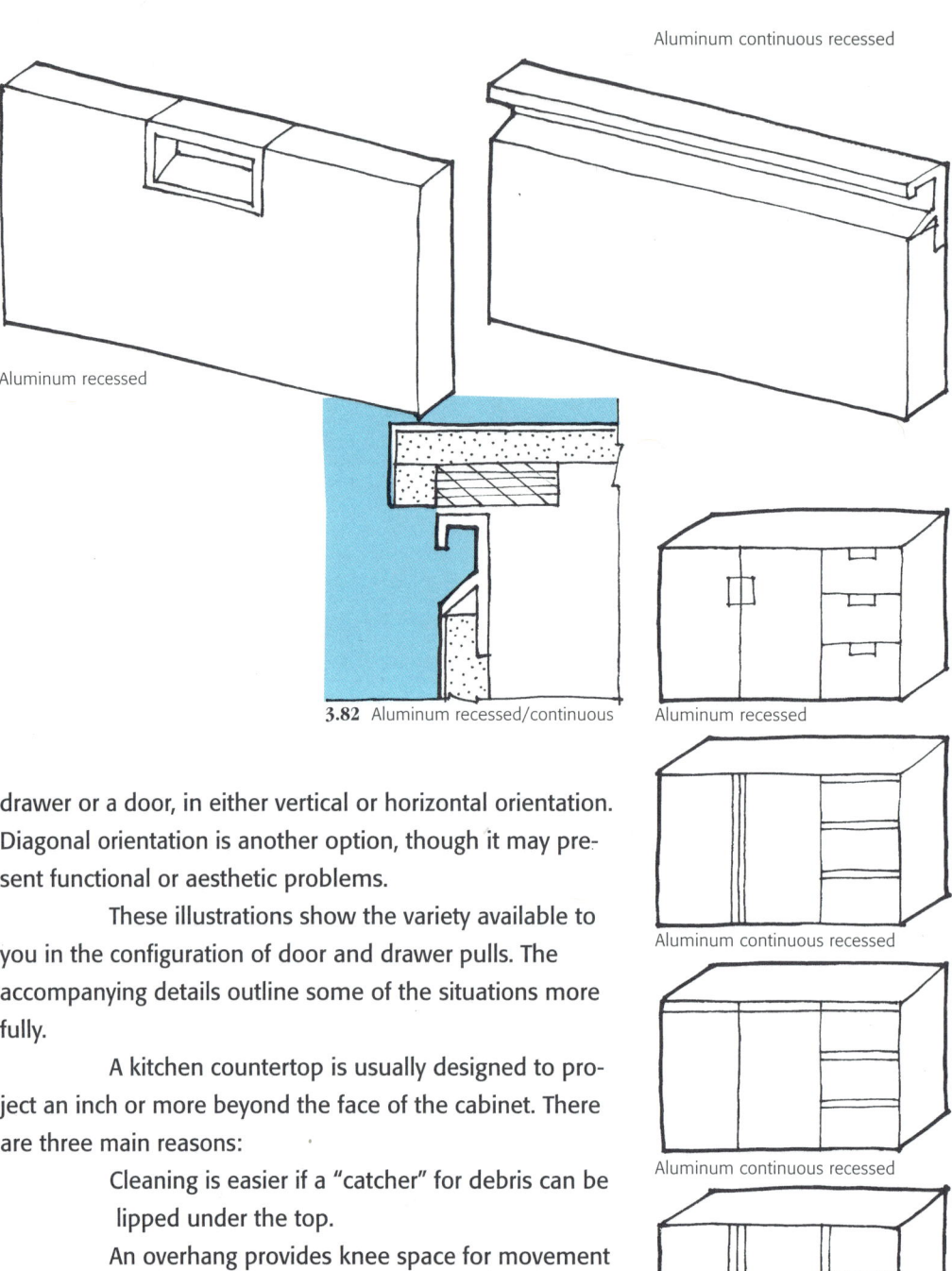

3.82 Aluminum recessed/continuous

drawer or a door, in either vertical or horizontal orientation. Diagonal orientation is another option, though it may present functional or aesthetic problems.

These illustrations show the variety available to you in the configuration of door and drawer pulls. The accompanying details outline some of the situations more fully.

A kitchen countertop is usually designed to project an inch or more beyond the face of the cabinet. There are three main reasons:

- Cleaning is easier if a "catcher" for debris can be lipped under the top.
- An overhang provides knee space for movement beyond the front of the body.
- An overhanging countertop protects users from projecting hardware.

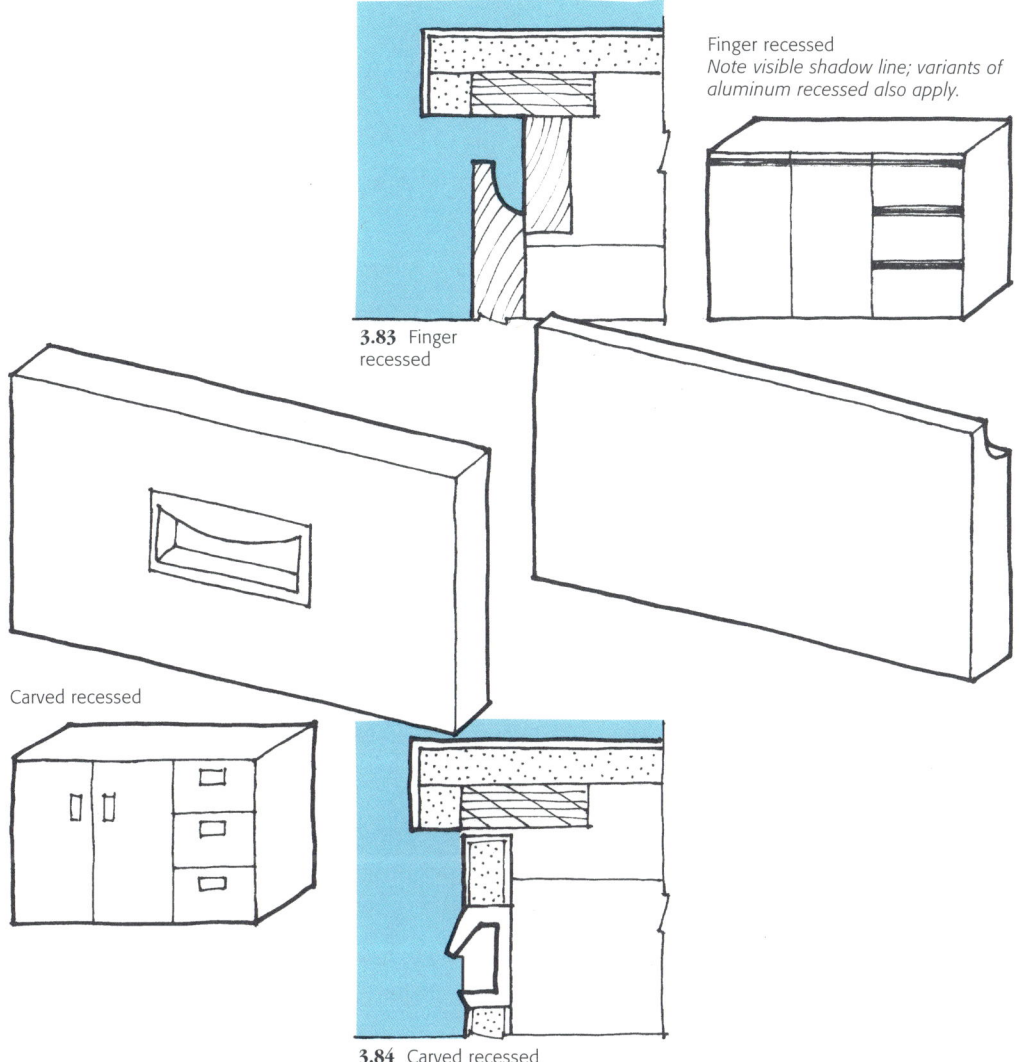

Finger recessed
Note visible shadow line; variants of aluminum recessed also apply.

3.83 Finger recessed

Carved recessed

3.84 Carved recessed

Therefore, the dimension from the front of the cabinet to the front edge of the top is relevant when selecting hardware.

Recessed pulls, on the other hand, do not affect this dimension. If the cabinet is not regularly used as a working counter, designers frequently specify recessed pulls and bring the cabinet face flush with the edge of the countertop—to arrive at a cleaner, sleeker appearance.

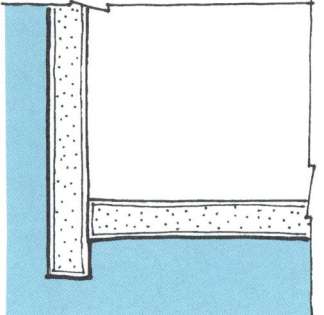

3.85 Finger pull on upper door

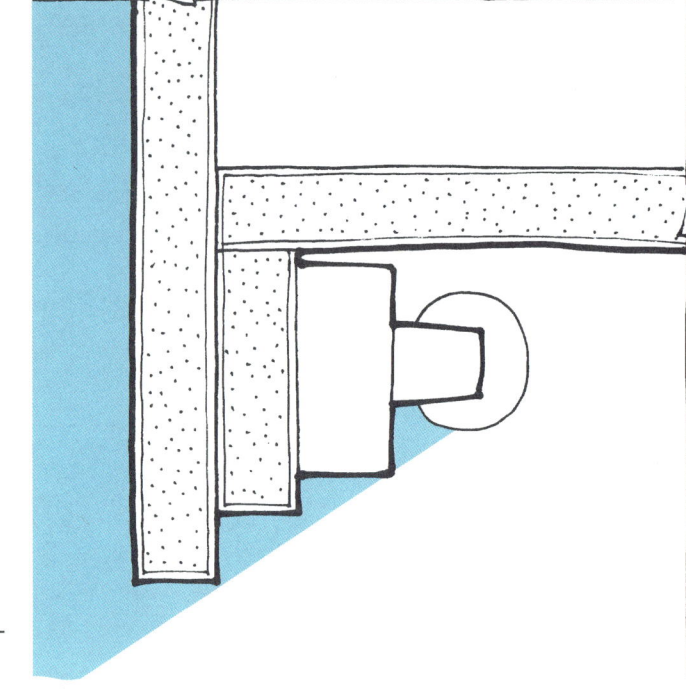

3.86 Upper door with raised shelf for under-cabinet lighting

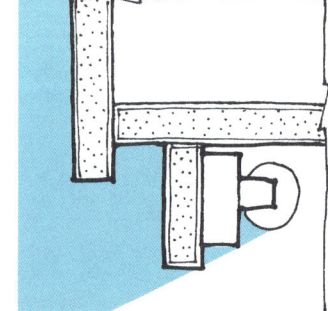

3.87 Variant w/lighting further back

Doors on upper cabinets can easily be treated with finger pulls by lengthening the bottom edge to a point below the underside of the cabinet.

Detail 3.86, a variation of 3.85, shows the bottom shelf raised up to allow for under-cabinet lighting. Positioning lighting near the front edge rather than at the back is less likely to cause veiling reflection on the countertop.

Detail 3.87 is another variation for a slightly different visual effect.

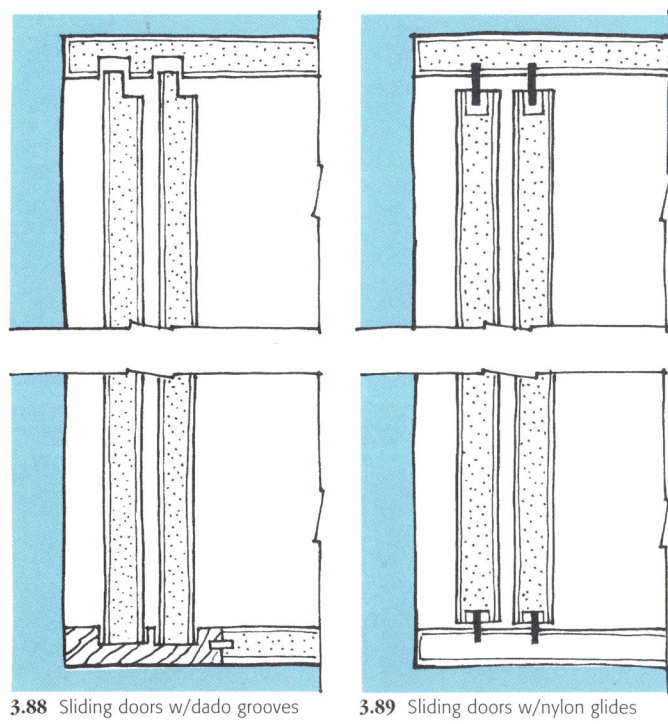

3.88 Sliding doors w/dado grooves

3.89 Sliding doors w/nylon glides

Detail 3.88 is an inexpensive method of accommodating sliding doors. In 3.89 the dark strips are nylon-impregnated fiber which are fitted into grooves in the cabinet. Details 3.90 and 3.91 are two variations using manufactured E-shaped steel and extruded aluminum channels.

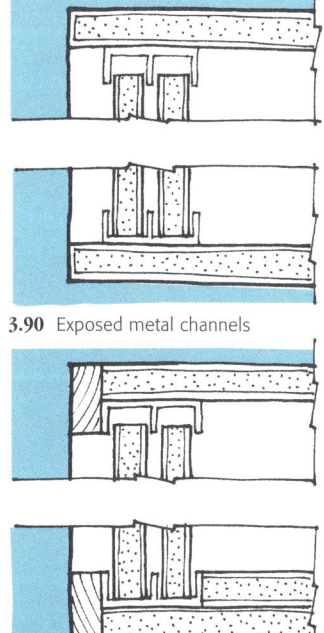

3.90 Exposed metal channels

3.91 Metal channels w/cover strips

Sliding Doors   There may be instances when you might find sliding doors preferable to hinged doors. Here are some of the various ways to detail for sliders.

Detail 3.88 is fairly typical of an inexpensive method of accommodating sliding doors. The bottom piece should be solid wood so that dado grooves can be smooth and, because one of the doors is set back so as to slide behind the other, there is also a fair amount of this piece showing. The grooves may be sanded smooth and waxed for good sliding, or a vinyl channel can be installed in each groove. There must be enough room between the top of the door and the upper groove to provide clearance when lifting the door free from the bottom groove while installing or removing the doors.

In 3.89 the dark strips are nylon-impregnated fiber which are fitted into grooves in the cabinet. Two or three "shoes" of matching material, a couple of inches wide, are inserted in the bottom edges of the doors. These pieces have been formed with a concave slot which rides on top of the strips inset into the grooves. Usually the upper strips are not glued in place but are simply a "tight fit." This allows them to be taken out when the doors are installed or removed. Variations 3.90 and 3.91 show manufactured E-shaped steel and extruded aluminum channels. Hardware units with ball bearings are also available for heavier doors and for use with glass doors.

Tambour Doors

Tambour door is the name given to the type of enclosure with which we're familiar on roll-top desks—interlocking strips of wood which slide up or aside into a hidden pocket, revealing the cabinet interior. Today's tambour door is made of either a manufactured door material or a custom-designed one. Wood, plastic laminate, or metal laminate strips may be glued to a canvas backing sheet, or plastic strips may be designed to interlock. As well, some plastic laminate manufacturers offer lines of factory-made tambour door materials.

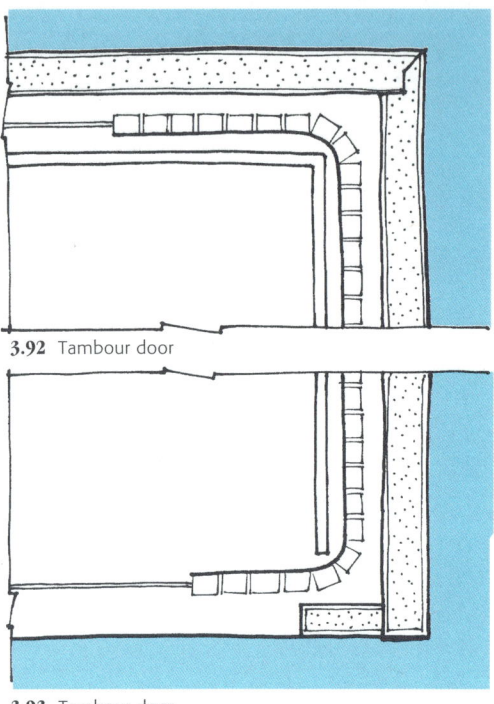

3.92 Tambour door

3.93 Tambour door

There are some basic details about tambour doors that you should keep in mind. While the details here are shown in plan view, they could be rotated into vertical view and still apply.

Details 3.92 and 3.93 show the groove which holds the tambour door, and the inner case. The curve for the groove will be dictated by the turning radius required by the door design you have chosen or devised. An inner case is advisable so that objects stored within the cabinet do not interfere with the smooth operation of the door. An optional cover strip is shown to point out the view down the side, which you might want to obscure.

Details below illustrate that there is a variety of profiles available to you in designing such a door.

 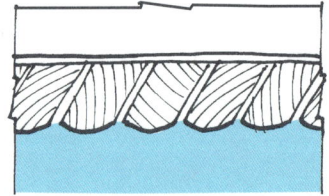 

3.94 Tambour slats

3.95 Metal shelf standard **3.96** Plastic shelf standard **3.97** Bored holes for pin shelf-rest

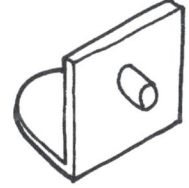

Adjustable Shelves Since it is not always possible to know the height of all the objects that might be stored in a cabinet it has become common practice to use adjustable shelves in at least some part of the unit.

Detail 3.95 illustrates a flush-mounted, steel shelf standard with adjustable support clips. The slots are usually on 1" centers. This system is available for surface mounting as well. Detail 3.96 shows a plastic strip that is simply hammered into a groove. Self-locking plastic clips are used with it.

Detail 3.97 shows a system in which precise holes are drilled in a vertical line for the pin-type shelf brackets. The advantage of this system is that you can decide at what increments you want to place the holes; they need to be drilled only where they would be useful. . . a space of one or two inches between shelves is not normally of any value. Frequently a metal grommet is inserted into each hole to prevent wear.

The advantage is that either system is readily available; your choice can be relative to the requirements of your project.

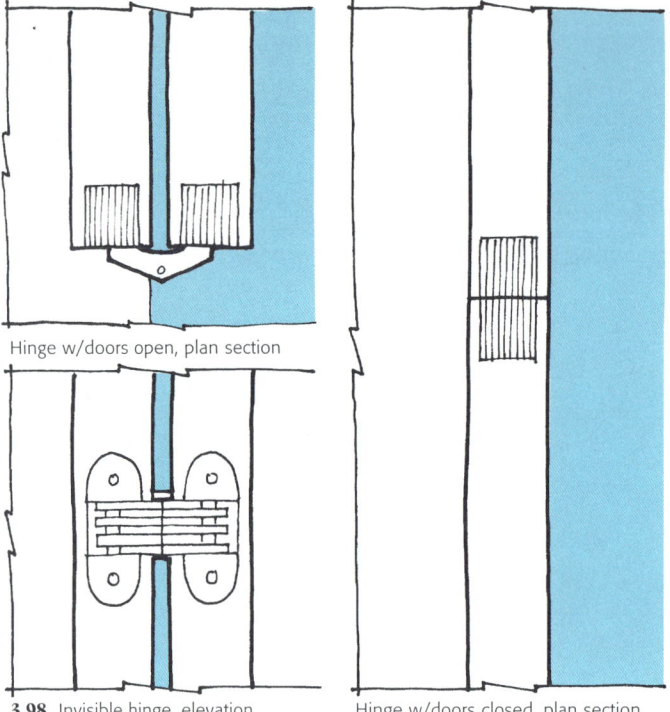

Hinge w/doors open, plan section

3.98 Invisible hinge, elevation

Hinge w/doors closed, plan section

The invisible hinge is inserted into the edges of the door and adjacent frame. It is completely concealed when the door is closed.

Hardware There are cabinetry hardware catalogs that are thicker than this book, and a vast array of general and specialized manufacturers. It is intriguing to leaf through the catalogs, assessing the various pieces, and trying to figure out ingenious ways of using them.

Here we describe a few basic types of hinges and closures. Whichever method you choose for hanging and holding open or securing the doors on your cabinet will have a profound effect on the design of the details.

The pivot hinge exposes the tip and pivot point either at the top and bottom of the door or in saw cuts on the hinged edge of the door.

Pivot hinge, plan

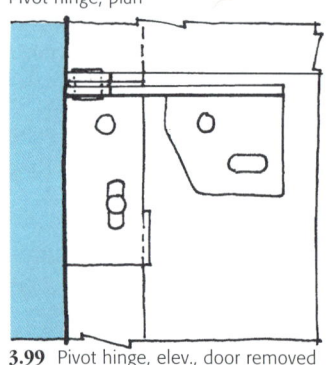

3.99 Pivot hinge, elev., door removed

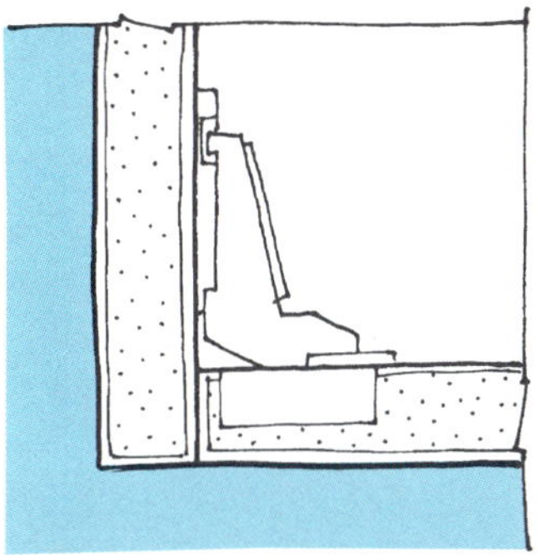

3.100 Inset adjustable hinge in plan

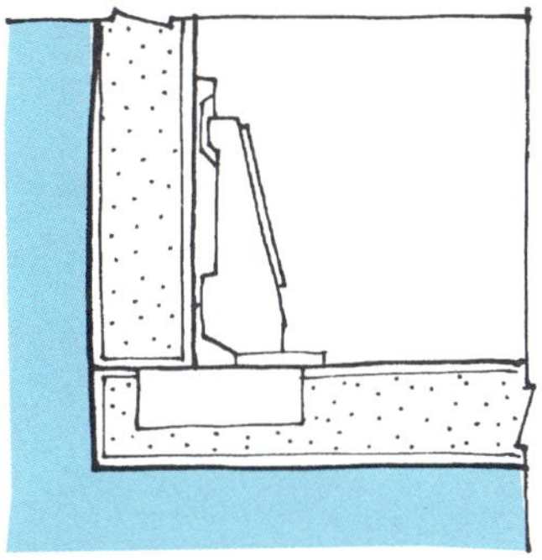

3.101 Overlay adjustable hinge

Another style of concealed hinge, 3.100–.101, is available for use with many door-to-frame constructions, allowing openings from 90° to 180°, with or without door close-and-stop capabilities. A door catch is not required with this style of hinge. A variety of mounting blocks for the cabinets allow different door-to-case configurations.

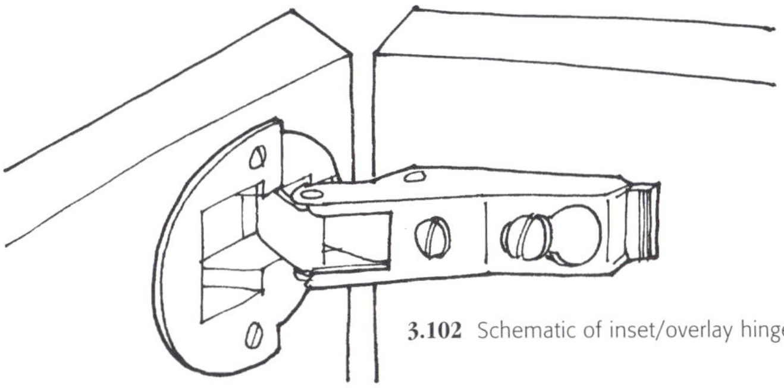

3.102 Schematic of inset/overlay hinge

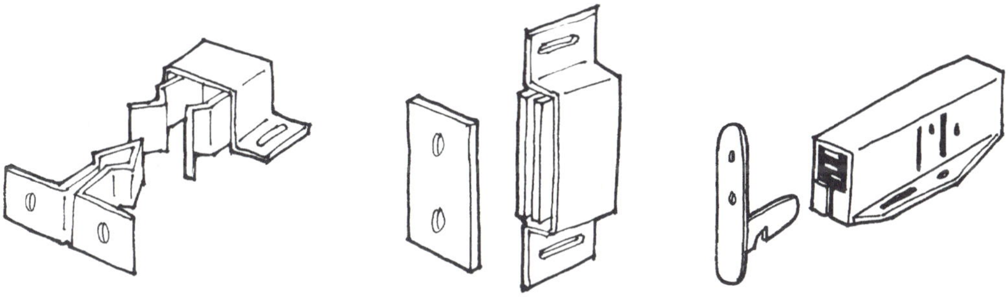

3.103 Friction catch

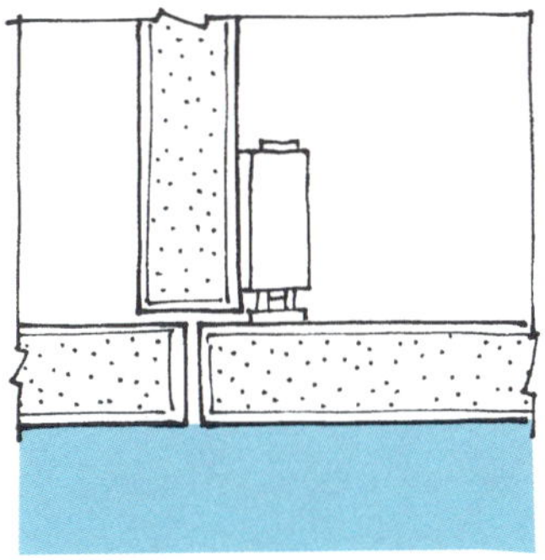

3.104 Magnetic catch

3.105 Touch latch

In the friction catch, above, the striker is fixed to the back of the door while the spring-clip holder is attached to the cabinet.

In magnetic catches like the one shown above, the striker plate is attached to the door and the magnetic unit is attached to the cabinet.

In the touch latch the body of the unit is attached to the cabinet and the striker is mounted on the back of the door. A push on the face of the door forces the striker into the unit, releasing a spring which pushes the door open. Another gentle push on the door catches the striker in closed position again.

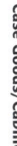

Case Goods/Cabinetry

79

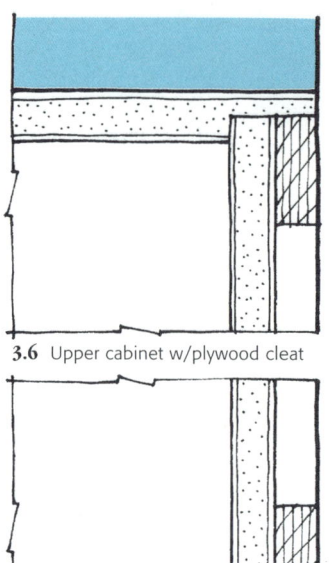

3.6 Upper cabinet w/plywood cleat

3.7 Lower cabinet w/plywood cleat

Wall-Hung Units

In the basic kitchen cabinetry shown at the beginning of this chapter, the upper cabinet is a wall-hung unit. The typical details at the rear top and bottom (3.6–.7, page 49) are repeated for reference above.

The framing members that are fixed to the wall are often referred to as *cleats.* You will note that the top edge of the cabinet covers the cleat with the same detail as the bottom edge. Since the top is well above eye level, this detail is not necessary for visual effect but is less expensive to do since the machinery is already set up to mill the bottom.

In wall-hung units where the top is exposed to view it is necessary to conceal the supports. The cleats are fixed securely to the wall, with the outer face true vertical; the cabinets are then securely attached to the cleats.

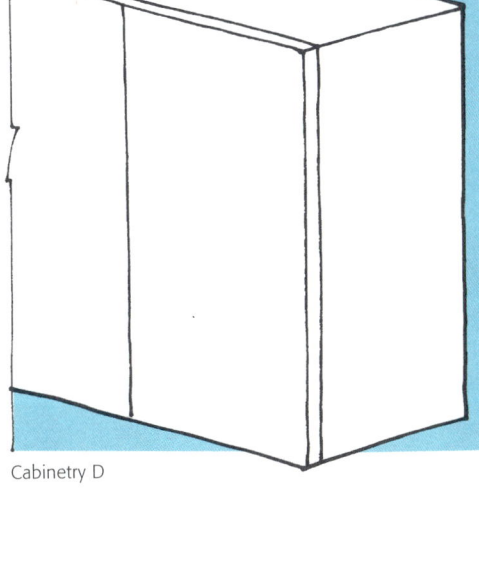
Cabinetry D

Cabinetry E

Details 3.6–.7 on the facing page then become typical for lightweight wall hung units, that is, light in their own weight and neither subjected to heavy weight inside the unit nor heavy pressure on the top. Lightweight construction such as this is usually used on cabinetry that is higher than it is deep, such as **cabinetry D.**

The greater the cantilever out from the wall, such as **cabinetry E,** the heavier a framing system required— 2 x 4s instead of 1 x 4s.

Thus, cabinetry D could be constructed with details 3.6–.7, and cabinetry E might require details 3.106–.107 which have the added support of 2 x 4 cleats. If further strengthening is necessary, metal brackets could be used instead of cleats.

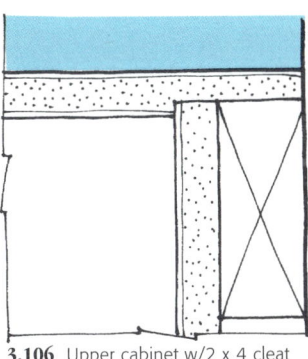
3.106 Upper cabinet w/2 x 4 cleat

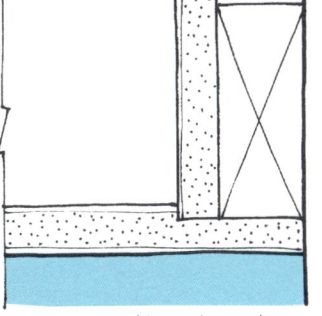
3.107 Lower cabinet w/2 x 4 cleat

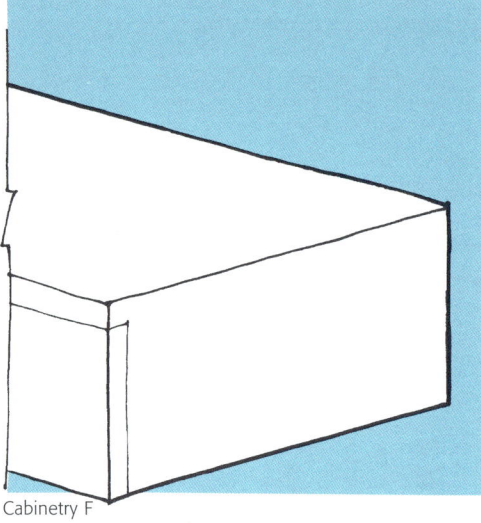

Cabinetry F

In cabinetry F the cantilever is great, that is, the depth of the unit is much greater than its height, and it is hung low enough that a visitor might decide to sit on it, which makes some form of steel support necessary.

The steel angles in 3.108 could be continuous or could be 3"-wide pieces installed approximately every two feet along the length of the unit. The T-brackets in 3.109 and 3.110 would be placed at suitable intervals in the same manner.

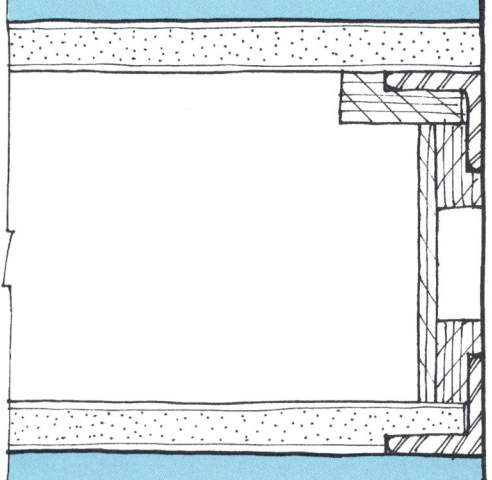

3.108 Cantilevered cabinet with steel angles and cleats

Detail 3.108 shows the use of two steel angles, one at top, one at bottom, each fixed securely to the wall, then the cabinet fixed to the angles.

The details at right illustrate the use of T-brackets which are fixed securely to the wall and extend well out under the cabinet top, 3.109, or shelf top, 3.110.

Because they are generic, the details on these pages lack information where cabinets meet walls, and regarding wall construction. The detail for cabinet-to-wall installation could be scribed as shown in 3.108 and 3.109, or have a recess, 3.113, or applied molding, 3.114. The choice of scribing detail may depend on your specifications for the wall finish. This will be discussed further in chapter 5, page 119. The selection of support system may depend on the construction of the wall, a subject which will be investigated in chapter 4.

Support variations other than those shown here are possible. The plumbing "chair", for instance, is extremely strong. It is composed of a T-bracket at the intended top edge, a pipe support extending from there down to the floor, and a T-bracket foot which is usually cast into the flooring material. Everything is concealed within the wall and floor construction except for any T-brackets which are used to support the object.

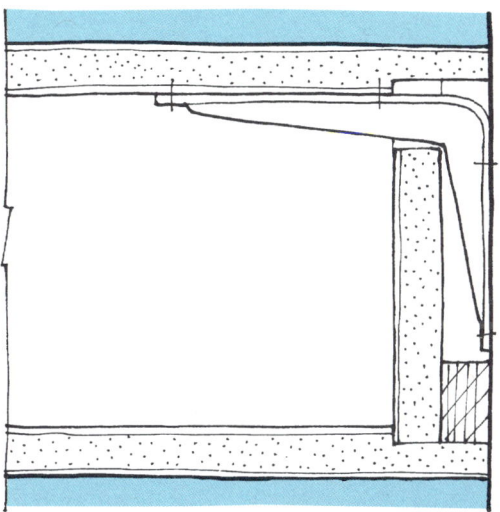
3.109 Cantilevered cabinet with T-bracket and cleat

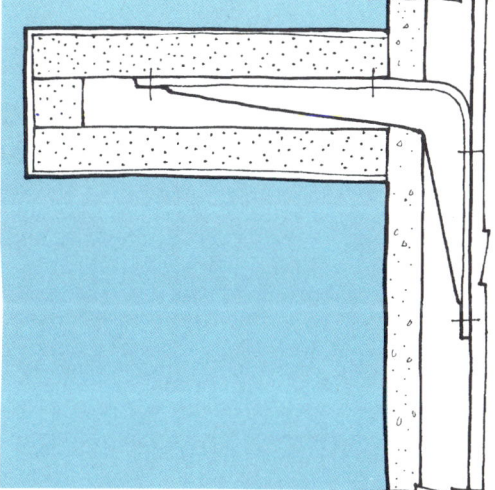
3.110 Cantilevered shelf with T-bracket

3.111 Cabinet-to-wall w/recess

3.112 Cabinet-to-wall w/molding

If you wish to have the cabinets demountable there are several possibilities open. The previous support systems could be used, with nuts and bolts rather than more permanent attachments. One of the following could also be used.

In detail 3.113, a shaped wood cleat, A, is fixed to the back of the unit and slides down to lock on cleat B, which is fixed to the wall. Cleats A and B are usually continuous across the length of the unit. Detail 3.114 shows a metal clip, C, fixed to the back of the unit, with a bracket, D, fixed to the wall. Sets of C and D are suitably spaced along the length of the unit; in any case no fewer than two would be used.

On occasion, designers have chosen to wall-hang both the upper and lower cabinets in kitchens. Using this method for lower cabinets obviously does away with the base. The bottom edge of the lower cabinet is usually raised eight or nine inches from the floor so that a greater floating effect is created (and for ease of cleaning).

By using a demountable support system, it is possible to adjust the height of the cabinet top to suit the user. A tall person might want a countertop higher than the standard 36", while a short person or one confined to a wheelchair might prefer or need a lower work-top. Flexible

3.113 Locking wood cleats

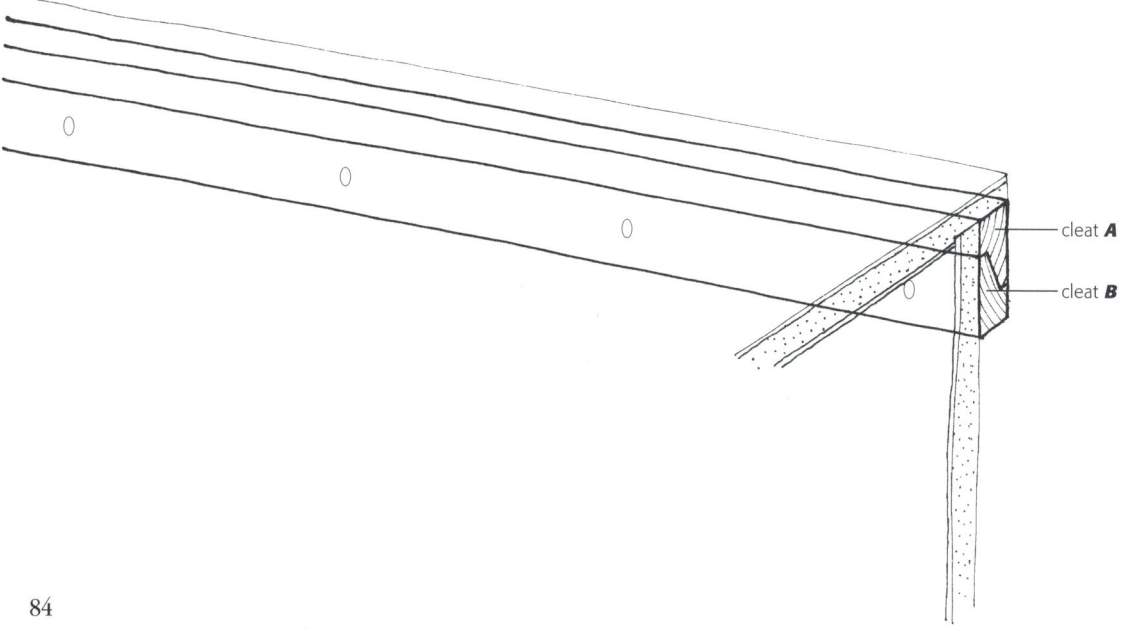

attachments for water and sink pipes are available for use in such cabinets.

Before detailing demountable kitchen cabinetry, several factors should be considered.

- It is more expensive.
- The adjacent wall treatment must be taken into account.
- The scribing detail would most likely be the reveal type.
- The cabinets would have to be modular.
- The counter tops would likely be in several pieces, which would require a non-solidifying type of caulking for the joints.

These factors are given here not to discourage you from using demountable cabinetry but to remind you that careful consideration and research is required before making a decision on the idea.

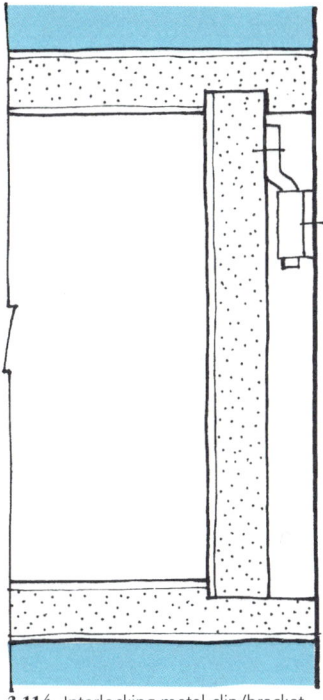
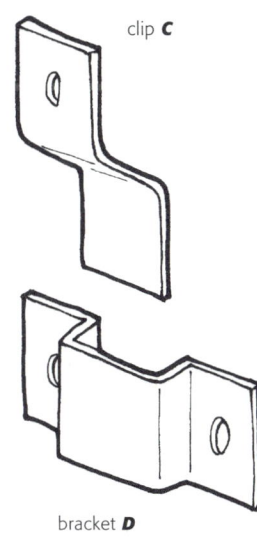

clip **C**

bracket **D**

3.114 Interlocking metal clip/bracket

Connections: Floors/Walls/Ceilings

CHAPTER 4

**ince this is a book on interior detailing** rather than on building construction the following details on floors, walls, and ceilings will be generic. There are many possible flooring and ceiling constructions; some are more likely to appear in residential projects, others in commercial. For our purposes, we refer mainly to the finish portions. Study the details, understand them, and you will be able to apply the knowledge regardless of the project type or location.

The significance of these details is in their similarities and differences. The three basic floor types show flat surfaces for receiving finish floor materials. Detail 4.2 uses wood, probably particle board, as a subfloor, which can be damaged by certain liquids and may need reinforcing if the applied finish is heavy or cannot withstand flexing, for example a stone or ceramic tile floor. In contrast, details 4.4 and 4.6, having concrete as a subfloor, are impervious to liquids and are very strong.

Details 4.1, top, and 4.2, bottom, show wood ceiling joists, a 2 x 4 wood stud wall, and subflooring on wood joists—typical of *residential* construction.

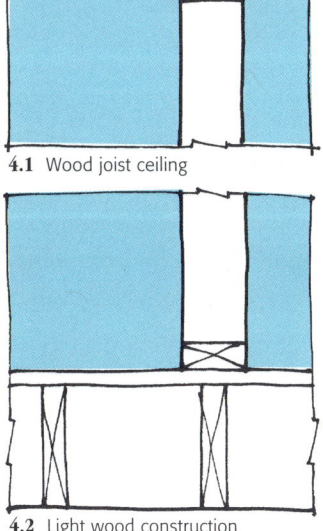

4.1 Wood joist ceiling

4.2 Light wood construction

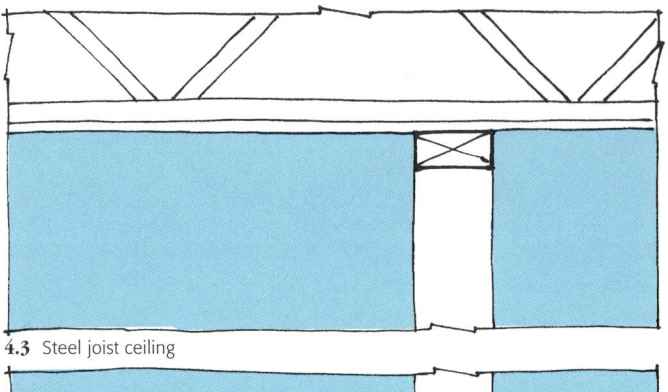

4.3 Steel joist ceiling

In the detail at the left, 4.3, top, and 4.4, bottom, show a steel joist, a wood stud wall, a concrete floor on steel pan over steel joists—typical of *light commercial* construction.

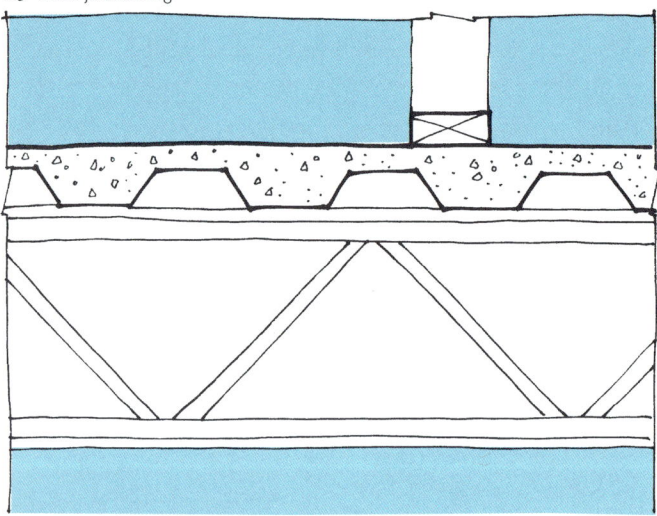

4.4 Light commercial construction

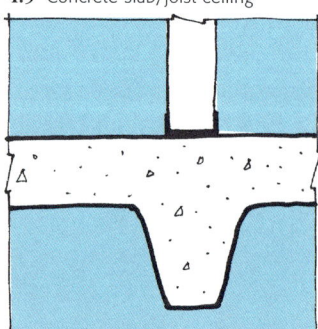

4.5 Concrete slab/joist ceiling

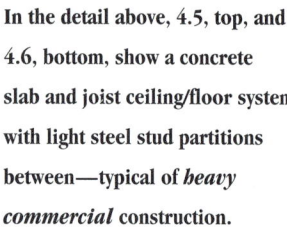

4.6 Heavy-duty construction

In the detail above, 4.5, top, and 4.6, bottom, show a concrete slab and joist ceiling/floor system with light steel stud partitions between—typical of *heavy commercial* construction.

In detail 4.3, where the underside of steel joists is the ceiling location, the ceiling must be wired to the bottom of the joist or hung on wires from the underside of the floor above. The latter method would also be used for the concrete slab/joist system as shown in 4.5. These methods allow many design possibilities regarding the form and height of ceilings as well as their corner relationships to adjacent walls. Not nearly as flexible to design concerns is detail 4.1, where the underside of ceiling joists is wood, and the ceiling finish is normally applied directly to it.

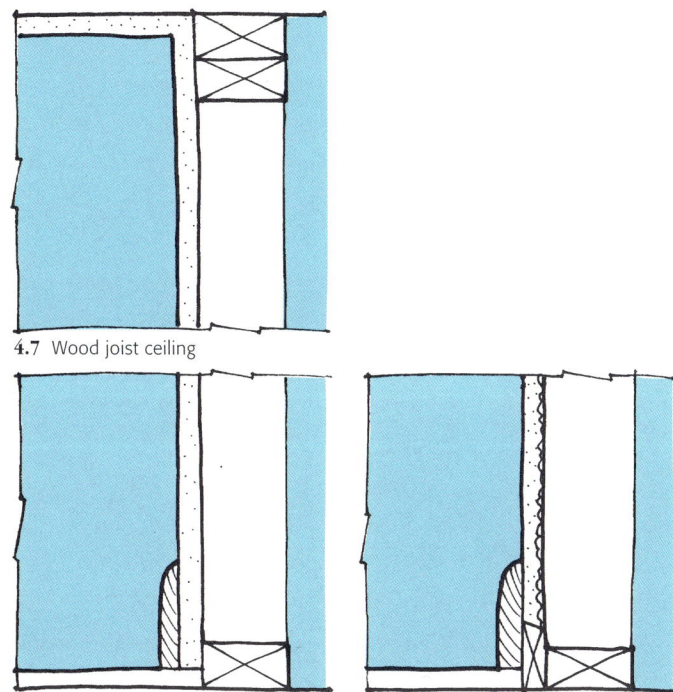

4.7 Wood joist ceiling

In the details at right, 4.7 and 4.8 show typical drywall finishes. Detail 4.9 shows a wall-to-floor variation, with wet plaster and wood baseboard.

4.8 Drywall finish

4.9 Wet plaster finish

Light wood construction, so typical of residential construction, is the subject of our first discussion in this chapter.

The finishes described in details 4.7 and 4.8 are applicable to 4.1 and 4.2. On the wood 2 x 4 wall and on the wood joist ceiling the finish indicated is gypsum board, commonly called *drywall*. (The term drywall refers to a dry finish for a wall, as opposed to plaster which is a wet finish.) Any installation where gypsum board is used is referred to as drywall, even if it is a ceiling: confusing until you become accustomed to it.

The ceiling-to-wall connection would look the same whether done in drywall or applied wet plaster. The wall-to-floor connection for wet plaster would be slightly altered, as shown in 4.9. The shaped block fixed to the wall frame at the bottom edge of the plaster is called a *screed* or *plaster stop*. Its purpose is to provide a surface guide to which the plaster can be leveled. It is attached with its beveled edge facing the wall, which holds the plaster against the wall structure and stops the plaster edge from crumbling away.

The drywall in 4.8 might be 3/8", 1/2", or 3/4"—usually a double layer of 3/8". The plaster in 4.9 might be three layers of plaster on metal lath, totalling 3/4" in thickness, or 3/8" plaster on 3/8" gypsum lath for a total of 3/4".

Baseboards

A baseboard is used for several reasons: it conceals the connection and finishing where wall meets floor; it protects the wall finish from damage by floor cleaning devices such as mops, brooms, and vacuum cleaners, and it provides a finished appearance.

Any change of plane, material, color, or finish on a wall creates a visible line, often referred to as a design line. A baseboard creates such a line; its height, depth, shape, and color have a visual effect. Heights of baseboards vary, but are usually between 2 1/2" and 6".

Detail 4.9 shows an **applied baseboard** in wood, which could be plain or molded as in traditional interiors. Detail 4.10 shows an applied rubber or vinyl baseboard.

Detail 4.11 illustrates a **flush baseboard,** showing a reveal between the top of the baseboard and the finish surface of the drywall. This gives a slightly different, somewhat less dominant, appearance than that in 4.9. Note that the reveal occurs against the inner sheet of drywall and that the edge of the drywall has been protected with a J-stop, a piece of bent thin metal which runs continuously along the lower edge, concealing the drywall's cut edge and protecting it from damage. The baseboard could abut the J-stop but the line where they meet would be apparent and would look like a crack in the wall. To prevent this, a reveal is often used. This deliberate design approach is sometimes referred to as "designed-in cracks," as opposed to unplanned but predictable cracks, and is particularly necessary for plaster, which is hand-applied when wet and therefore never perfectly straight.

Detail 4.12 shows a **recessed baseboard.** Again the lower edge of the plaster or drywall needs to be protected with a J-stop, but a reveal is unnecessary because the butt connection (where the bottom of the wall finish

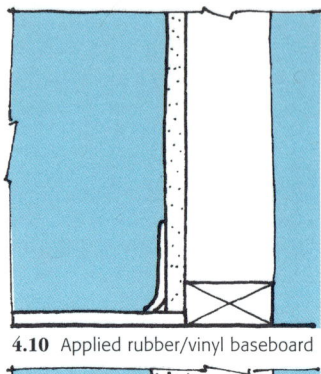

4.10 Applied rubber/vinyl baseboard

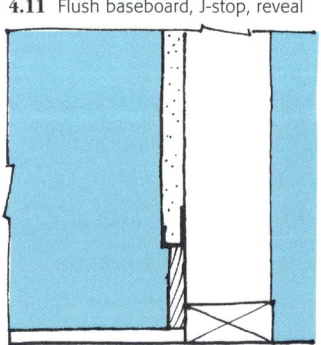

4.11 Flush baseboard, J-stop, reveal

4.12 Recessed baseboard, J-stop

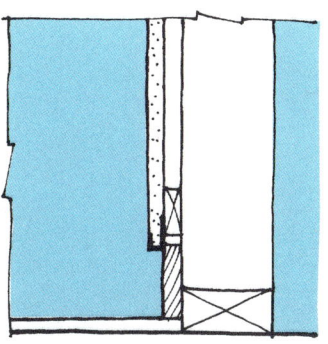

4.14 Recessed baseboard

The drywall shown above has been built out from the wall structure on strapping so that the baseboard may be recessed. Strapping is usually 3/4" solid wood or plywood, 2 1/2" or 3 1/2" wide and applied horizontally at 16" centers. (An explanation of strapping occurs on page 96.)

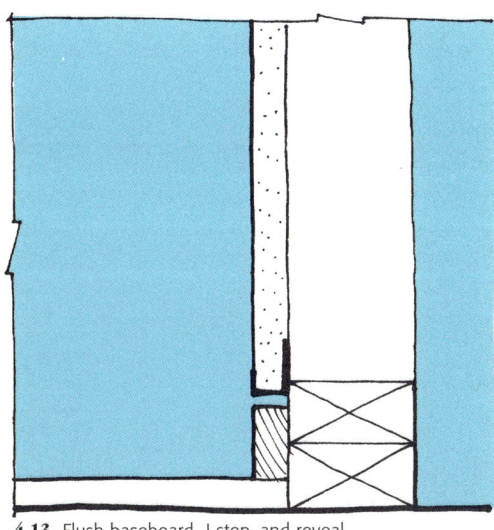

4.13 Flush baseboard, J-stop, and reveal

In detail 4.13, above, a double plate has been used at the bottom of the wall construction to act as a back-up for the reveal. The face of the reveal could be painted, veneered, or covered with plastic laminate, a metal strip, or other material. Another variation would be to fit a metal or vinyl channel into the reveal.

meets the baseboard) is out of sight. This detail calls even greater attention than the previous detail to the line of the wall bottom and plays down the existence of the baseboard. Do a small three-dimensional sketch of each of these three baseboard details and notice how the plane relationship of the baseboard to the wall changes the visual effect and the order of dominance of the elements in each.

In both 4.11 and 4.12 the thicknesses of the wall finish material and the baseboard must be taken into account. For instance, if a single layer of 3/8" or 1/2" drywall is being used then the construction might have to change to provide sufficient backing. Examine details 4.13 and 4.14 to see how this might be handled.

Ceiling-to-Wall Connections

The ceiling-to-wall connection may be a simple right-angle butt joint as was shown in 4.7. This is the easiest and most common treatment. However, as with baseboards, it is possible to vary the treatment at the top of the wall. Just as it is possible to use a molded baseboard, so it is possible to make the upper corner connection with a crown molding or other traditional shape.

There are more possibilities for varying the ceiling-to-wall connection where a hung ceiling is used, as is the case in most commercial spaces. But first let us look at wall constructions which support the finishes and connections.

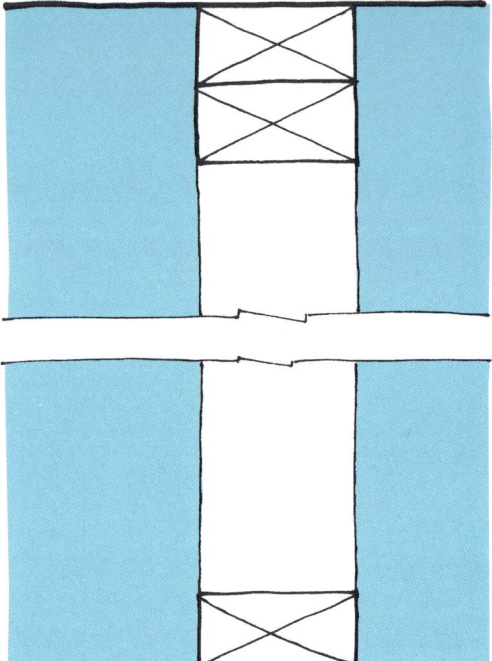

4.15 Wood stud wall construction

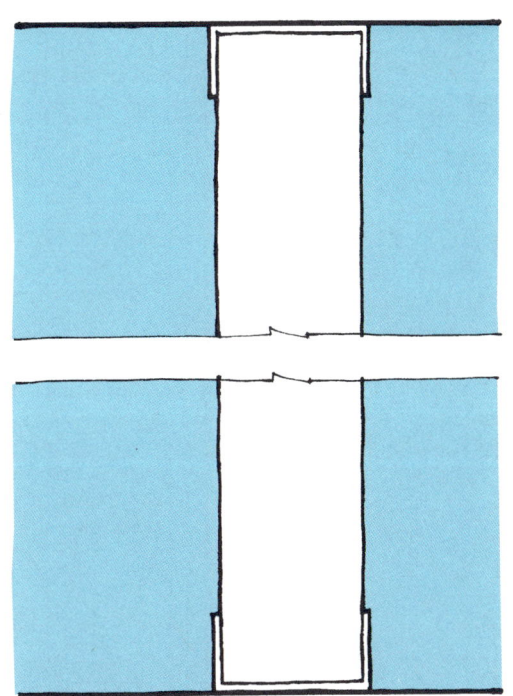

4.16 Steel stud wall construction

Basic Commercial Wall Construction

The three most common basic partition constructions for commercial spaces are shown here and on the following page. Each is a nominal 4" thick; remember that 2 x 4s are actually 1 1/2" x 3 1/2".

Wood studs (4.15) are used in the same manner as in residential construction—vertical 2 x 4s at 16" centers, firmly toe-nailed into 2 x 4s which have been nailed to the joists. **Steel studs** (4.16) are 1 1/2" x 3 1/2" and sit inside runner channels screwed or nailed to the floor below and the joists above. The steel stud is simply a C-shaped light steel channel manufactured to replace the wood stud. It is lightweight, easy to install, and fireproof. However, its light weight can also be a disadvantage: it forms a rather flimsy wall that in many instances, other than in ordinary wall construction, needs extra bracing.

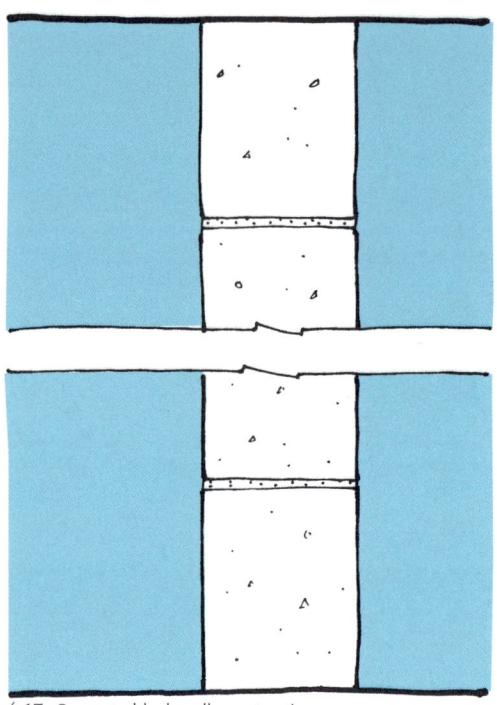
4.17 Concrete block wall construction

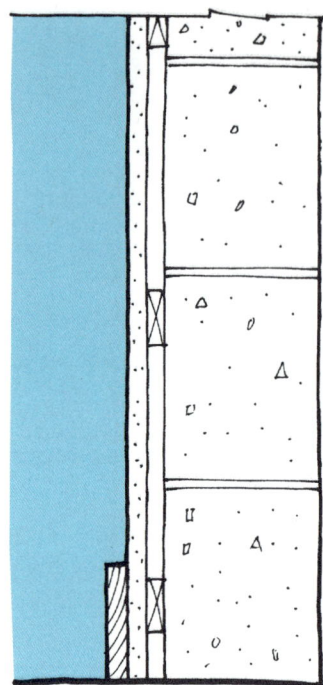
4.18 Strapping on concrete block

Concrete blocks (4.17), even the so-called "lightweight" type, are massive, heavy, and strong. A concrete block partition is laid in place by hand, seldom producing a smooth, even, perfectly vertical wall, and thus needs the addition of a layer of **strapping** between the wall and the finishing material; this is usually 1 x 2, 1 x 3, or 1 x 4 strips of wood or plywood which are nailed onto the concrete blocks at 12" or 16" centers either horizontally, vertically, or in both directions, depending on the requirements of the finish material. Strapping is shimmed with tapered pieces of wood (usually pieces of wooden shingles) until the front face is true and vertical. Sometimes, to avoid adding the thickness of strapping, strips of wood are laid into the edge of the mortar joint between blocks, and then used as nailing points. This is not as effective a system, however, since it may not correct the unevenness of the wall.

Apart from the leveling requirement, nailing into

Conventional strapping is horizontally applied to a concrete block wall, with applied drywall and baseboard.

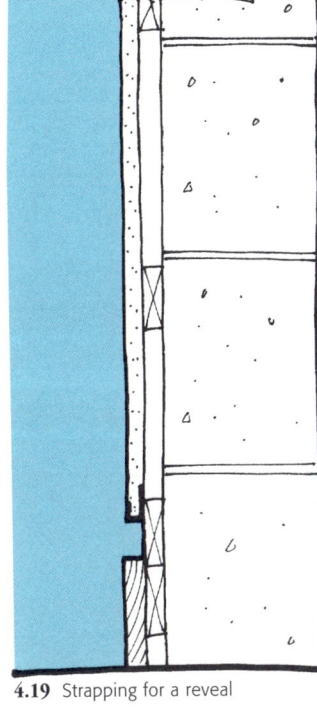

4.19 Strapping for a reveal

4.20 Strapping for baseboard recess

For a recessed baseboard such as at left, the strapping for the baseboard may be the usual 3/4" thick (expressed as 1x—"one by"–but actually cut to the smaller dimension) but the strapping for the wall surface material must be of 2x so that it protrudes beyond the baseboard. Obviously this is a slightly more expensive detail. However, don't be discouraged from using it since the cost of your baseboard and/or wall material may be flexible enough to make the detail cost insignificant.

The detail above is similar to 4.18 but has an extra row of strapping applied as back-up for a reveal.

concrete block requires a great deal of force (usually with a power gun). This would damage the face of any material being secured so the strapping also acts as a cushioned nailing strip and prevents damage to the finished surface material.

Deciding which wall construction to use depends on a variety of factors:

    Fire rating requirements
    Acoustic factors such as sound transmission loss,
     attenuation, reverberation, and so on
    Desired finish treatment
    Planned wall fixtures and attachments
    Height
    Permanence

Baseboard details for a steel stud wall would be essentially the same as details 4.8 through 4.14 for wood stud construction. Examine 4.18 to 4.20 when detailing for baseboards applied to a strapped concrete block wall.

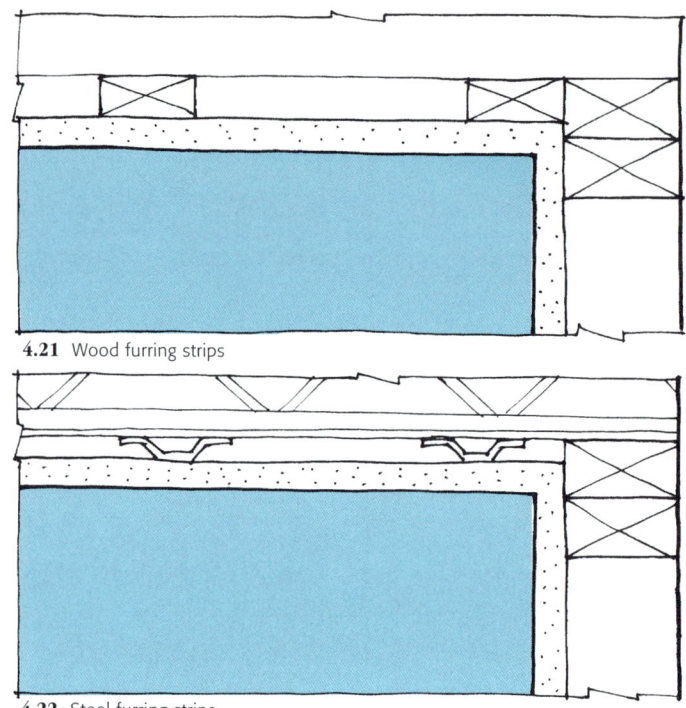

4.21 Wood furring strips

4.22 Steel furring strips

In detail 4.21, wood furring strips mounted between the wood joist and the ceiling material allow tracks for lighting or drapery to be recessed into the ceiling. The detail indicates 1x furring but this dimension can be increased to suit requirements.

Detail 4.22 is used infrequently since steel joists are usually installed further from the floor than the traditional ceiling height to permit mechanical ducts to run between the joists and the ceiling.

Ceilings For residential ceilings, the finish material may be applied directly onto the bottom of the ceiling joists. However if more distance is required between the underside of the joists and the ceiling finish material either furring strips are added or a suspended ceiling system is used. Details 4.21 and 4.22 show wood and steel furring strip installations; these may be used interchangeably unless fire codes require the use of steel. Commercial ceilings however are usually hung on steel wires some distance below the bottom of the joists.

Basic Suspended Ceiling Systems

Before investigating ceiling-to-wall details further, you need to know something about the types of ceiling systems that have been devised to suspend ceilings in commercial construction.

Basically, ceiling components are hung from steel wires fastened to the underside of a floor (or roof) structure above. If the construction is concrete, ring nails are fired into the concrete with a "ram set" power gun. (A ring nail is simply a nail with a ring on the head.) Steel wires are then inserted into each ring and twisted, much as a twist-tie on a trash bag. If it is steel joist construction, the wire is wrapped around the bottom chord of the joist and twist-tied. The wires are then cut to a suitable length, allowing the ceiling to be suspended at the appropriate height with enough wire left to twist-tie around the ceiling suspension members.

The suspension members have various names but essentially are two types, carrying channels and furring channels. Carrying channels are usually 3/4" x 1 1/2", are attached to the steel wires, are spaced on approximately 4' centers, and carry the weight of the ceiling. The furring channels may be 3/4" x 3/4", are installed 2' apart at right angles to the carrying channels and are wire-clipped to them. The ceiling material is then attached to the underside of the furring channels.

There are many variations of concealed, semi-concealed, recessed, and exposed bar systems as well as other ceiling material systems. Virtually all ceiling systems will be variations of 4.23 to 4.25. Reference books and manufacturers' catalogs are excellent sources for information on options.

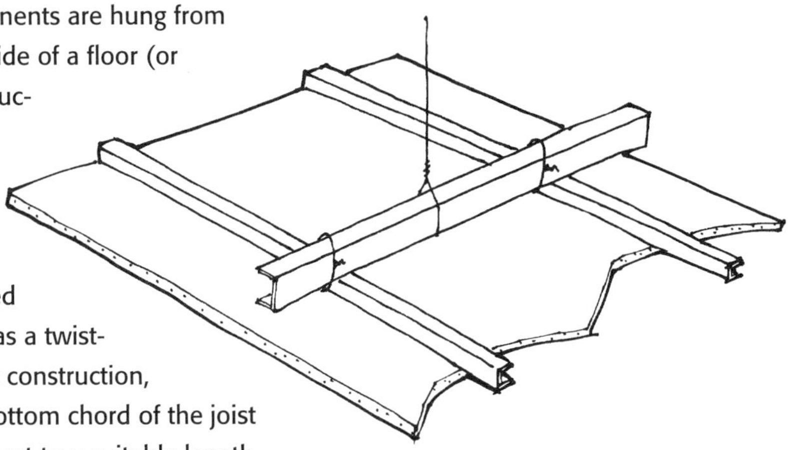

4.23 Suspended drywall ceiling

This detail shows a suspended ceiling in which drywall is screwed onto the underside of the furring channels. The furring channels are wire-clipped to the carrying channels that are wired to the slab above. The ceiling's connection to the wall may be taped and filled as in any joint between pieces of drywall, or a reveal may be used, similar to the ones that are discussed for the other ceiling systems.

4.24a Section at wall

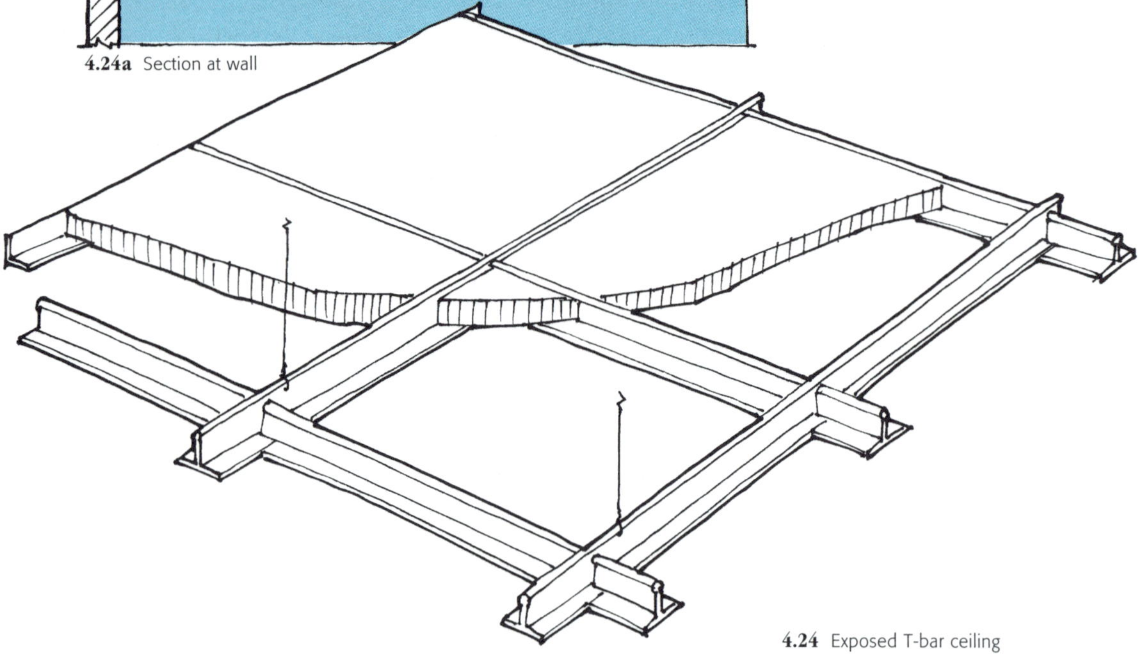

4.24 Exposed T-bar ceiling

Construction of this hung ceiling is composed of exposed T-bars with lay-in acoustic tile panels. This ceiling system, as shown or with slight variations, is the most commonly used. The wall molding, or angle trim, will feature prominently in the details to be discussed later in this chapter.

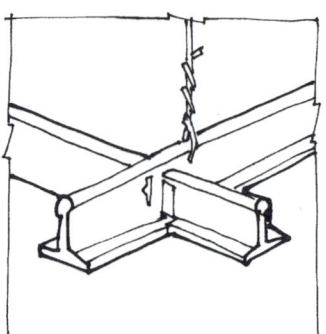

4.24b Detail of suspension point

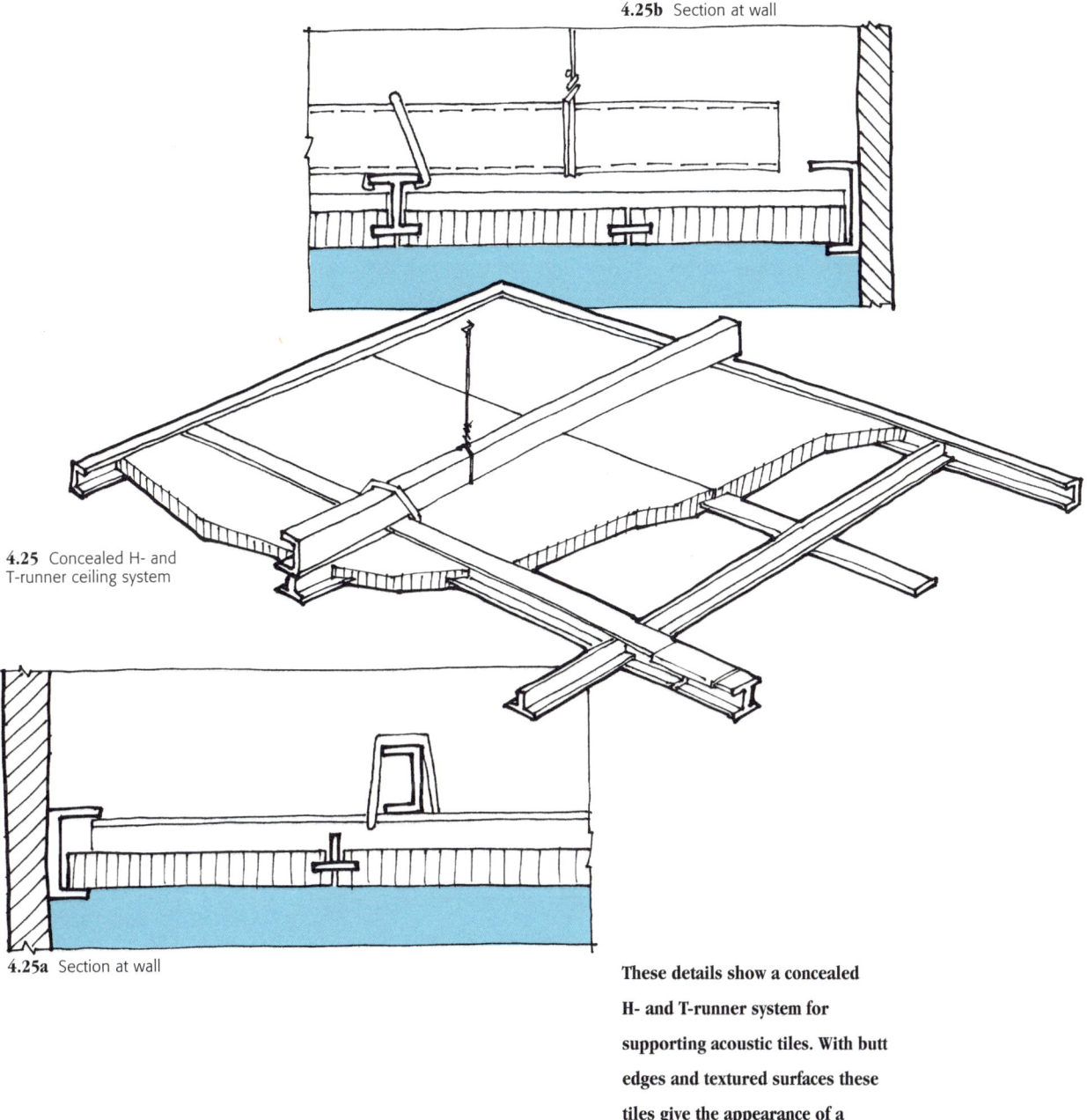

4.25b Section at wall

4.25 Concealed H- and T-runner ceiling system

4.25a Section at wall

These details show a concealed H- and T-runner system for supporting acoustic tiles. With butt edges and textured surfaces these tiles give the appearance of a homogeneous ceiling similar to lightly textured plaster. A wall molding—as in detail 4.24a—has been used.

Where the Wall Meets the Ceiling

It is important to note that almost all ceiling systems use an angle trim or wall molding, primarily to conceal the edge of the tile. Because tiles come in pre-cut sizes which rarely fit the dimensions of the room or space into which they are being installed, such a cover trim is needed. The designer's problem is deciding on how that trim should meet the wall.

Detail 4.26 shows a typical angle trim fixed to the wall and covering the cut edge of the tile. The steel or aluminum angle is flexible enough to conform to the shape of the wall fairly well but occasionally can leave gaps. Depending on how close the viewer is, and the colors of the ceiling and wall, this may or may not be a serious problem. If it is particularly obvious, it conveys a somewhat sloppy look to the detail and the workmanship of the interior. Use of a reveal on the ceiling plane as shown in 4.27 is one attempt to overcome the problem. Detail 4.28 uses a reveal on the wall plane to bridge and disguise the gap. Detail 4.29 shows a wall-mounted molding.

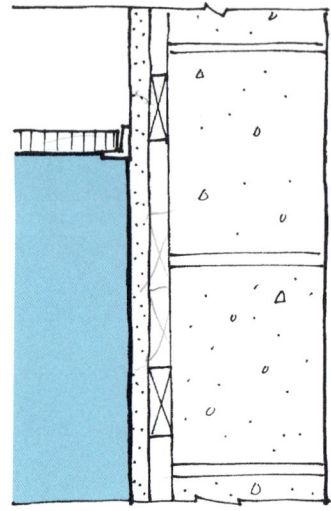

4.26 90° butt joint, angle trim

Considerations Before Detailing

Which detail to use? Your decision will depend on both circumstance and choice. In some situations the partition walls continue up to the underside of the slab above, while in others, the partitions stop at the underside of the hung ceiling, therefore 4.27 would be easier to use in the first instance and 4.28 in the second. However, it is possible to create a custom detail to surmount the problem once you understand the reasons for, and are aware of, any construction constraints.

Now let us consider choice for a moment.

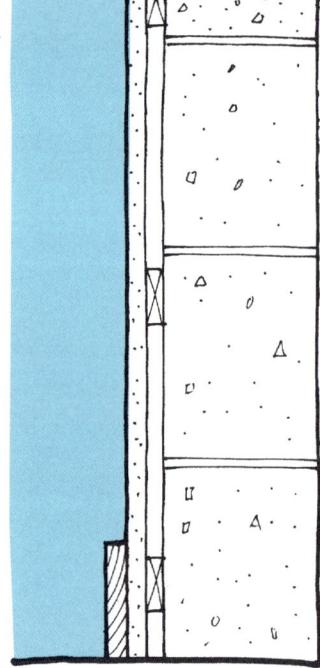

4.18 Applied baseboard

What visual effect do you wish to create? Consider the visual perceptions when making your decision. If the reveal is on the ceiling plane it gives the impression that the ceiling is bound by walls which continue upward out of sight, unlimited; if the reveal is on the wall plane it appears

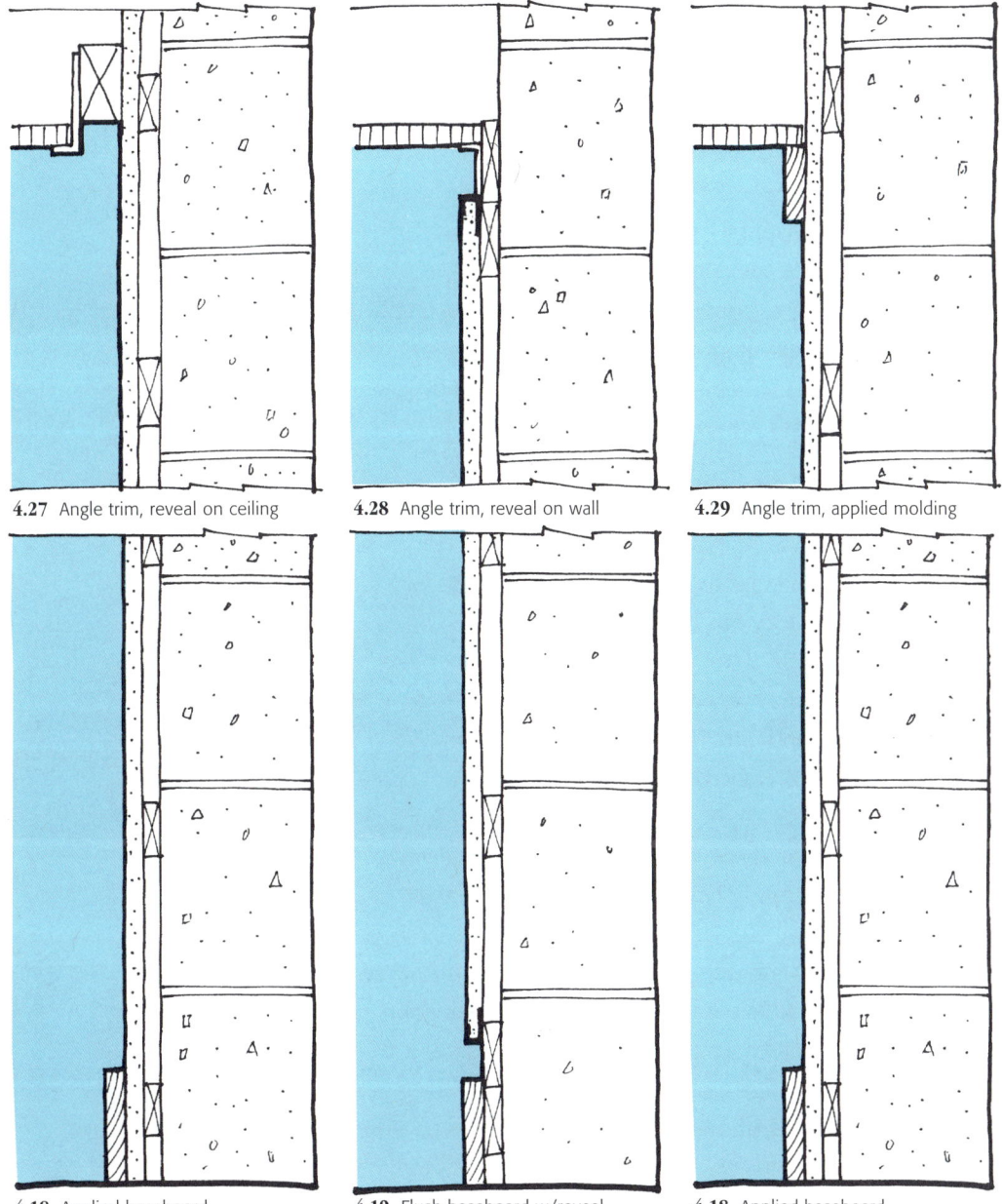

4.27 Angle trim, reveal on ceiling

4.28 Angle trim, reveal on wall

4.29 Angle trim, applied molding

4.18 Applied baseboard

4.19 Flush baseboard w/reveal

4.18 Applied baseboard

that the walls are mastered by a ceiling which carries on indefinitely, beyond view. The proportions of the reveal will lessen or magnify the effect. Generally the wider and deeper the reveal, the greater its effect. If it becomes too wide, however, it begins to look like a border, not a reveal.

Which ceiling/wall relationship do you wish to convey?

If the room is relatively small you might want to give it greater lateral feeling and therefore place the reveal on the wall, indicating horizontal continuity of the ceiling. If the ceiling is particularly low, a reveal on the ceiling plane allows the walls to appear to continue upward, giving a feeling of added height. Reveals in other dimensions can suggest other things as well. This will become more apparent when discussing the details for wall paneling.

Where the Wall Meets the Floor

The detail selected for the baseboard is another factor to be taken into account. Refer to the illustrations here and on the previous two pages for this discussion.

Detail 4.26 at the ceiling with 4.18 at the baseboard is a standard combination. Detail 4.27 used with 4.18 is also fairly common and they are not at odds with one another. Detail 4.28, a reveal into the wall, would not relate as well to 4.18, because the finish being applied at the bottom is in front of the wall plane, whereas the reveal at the top suggests a layer in back of the wall plane. However, 4.29 with an applied cornice trim that matches the baseboard in 4.18 gives the wall a substantial appearance. Draw a three-dimensional sketch of the 4.29/4.18 combination and see how the wall becomes a lateral band set behind the base and cap planes.

Now study baseboard detail variations 4.19 and 4.20. The flush base/reveal of 4.19 harmonizes with the ceiling detail 4.28 on the previous page. Combining 4.19 with ceiling variation 4.30 as shown at right gives a different visual effect to the wall.

In 4.31 the wall cap matches the recessed base of 4.20, which again changes the emphasis of the wall.

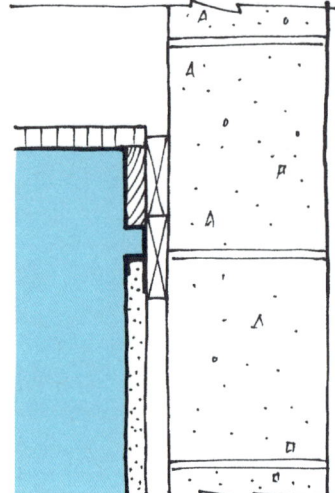

4.30 Flush molding, reveal on wall

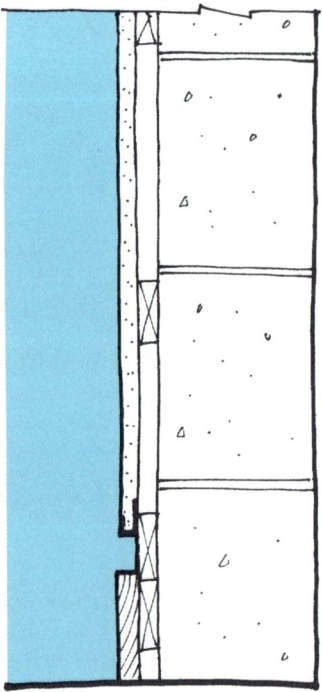

4.19 Flush baseboard w/reveal

Further, if the material, color, or value of the base and cap pieces are different from each other or the wall material, other effects will be created.

As you can see from these few examples, the pairing of ceiling and floor details combined with variations of material, color, value, finish, gloss, and so on affects not only the design of the wall but the relative importance of the wall as object, place, barrier, or boundary.

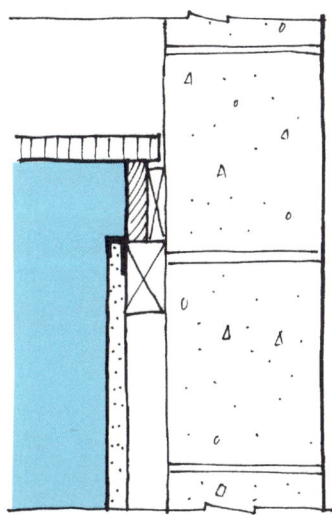

4.31 Recessed wall cap

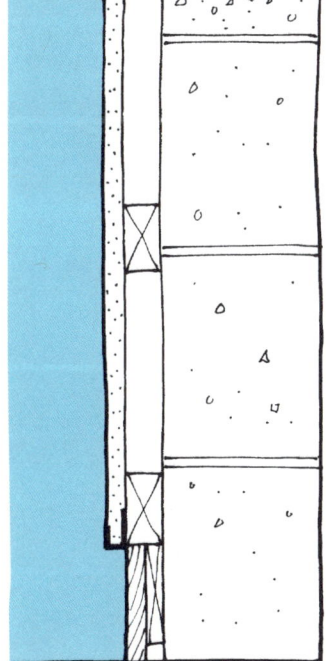

4.20 Recessed baseboard

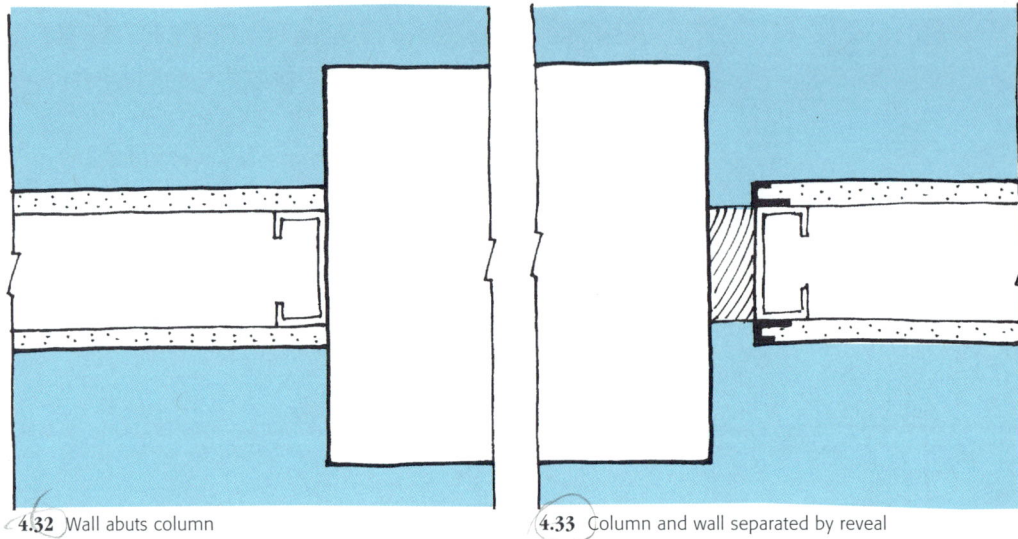

4.32 Wall abuts column

4.33 Column and wall separated by reveal

The drywall finish in 4.32 flows directly from the wall into the column—visually unbroken. Within this interior it will appear that there are shallow pilasters on the walls.

In 4.33, the wall stops short and a reveal with filler attaches it to the column. In this interior the visual message is that there are wall surfaces which fill in the spaces between structural columns.

Other Wall Situations In non-residential projects particularly, you may be faced with butting a wall against a column and/or a curtain-wall window frame. Each situation presents peculiarities which must be addressed but the following generic examples describe the basics.

When butting a wall into a column it is necessary to consider several aspects:

    The shape of the space created
    The finish materials
    The size of the column relative to the thickness of the wall
    The visual definition of the wall/column relationship

The concept of the column-to-wall relationship will be defined by the details you use to join them. Examine 4.32 and 4.33 for straightforward solutions.

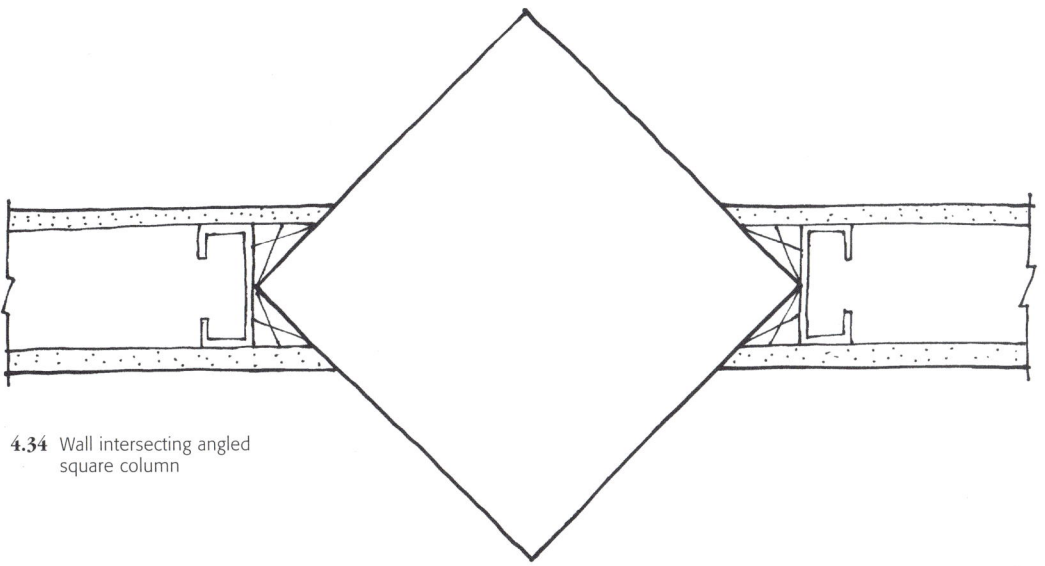

4.34 Wall intersecting angled square column

When the connection must occur on the corner of the column, the detailing becomes more challenging. One of several alternatives may suit your design concept. In 4.34 the column becomes a triangular pilaster on the wall. Detail 4.35 illustrates a reveal connection that clearly separates the column from the wall and proclaims the column as an entity unto itself. The connection illustrated in 4.36 increases the panel effect of the wall and ensures that the wall reads as a barrier between columns.

In 4.36, note the **corner bead,** a 90° metal angle trim on the outside corner of the wall. Like a J-stop, the corner bead covers the exposed cut edges of drywall; in addition it gives strength to a corner's edge.

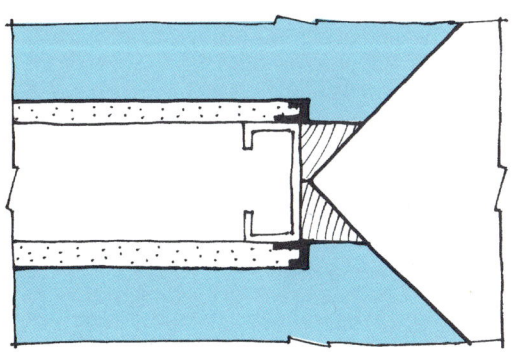

4.35 Wall intersecting angled square column, w/reveal

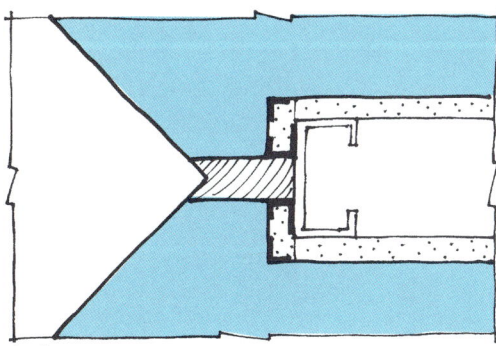

4.36 Wall intersecting angled square column, w/reveal var.

When the wall meets a column at an odd angle, or when two walls at 90° meet at an angled column, different design opportunities arise.

Detail 4.37 uses the panel/reveal/column arrangement but the connection is angled so that the wall intersects the column at 90°, avoiding an acute angle at the inside corner, which would be more difficult—thus more costly—to construct.

In some situations it might be better to use a detail such as 4.38 where the angled space has been concealed by furring out one or both walls so that they arrive flush with the column face.

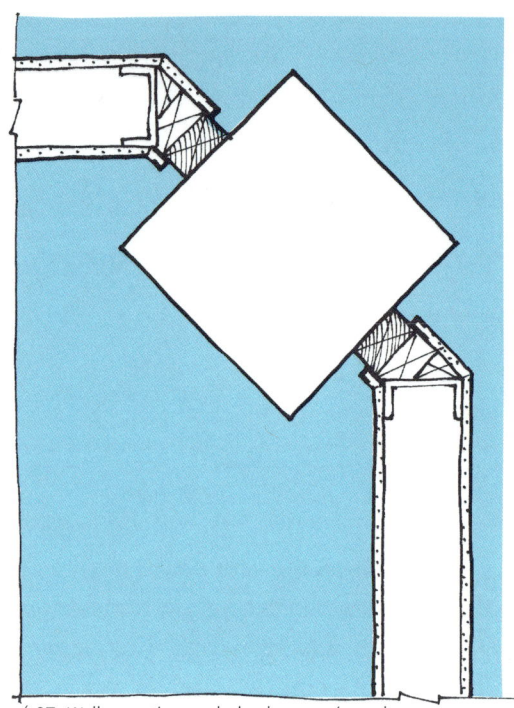

4.37 Walls meeting angled column, w/reveal

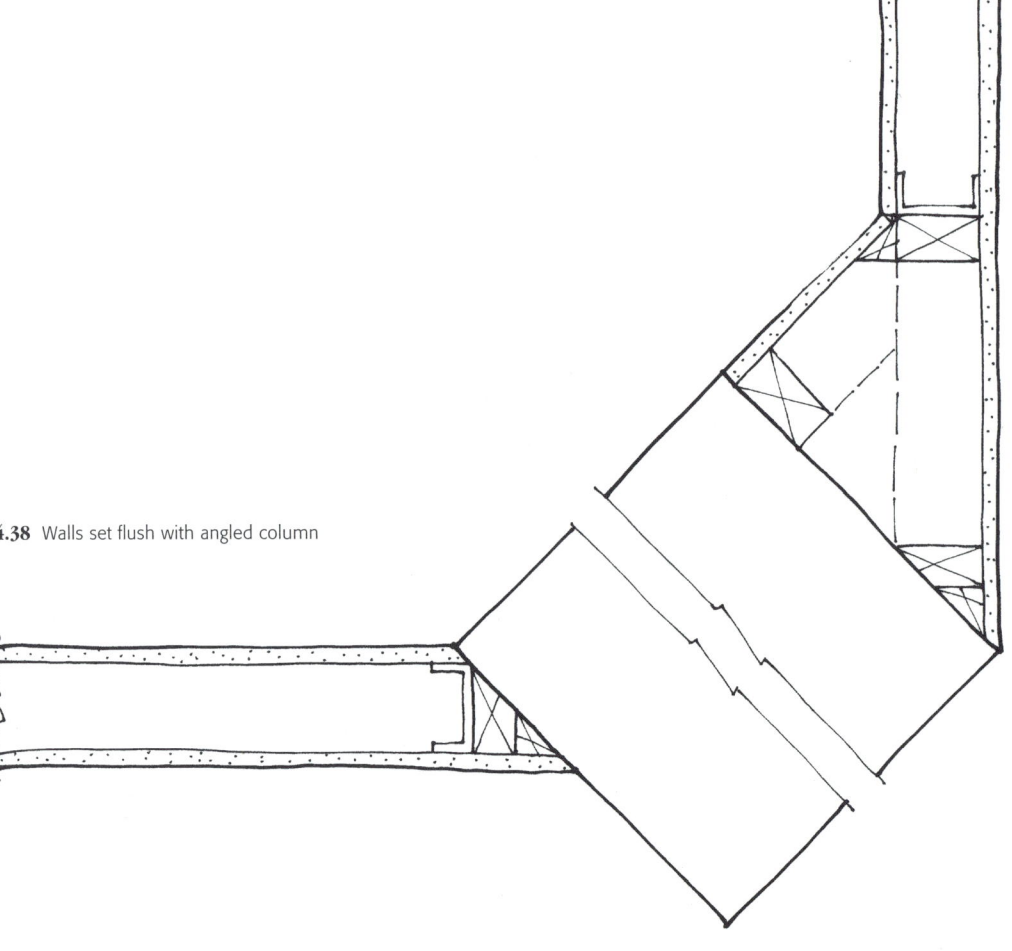

4.38 Walls set flush with angled column

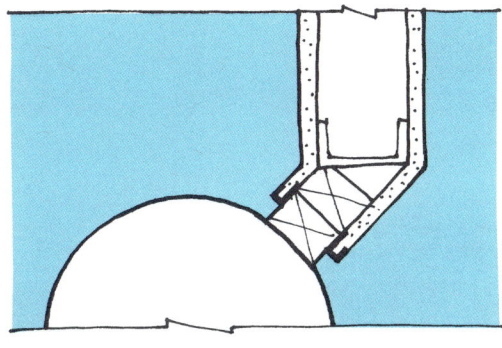

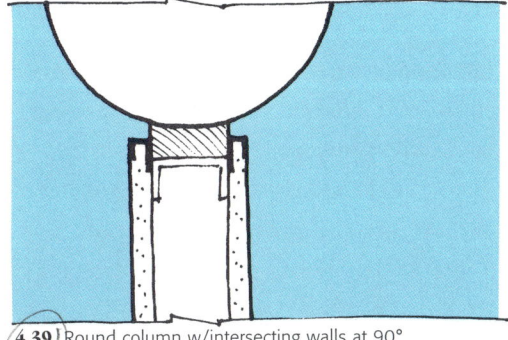

4.39 Round column w/intersecting walls at 90°

Whether the wall intersects the center line of the column or at another angle, the connection itself looks best if it meets the column at a right angle.

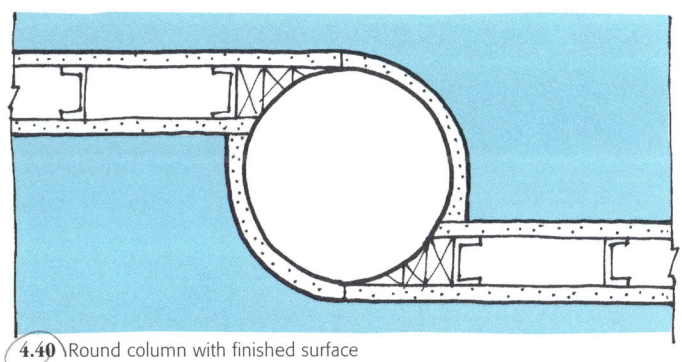

4.40 Round column with finished surface

When butting a wall into a round column, such as shown in details 4.39 and 4.40, you might find the approaches used in 4.35 and 4.37 most workable.

All of the wall-into-column details from 4.32 to 4.39 can be used whether the column is finished with plaster or drywall, or left as exposed concrete. Only 4.40 requires that the column have an applied surface.

With careful work and a good taping job, the drywall or plaster can flow smoothly into the rounded surface of the finished column. Success with this detail depends on a fairly large-sized column and good finishing craftsmen; it is not recommended for ordinary situations.

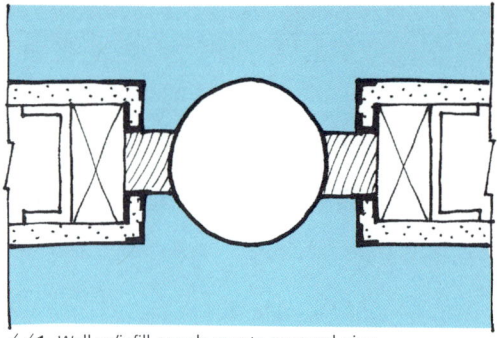
4.41 Wall w/infill panels meets exposed pipe

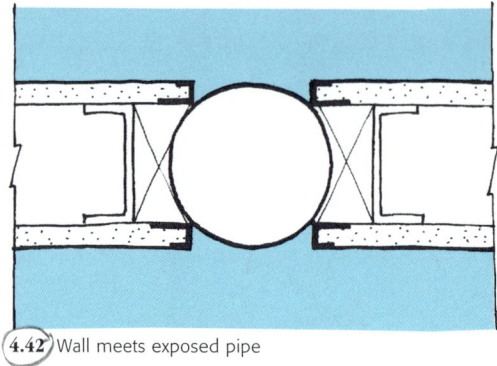
4.42 Wall meets exposed pipe

Exposed steel pipe or H-columns pose somewhat different problems but they can be handled similarly.

The two variations above convey slightly different messages. Detail 4.41 indicates panel walls mounted between structural elements—largely an expression of structure with subordinate infill panels. Detail 4.42 expresses a wall but lets the viewer know that structure is also an element of the design—a more subtle expression than 4.41. Examine the details at right, which are varying solutions to walls meeting H-columns.

In detail 4.43, a strong expression of structure is conveyed on one side of the wall and concealed on the other.

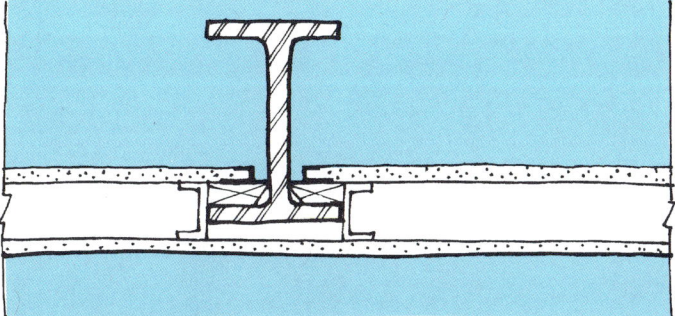

4.43 H-column exposed on one wall, covered on the other

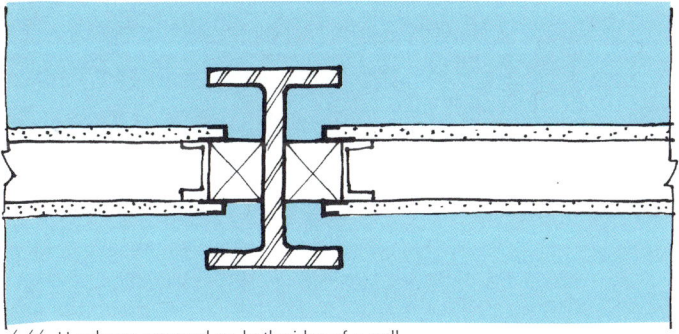

4.44 H-column exposed on both sides of a wall

This detail can express structure on both sides of the wall if the column is of sufficient dimension to be featured.

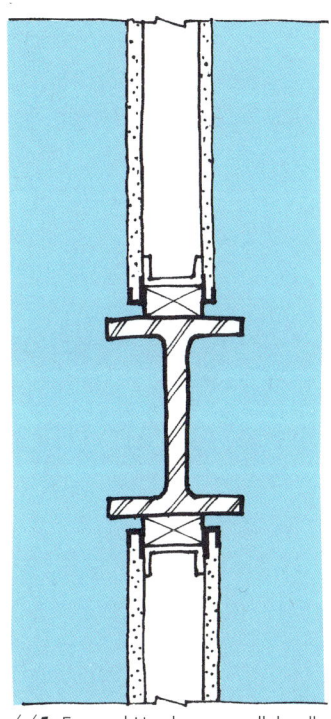

4.45 Exposed H-column, parallel wall

Detail 4.45 shows one way of handling an H-column where a wall runs in the same direction as the column web.

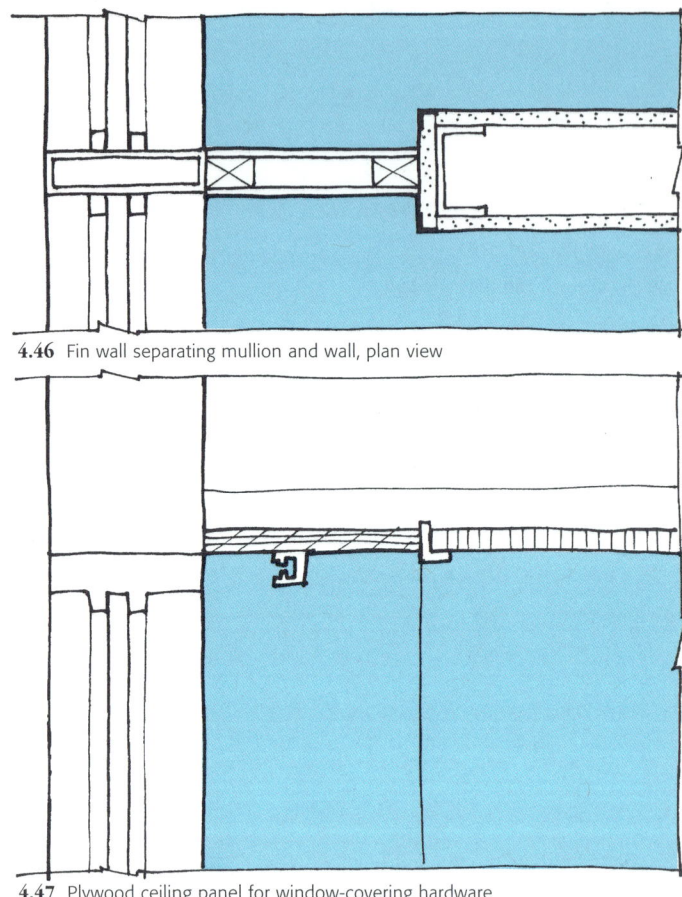

4.46 Fin wall separating mullion and wall, plan view

4.47 Plywood ceiling panel for window-covering hardware

Where the Wall Meets a Window

The designer's problem when butting a wall, usually a thin element, into a column, most often a thick element, is maintaining the integrity of the combination. In butting a wall to a window mullion, integrity is still important but now the thickness of the *wall* is greater than the element to which it abuts.

For example, a partition wall abutting a window mullion at right angles is often thicker than the mullion. Detail 4.46 illustrates a simple way to reduce the wall thickness from 4 1/2" to 1 1/2" by using a "fin" wall. The width of the fin wall can neatly coincide with the depth of the heating system at the floor level, or perhaps with the dimension of the area at the ceiling which accommodates the window covering.

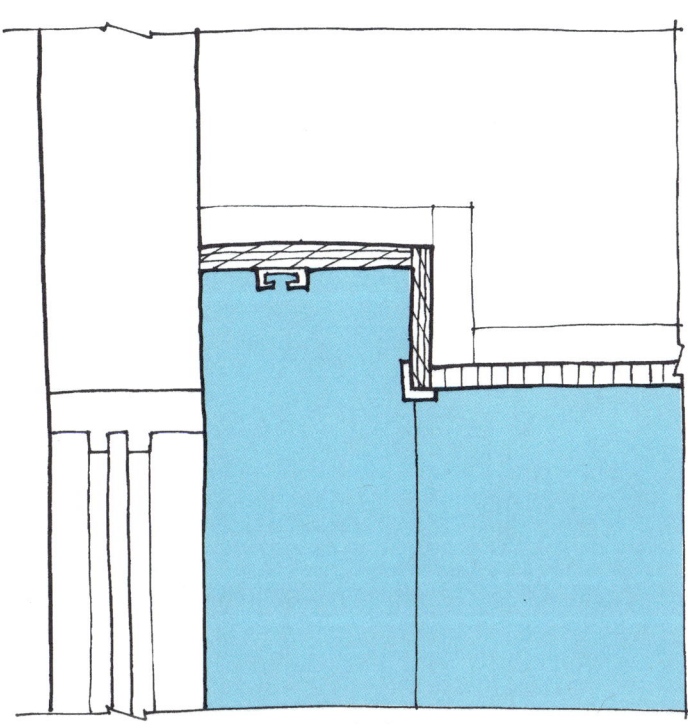

4.48 Ceiling recess for window-covering hardware

Planning for Future Window Treatments Details 4.47 and 4.48 illustrate fairly typical situations found in commercial buildings where the ceiling height is the same as the top of the window frame. For drapery track (or other window covering hardware) it is important that the mounting surface be secure and strong enough to withstand the strain applied over time. Therefore, the typical relatively soft acoustic ceiling tile has been replaced with plywood above the track, as shown in 4.47. It is only logical that such changes align with or in some way relate to the change of plane on the adjacent wall.

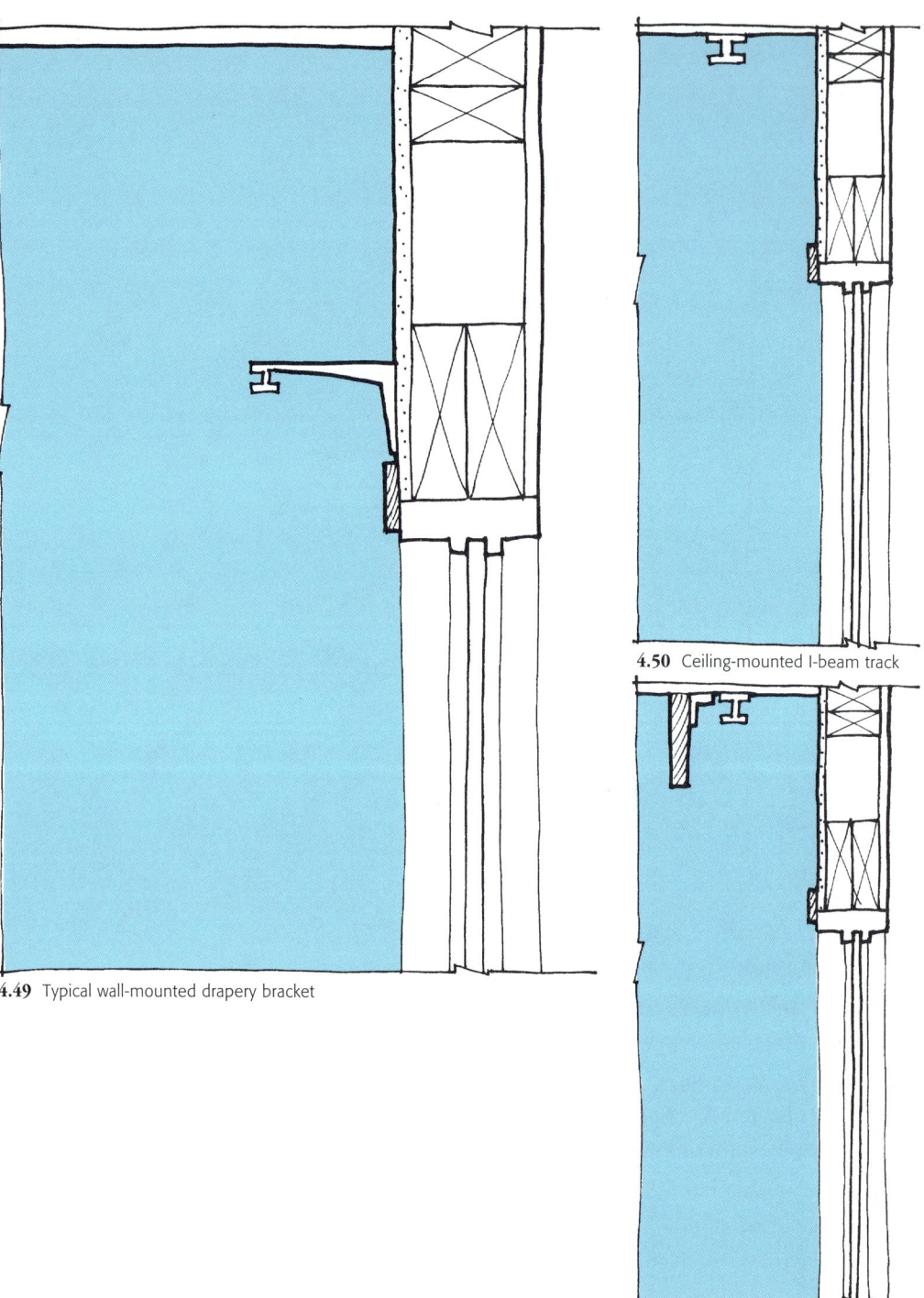

4.49 Typical wall-mounted drapery bracket

4.50 Ceiling-mounted I-beam track

4.51 I-beam drapery track w/valance

In a residential situation the details would be somewhat different. Depending on your concept of window treatment for a particular project, you may wish to mount drapery track on either wall- or ceiling-mounted brackets. Detail 4.49 shows a typical wall-mount installation. The length of the bracket arm is determined by the situation at the bottom of the drapery. If the fabric is thick and/or particularly heavy, the folds of fabric may be quite deep and therefore require a long bracket arm. The location of heating units would also affect the distance of the drapery from the wall. Note that a too-long bracket will sag in an unsightly fashion with the weight of the fabric. In such cases a ceiling-mounted track might be preferable. Detail 4.50 shows an installation of a ceiling-mounted I-beam track, which can be mounted at any distance out from the wall. The track and top of the drapery may be concealed behind a valance as shown in 4.51.

Detail 4.52 illustrates the use of a different style of track—a C-track—which, though also available for surface mounting, is specifically made for recessing into the ceiling, which minimizes its visibility.

Many other types of hardware are available for various fabric-based window treatments, as well as for other methods of treating windows. Explore all the possibilities, perusing manufacturers' literature for detail ideas that will best express your concept. You should have a clear idea of what will be used before finishing the construction details.

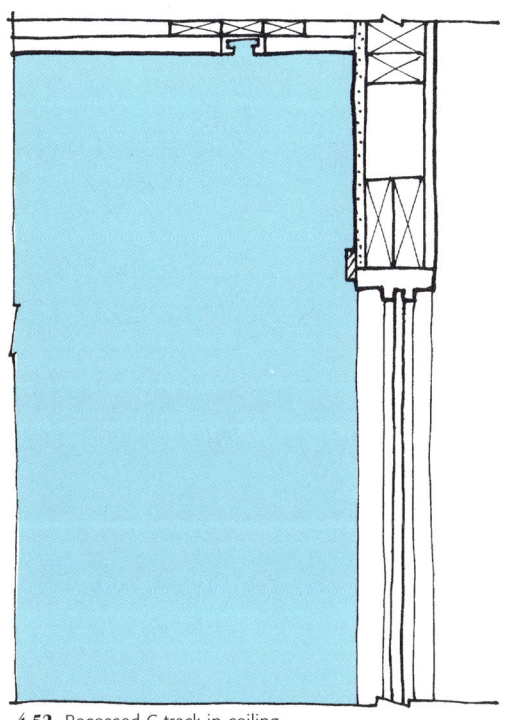

4.52 Recessed C-track in ceiling

Wood as a Wall Finish

CHAPTER 1 2 3 4 5 6 7 8

efore detailing any interior wall finish you must take a close look at the materials themselves—their colors, characteristics, patterns—and think about their applications: all the possibilities, the probabilities, and even what you consider downright impossibilities, which, interestingly, with adroit maneuvering sometime turn out to be possibilities after all.

Wood in particular is a wall finish material that requires and deserves careful examination. It would be useful to begin with a review of the section on wood, beginning on page 25. Study the stylized grain patterns used to illustrate the matched sets of plywood panels—running match, balance match, center match, and so on—and find examples in photographs or actual situations.

Let us look at some of the variables, and please do not get discouraged and decide to use a wood-grain plastic laminate instead. Even though it is composed of identical reproductions of a single panel, and is therefore easier to deal with, plastic laminate does not have the character and warmth of real wood.

Except for random matching, all veneered panels are manufactured in sequence for the run of each veneer flitch and are so numbered on the edge or back. Pre-manufactured sets of panels, usually 48" x 96" or 48" x 120", are numbered in sequence and vary in number of panels from 4 to 12 or more. If more than one set is required to complete a room, you will have to go to the supplier's warehouse and attempt to match up available sets as closely as possible. There is no guarantee of close matching between sets. In terms of your particular project, while you may specify a certain effect for pricing purposes, you must reserve the right to see and approve the flitch being provided before installation takes place.

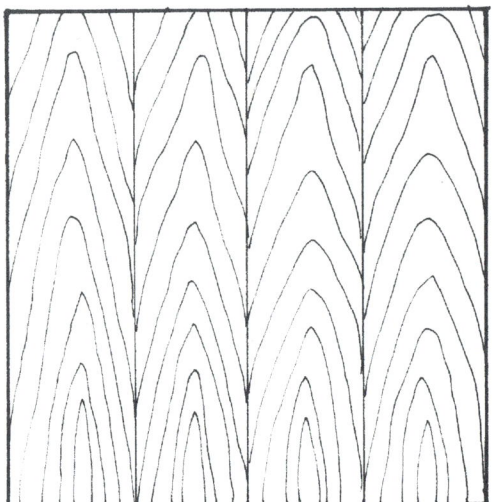

5.1 Running-matched veneer panels

In examining veneer panel samples, you should note that the inherent pattern of a wood species, particularly if it is strong, might dictate your design and detail choice. For example, study the **running-matched pattern** here. In this plywood pattern a dominant "cathedral" effect runs downhill until it is overcome by another dominant part of the grain pattern. The cathedral effect is

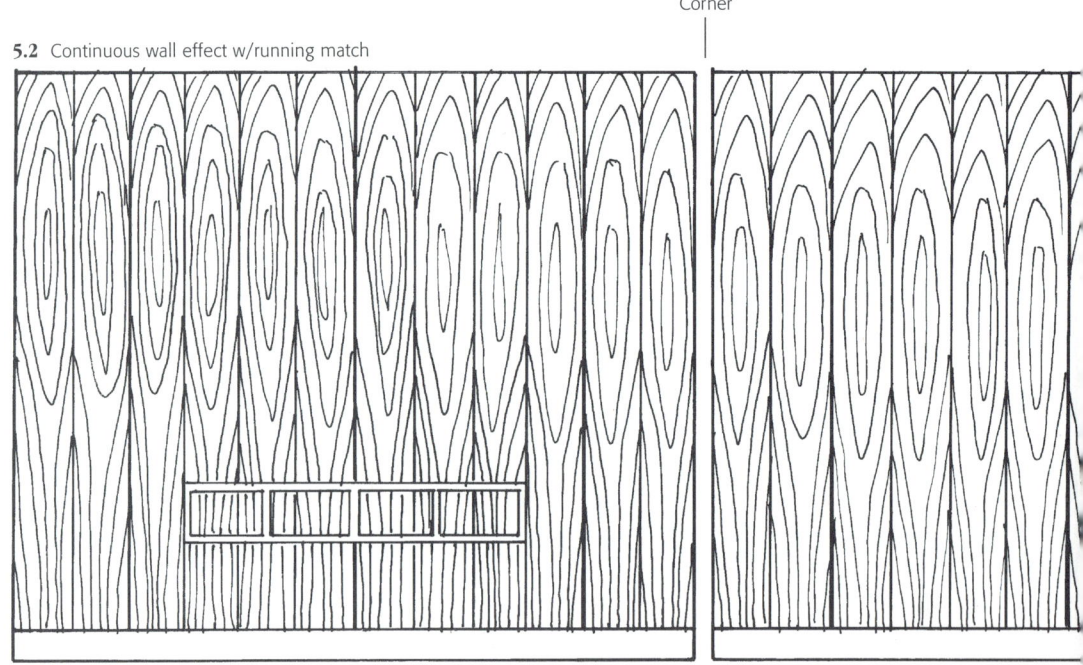

5.2 Continuous wall effect w/running match

caused by the fact that the annual rings which create the pattern are imperfect circles; the pattern runs downhill because the leaves of veneer have been cut from different levels of this varied pattern. If the particular wood you select normally has a very consistent color and even grain value, then a running match with butt-jointed full panels may be successful, assuming that you want a continuous wall effect like the one shown in figure 5.2. If the color and graining vary more than moderately you may be well advised to cut the panels to approximately the same size and separate each one so that they read as individual panels such as shown in figure 5.3.

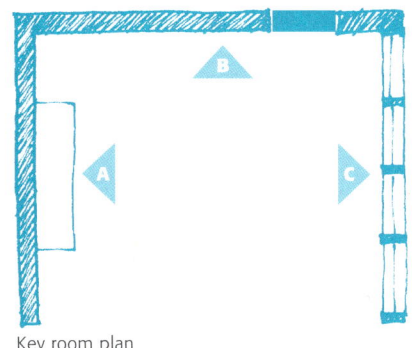

Key room plan

With a running match and butt-jointed panels this room would appear to have a continuous, unbroken wall surface. If you have the door custom-made the waste panel could be used on the door.

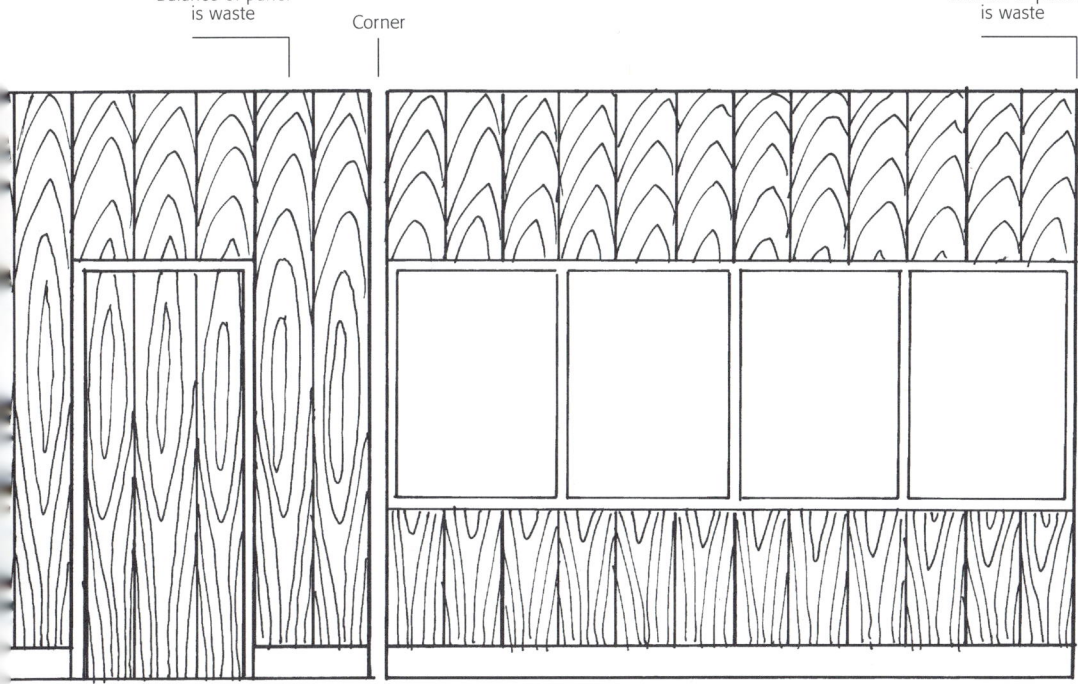

Balance of panel is waste Corner Balance of panel is waste

5.3 Panels cut and detailed to read separately

Compare details 5.2 and 5.3. In 5.3, where the joints are a noticeable part of the design instead of concealed as in 5.2, you can see how important it is to have the locations of the wall-hung credenza, the door, and the window relate to the panel joints.

Pre-manufactured sets of panels are the most economical way to panel a room or a surface with wood. More effective visually—but also more costly—is to specify that a uniform width and precise height be manufactured for the particular location. Unless specified otherwise, however, a door and credenza front such as shown above would not normally be finished with matching pieces of veneer.

To achieve maximum grain continuity over the whole area to be paneled, specify **"blueprint matched."** This system requires that doors and other attached units be matched in sequence. Particular leaves of veneer must be identified, marked accordingly, and delivered to the manufacturers of the doors and other attachments. If more than one flitch is needed to complete the project the supplier must carefully select flitches that are as closely matched as possible.

Corner

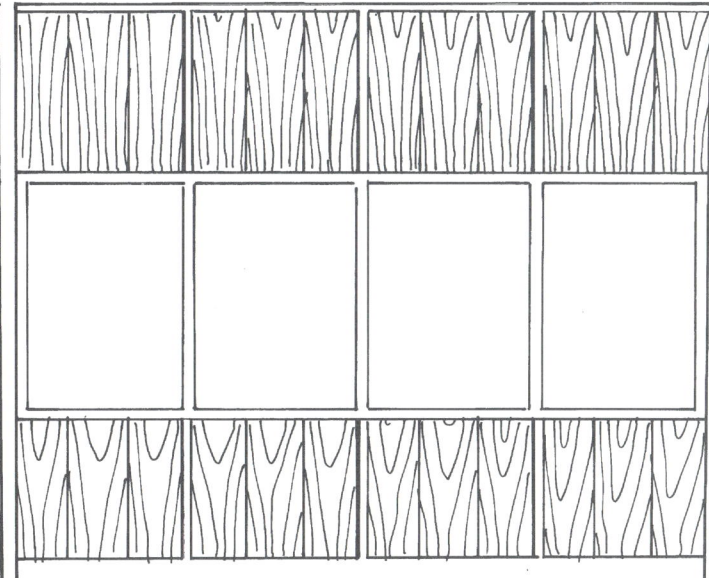

A recessed reveal or a raised molding at the panel joints would create a separate panel effect. A more aesthetically pleasing result has been achieved by reducing the width of the panels to achieve even widths per wall. Relative to the key room plan, the door was necessarily moved approximately one foot to the left.

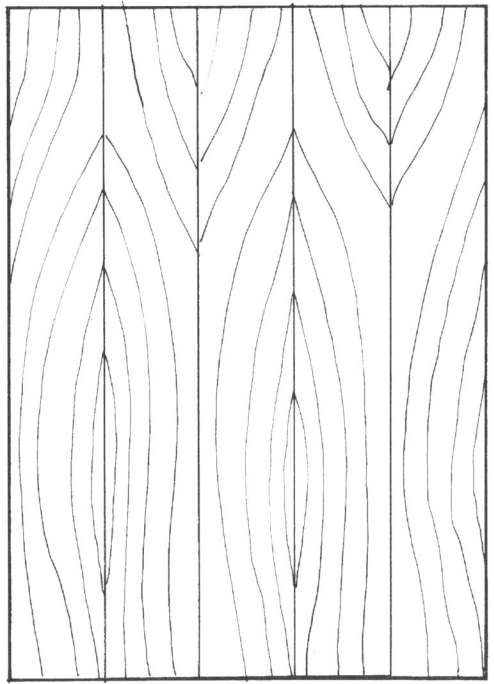

5.4 Balance-matched veneer panel

Balance-matched panels are made up of an odd or even number of veneer leaves that are equal in width. If the number is odd, as shown in 5.4, then the "pattern" effect becomes ambiguous. Cover one leaf at either side and observe how the focus of the pattern changes.

Center-matched panels have an even number of leaves, matched on either side of the panel's center line. The pairs of leaves may vary in width but because of the even numbers only complete grain patterns occur on the panel, as shown in 5.5.

Your design and detailing of the wall will influence your decision on which type of matching to specify. If you are planning to use visually separate panels the seam detail has an influence. If the separation is set off by a reveal you may be satisfied with the run-off grain pattern inherent in either running or balance match. If you are detailing each panel as a framed unit, you might prefer the symmetrical balance of center-matched panels, each complete and able to stand alone as a pattern/design unit.

Remember the many different ways to cut veneers and that each method produces a different grain pattern. Theoretically, the five ways to cut veneer and the three ways of matching in the lay-up of panels would give fifteen possibilities per wood species. However, not all wood species are cut in all five ways. While oak lends itself to various cuts, the most com-

---

Cost Comparison of Veneered Panel Sets
(from least to most costly)

–Pre-manufactured sets, running match

–Pre-manufactured sets cut to size, running match

–Balance match

–Blueprint-matched running match

–Blueprint-matched balance match

–Center match

–Blueprint-matched center match

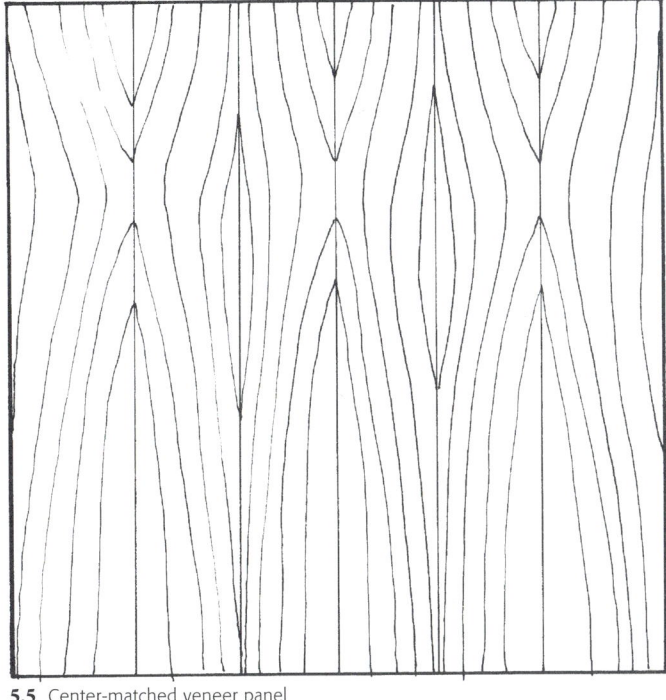

5.5 Center-matched veneer panel

mon cuts in other species are plain and quarter slicing, which still adds up to a great range of possibilities. Consider also that some grain patterns of a species are more attractive in one cut than another or, due to log size, are only cut in one way. For example, zebra wood, with its grain color ranging from charcoal brown to blond, or figured red gum, with its jazzy grain pattern, would be wastefully expensive in a center-matched cut because the color and/or pattern would obscure the matching system used.

Another point to remember is that occasionally the thickness of veneer changes with the species due to the nature of the particular wood or, sometimes, due to its rarity and value. Since veneers vary in thickness from 1/10" to 1/85" it is necessary to know this dimension when detailing. Don't assume that a 1/4" or 3/4" panel will be that thick. Its dimension depends on the veneer thickness and whether it is a pre-manufactured or custom panel, on plywood or particle board.

To summarize: before specifying a species of wood in a certain veneer cut and matching method check with the suppliers to discover what is currently available on the market and what is capable of being produced. Caution: Find knowledgeable suppliers. It
is better to acknowledge your ignorance and to learn through asking than it is to specify an impossible or outrageously expensive combination of wood, cut, and veneer match.

Fixing Panels to the Wall

As shown in the illustrations beginning on page 96 in chapter 4, wood strapping is used over concrete block to furr out a wall so as to make it a perfectly level vertical plane. When designing a space featuring fine wood paneling, regardless of the wall construction it is advisable to specify strapping since it is important that the back-up to the paneling be an even surface plane. The details below are useful when considering the application of paneling onto any type of wall construction.

Plywood panels are available in a variety of thicknesses: 3/16", 1/4", 3/8", 1/2", 5/8", 11/16", and 3/4". Hardwood-veneer-clad plywood is usually stocked in 1/4" and 3/4", in the standard width of 4'-0", and lengths of 8'-0" and 10'-0". Even when you are specifying custom matching or custom-length or -width panels you can also specify and use any of the stock thicknesses.

Permanent Mounting   Traditionally panels were nailed to strapping with small-headed finishing nails at 16" centers for 3/4" panels, or 12" centers for 1/4" panels. The nails would be countersunk and the resulting holes filled with putty-like material colored to match the finished wood.

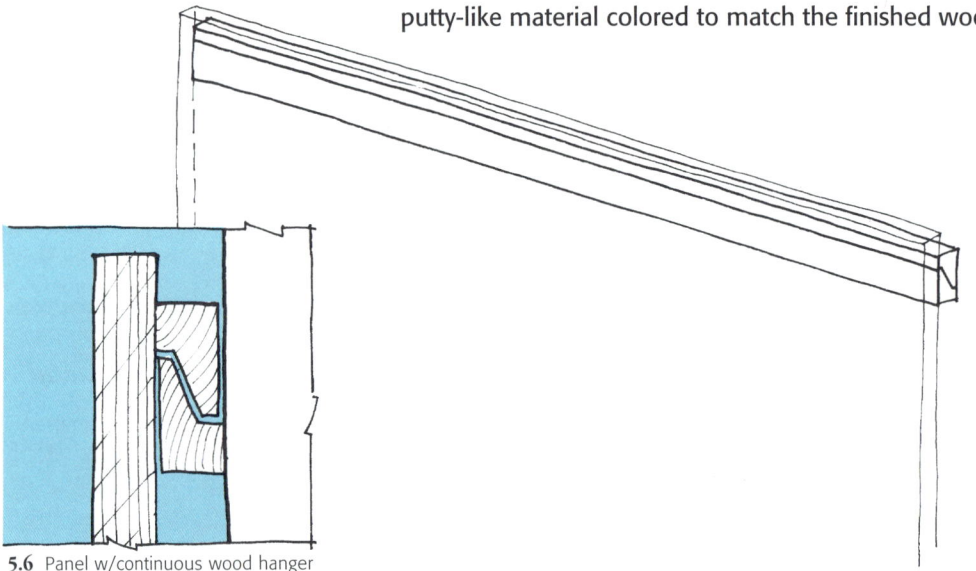

5.6 Panel w/continuous wood hanger

This system is still used but, given the excellent adhesives on the market today, it is possible to glue the panels in place, avoiding nail holes completely. However panels must be "held" until the adhesive sets. Thick panels may be tacked in place with nails driven into the edge (and nails removed once the adhesive sets); thinner plywood panels need to be angle-braced in place. Note that bracing may interfere with other trades working on the premises so such an installation must be planned well in advance. (As an aside, conditions on site must always be anticipated as you design/detail weeks or months before actual construction takes place.)

Another permanent mounting method, convenient when you are retrofitting or where acoustics are a factor in the wall construction, is to glue thin panels directly onto a drywall surface.

Flexible Mounting Instead of permanently fixing panels to the structure it is possible to hang them off the strapping with wood hangers or metal clips as shown below.

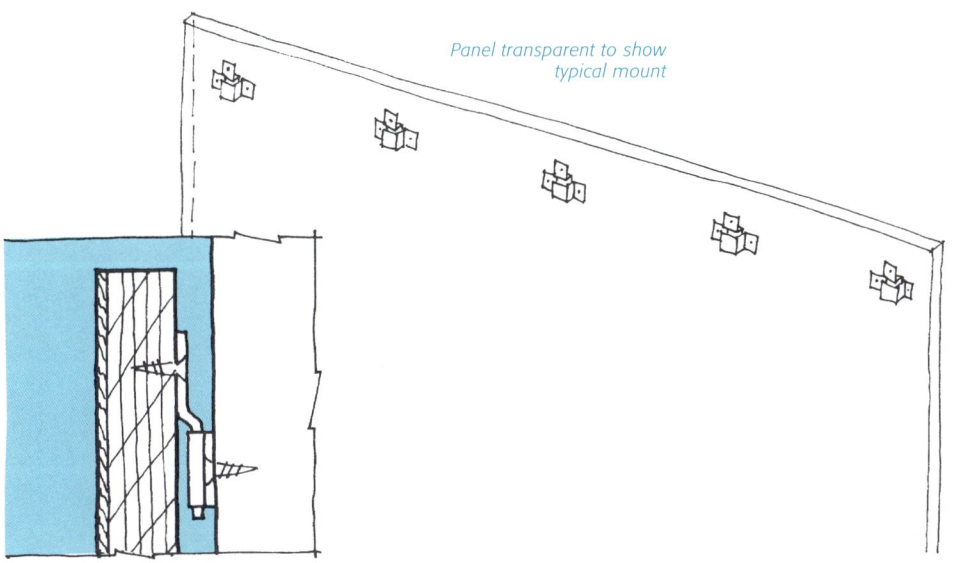

Panel transparent to show typical mount

5.7 Panel w/metal hanging clips

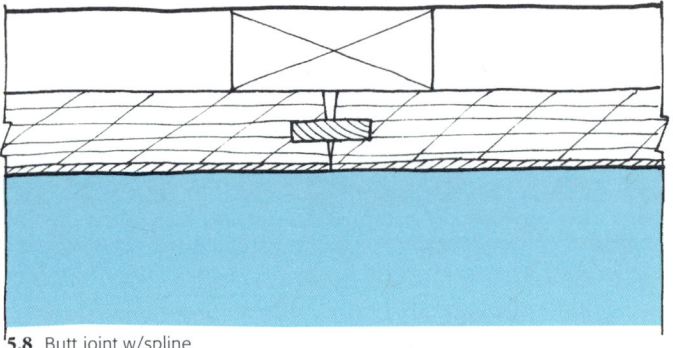

5.8 Butt joint w/spline

This detail shows a butt joint with a spline. If the panel is a thin one then the spline would be omitted.

Notice that the edges have been trimmed back at approximately 5° to allow them to gently touch without imperfections in the edges keeping them fractionally apart—which would cause a slight crack to be visible.

Side-by-Side Panel Relationships

It is possible to relate one panel to another in a variety of ways. Adjacent panels can

—butt together, for a continuous wood wall appearance with no visible joints
—use reveals of several types
—be joined with flush battens
—be joined with projecting battens
—use a combination of methods to connect.

Each of the reveal effects shown at right is quite different visually and needs careful thought. Imagine how the effect would change if the thickness of the panel were changed— a 1/4"-deep reveal is not nearly as visually impressive as a reveal 3/4" deep.

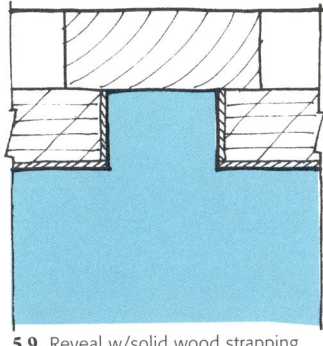

5.9 Reveal w/solid wood strapping

In a typical reveal such as shown at left, the edges of the sheet are veneered and the visible strapping is made of the same solid wood as the panel face.

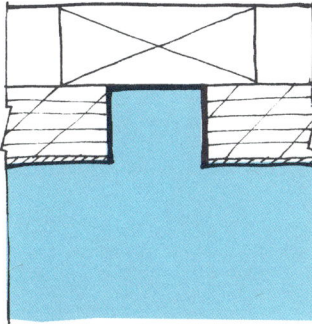

5.10 Reveal w/contrasting finish

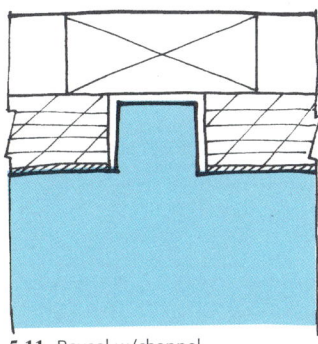

5.11 Reveal w/channel

At left, a channel is set into the reveal. The channel could be plastic or any metal.

The strapping in 5.10 is faced with either a veneer of the same face wood, or another material. Paint, plastic laminate, metal, another type of veneer, mirror, or anything else that you think is suitable could be used.

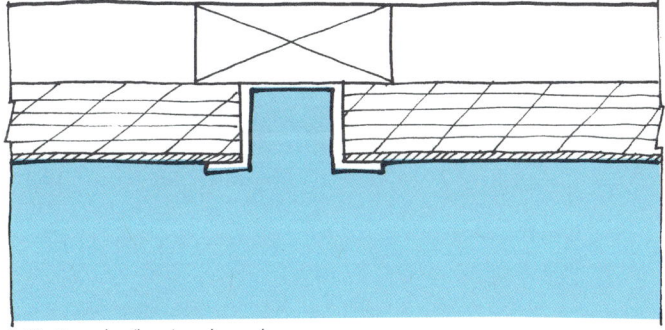

5.12 Reveal w/lapping channel

In 5.12, the channel effect is expanded by lapping the plastic reveal over the face of the panel.

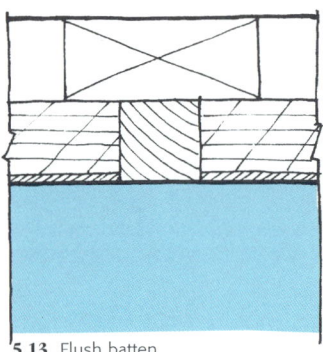

5.13 Flush batten

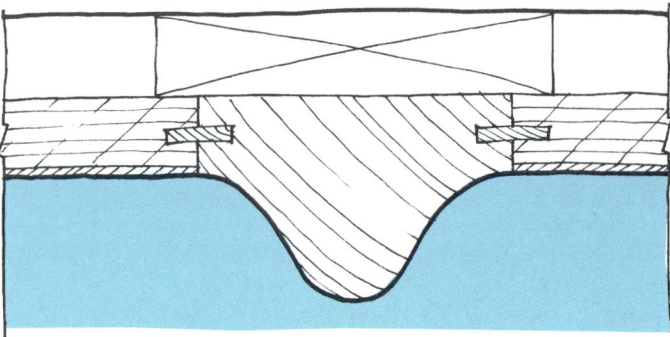

5.14 Curved batten

A flush batten such as shown in 5.13 has a different material inserted between the panels—a contrasting piece of wood, a metal or plastic bar, stone, mirror, ceramic tile, plastic laminate. What else can you think of?

In 5.14, the batten begins flush and then rises out from the surface in a voluptuous curve. Splines are recommended here to prevent the solid wood and plywood from separating.

The batten in 5.15 overlaps the panels to conceal any gap that might develop.

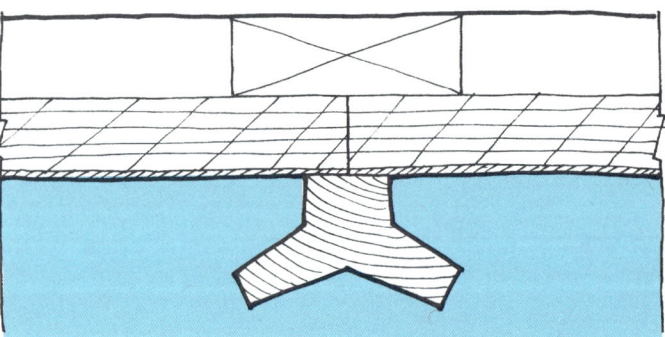

5.16 Custom-shaped batten

Here's a fanciful batten showing that the cross-section need not be a neat square or rectangle but can be milled to suit your imagination.

5.15 Overlapping batten

Detail 5.17 shows the combination of a reveal with a surface batten. This may be either a vertical or horizontal joint. If continued on all four sides, it becomes a frame for each individual panel.

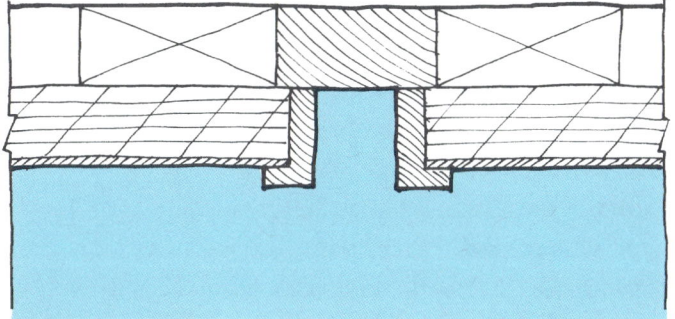

5.17 Reveal and batten

Inside and outside corners pose various challenges, and all must be considered in order to appear compatible with the panel joints.

For example, on a wall with wood panels butted together, as in 5.8 and repeated below center, details 5.18 and 5.19 might be used. Either joint could also be handled with a lock miter. The important feature is to have secure joints that will not open up and spoil the continuous effect of the wood treatment.

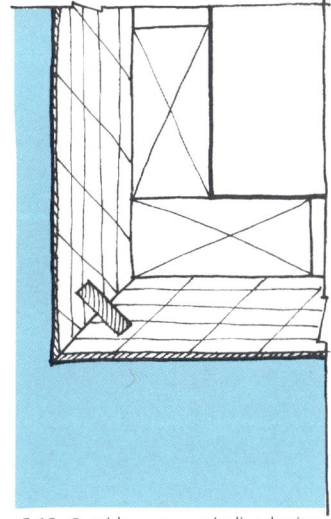 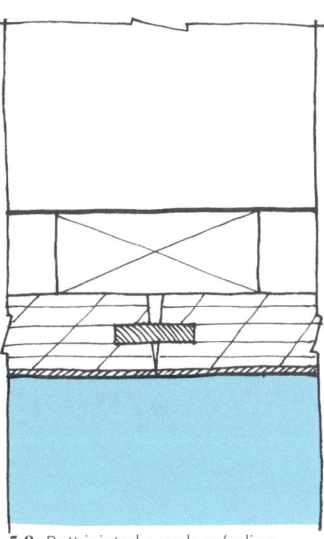 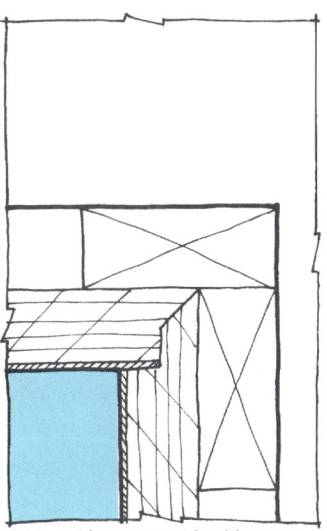

5.18 Outside corner w/splined miter   **5.8** Butt-jointed panels w/spline   **5.19** Inside corner w/shoulder miter

Details 5.20 to 5.22 correspond to detail 5.9 in which panels are joined with a reveal. Note the consistent use of dimension 'x' in keeping all the details relative. Outside corner detail 5.20 has the visual effect of the reveal in straight-on view. Inside corner detail 5.21 has the same dimension but in angled view, while detail 5.22 uses the straight-on view principle. This *seems* to be more appropriate with 5.20, however, since the sight line rarely falls perpendicular to the surface of an inside corner, this

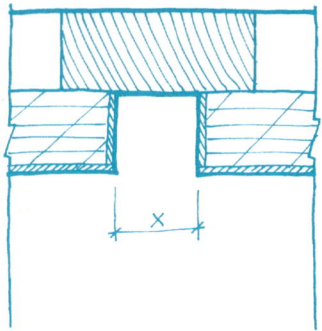

5.9 Reveal defines dimension 'x'

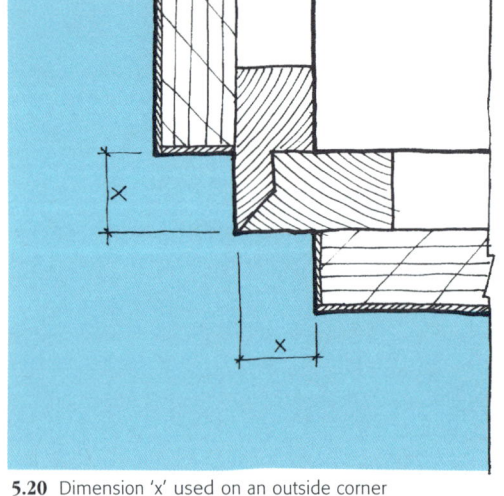

5.20 Dimension 'x' used on an outside corner

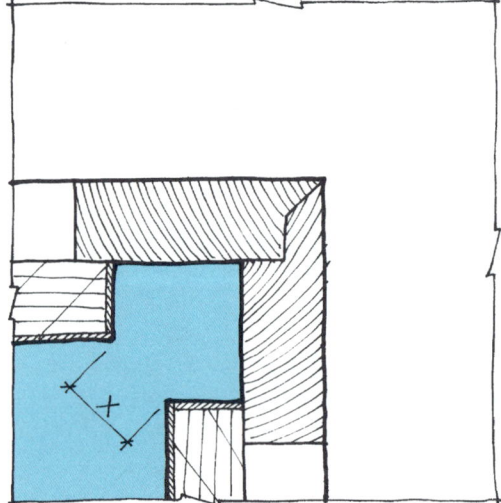

5.21 Dimension 'x' across inside corner

choice becomes an academic rather than a practical one. In reality, the corner is viewed from all angles; thus, maintaining dimension 'x' *across* the inside corner makes 5.21 most visually similar to 5.9 and 5.20; the proportion of the reveal appears to be consistent throughout all the details.

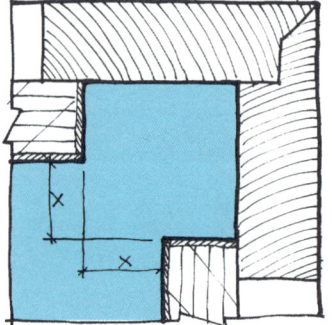

5.22 Dimension 'x' in straight-on view

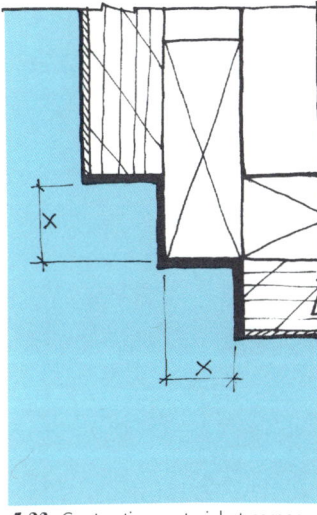
5.23 Contrasting material at corner

5.10 Contrasting material on reveal

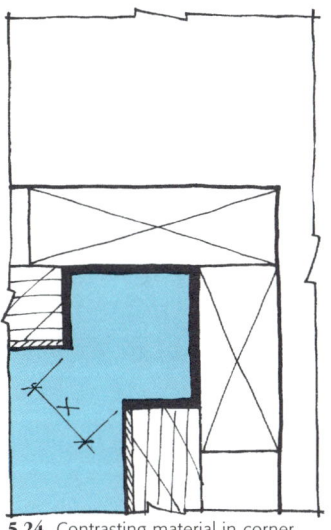
5.24 Contrasting material in corner

The details variations at left and right above would be suitable for the outside and inside corners to accompany 5.10, which is like 5.9 but with the reveal surface finished in contrasting material.

Note that 5.25, below left, unlike the variation above it, is a modified version of 5.20; the amount of reveal material has been reduced. Plastic or metal channel used in place of the veneer and wood of 5.20 would likely be too dominant.

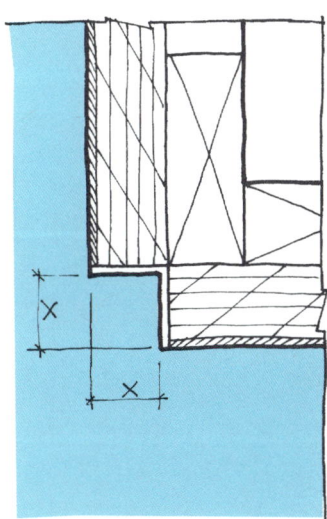
5.25 Outside corner w/inset channel

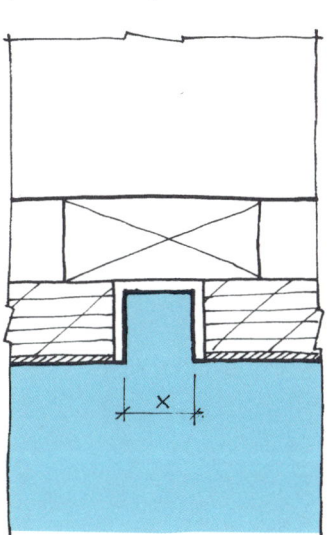
5.11 Panel reveal w/inset channel

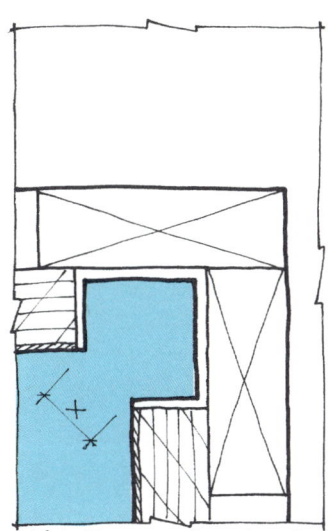
5.26 Inside corner w/inset channel

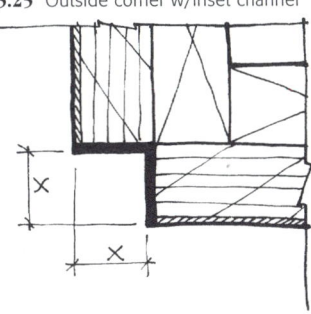

The simplified outside corner of detail 5.25 could be adapted as shown at left for use with panel joints 5.9 or 5.10.

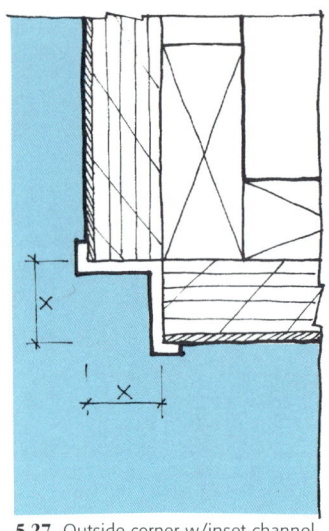 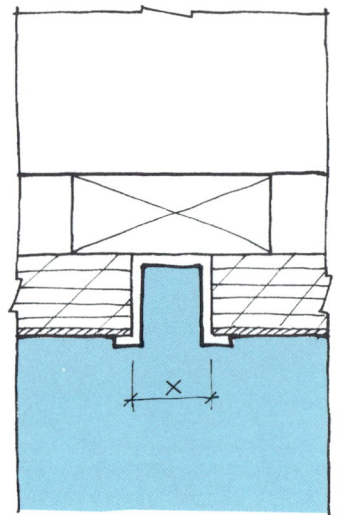 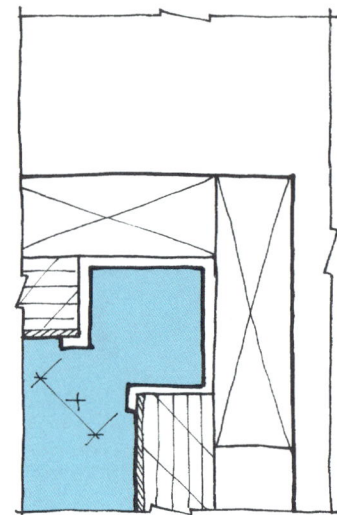

5.27 Outside corner w/inset channel **5.12** Reveal w/overlapping channel **5.28** Inside corner w/inset channel

The details at left and right above relate to panel joint 5.12—all featuring overlapping inset channels. They are variations on 5.25 and 5.26.

The details at left and right below have the same visual effect as panel joint 5.13, center. Maintaining dimension 'x' is the key factor for consistency.

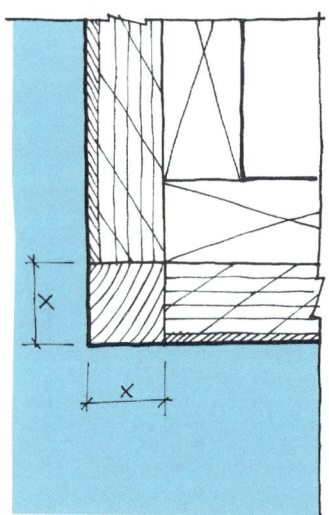 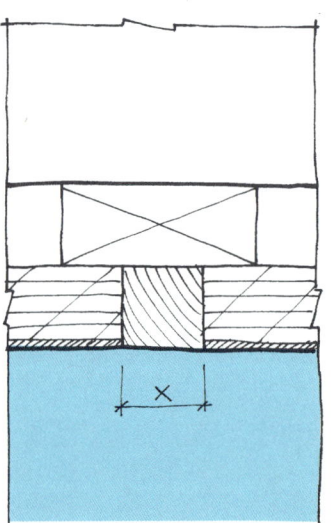 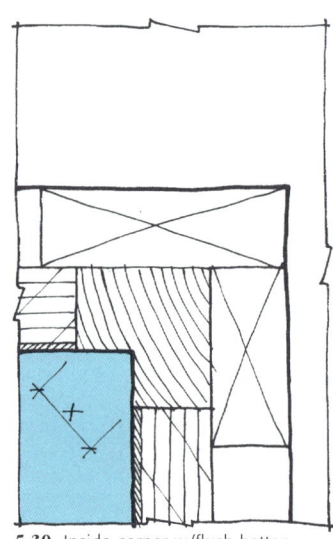

5.29 Outside corner w/flush batten **5.13** Panel joint w/flush batten **5.30** Inside corner w/flush batten

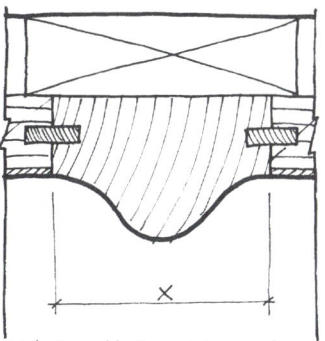

5.14 Curved batten joining panels

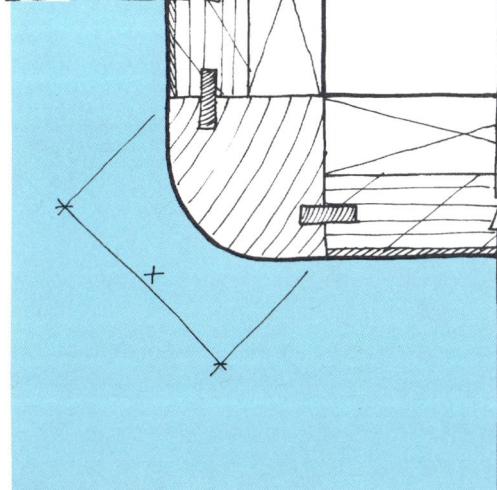

5.31 Outside corner w/curved batten

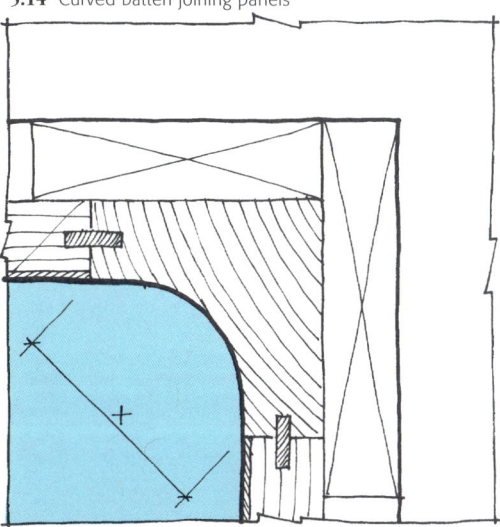

5.32 Inside corner w/curved batten

The rounded corners of 5.31 and 5.32 are the best solutions to match the curved batten that joins the panels, 5.14, top. Note that dimension 'x' comes into play again.

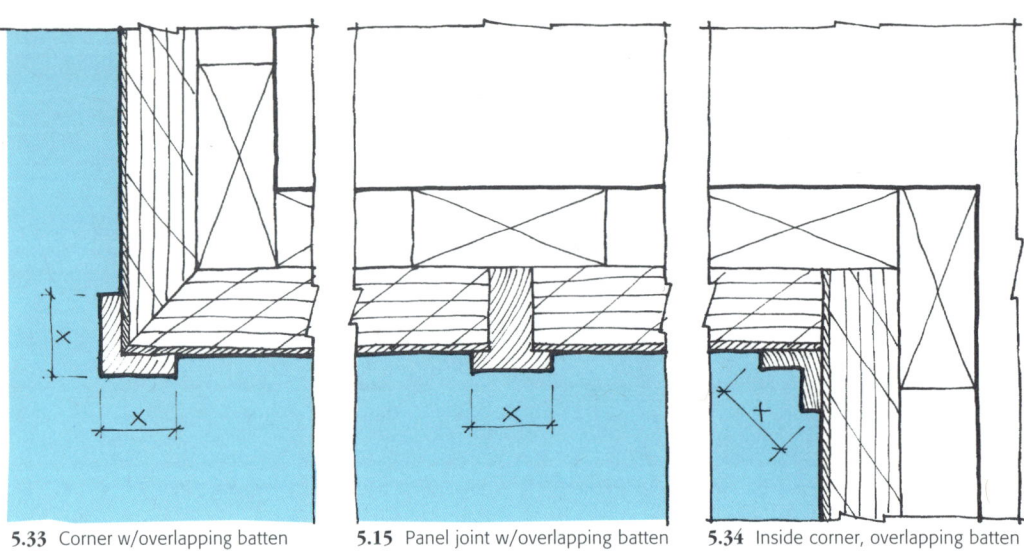

5.33 Corner w/overlapping batten **5.15** Panel joint w/overlapping batten **5.34** Inside corner, overlapping batten

Details 5.33 and 5.34 use dimension 'x' to match the discrete projection of the batten shown in 5.15, center.

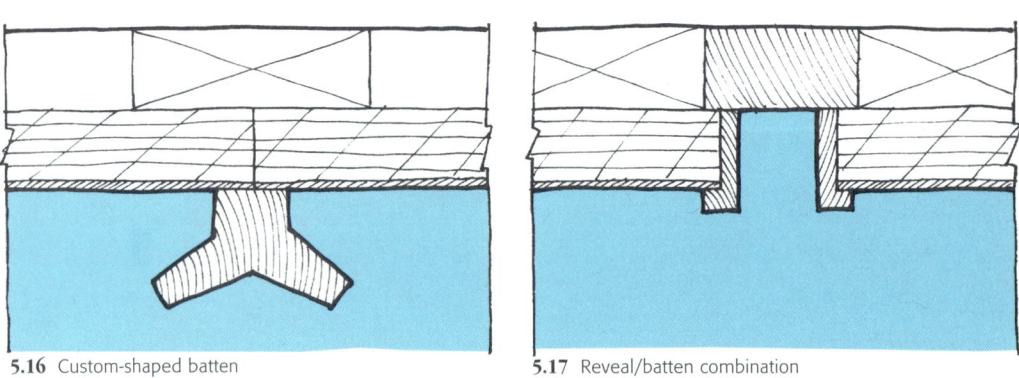

5.16 Custom-shaped batten **5.17** Reveal/batten combination

A custom-shaped batten such as 5.16 poses a slightly different problem. It is the type of dynamic design best used on a single surface, flat or curved. Corners would be downplayed, that is mitered as in 5.18/5.19.

The 5.17 combination reveal and batten would need similarly treated corners. Maintain dimension 'x' with 5.20 and 5.21 as models.

Vertical Connections

Now that we have examined the horizontal joints in a paneled wall, let us look back at the vertical joints involved in the floor/wall/ceiling connections. The simplified profiles on the following pages show the six basic ceiling/wall connections and the three wall/floor connections; for comparison the seven horizontal panel-to-panel joints are also included. Each detail is identified by its original number.

The design challenge is to match up one profile from each category to produce an aesthetically pleasing paneled wall design. As a demonstration, we have explored the concept of a continuous, joint-free wall in the chart on page 139 using panel-to-panel detail 5.8. Crosscheck the visual impact of various profiles when combined. Note that the choices of ceiling-to-wall and wall-to-floor profiles—combined on the chart with just one panel-to-panel profile—have resulted in ten variations. Other possible treatments, which vary widely in concept, are described beginning on page 140.

Ceiling-to-Wall Connections
(section)

4.26 90° butt   **4.27** Reveal on ceiling   **4.28** Reveal on wall

Wall-to-Floor Connections
(section)

4.12 Recessed baseboard

Panel-to-Panel Connections
(plan view)

5.8 Butt   **5.9** Reveal   **5.13** Flush batten

Examples devised to demonstrate specific ceiling-to-wall and wall-to-floor character relationships are discussed on the following pages.

4.29 Applied molding

4.30 Flush molding, reveal

4.31 Recessed cap

4.8 Applied baseboard

4.11 Flush baseb'd, reveal

5.14 Curved batten

5.15 Overlapping batten

5.16 Custom batten

5.17 Reveal and batten

Combining Connection Details
(on a descending scale from most compatible to acceptable)

Concept	Panel-to-panel Connection	Wall-to-floor Connection	Ceiling-to-wall Connection
Smooth, continuous, joint-free	5.8	4.8	4.29
			4.26
			4.27
			4.28
		4.11	4.30
			4.28
			4.26
		4.12	4.31
			4.28
			4.26

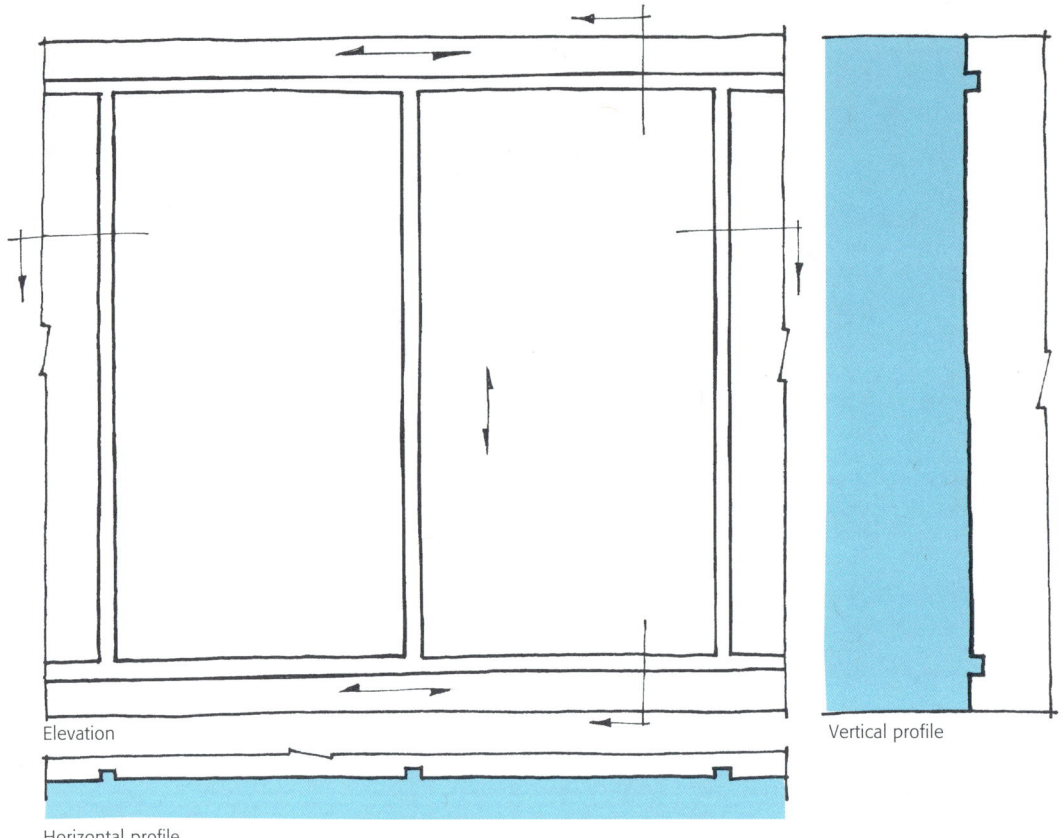

5.35 Low-profile paneled wall with reveals and flush base and cap

Wall Effects With Paneling
When choosing connection details remember that certain combinations are useful in achieving particular wall effects, some of which are described here.

Low-Profile Paneling In 5.35, because each panel is set off by shallow reveals, the details produce a flat, low-profile wall. Even though the grain direction of the baseboard and cap is perpendicular to that of the wall panels, the wall reads as a homogeneous plane from floor to ceiling, with the base and cap less obtrusive separate elements.

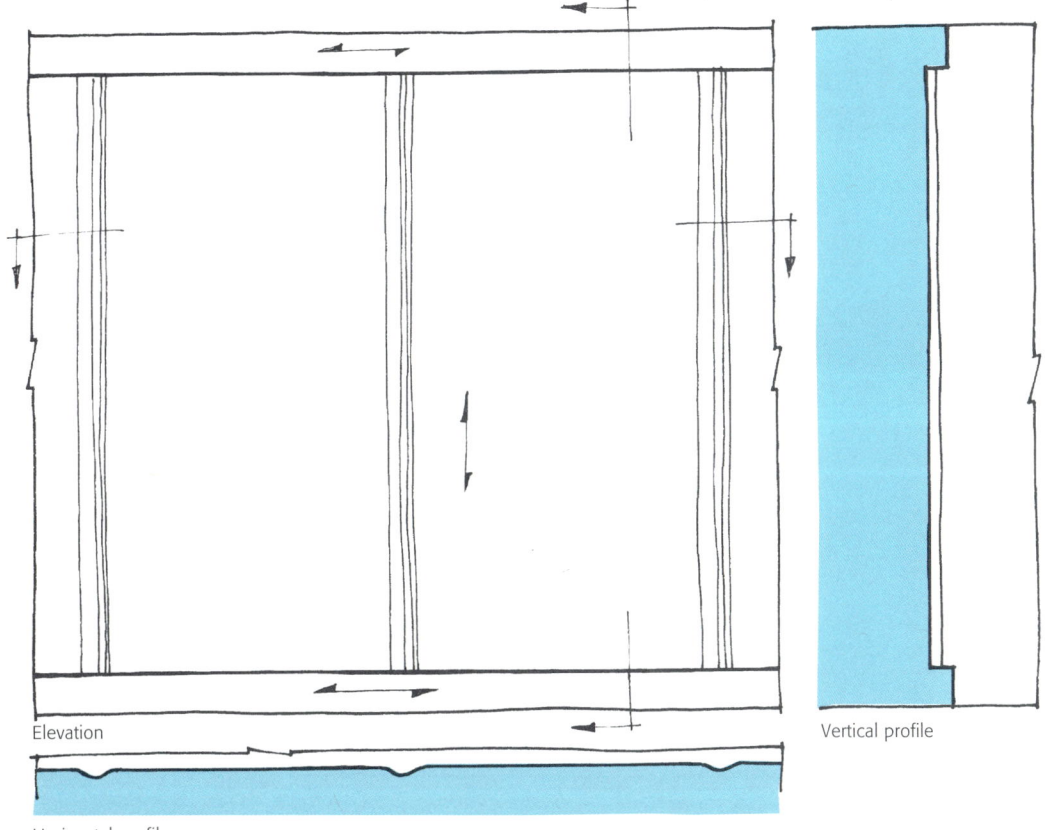

5.36 Applied paneling with curved battens and recessed base and cap

Paneled Wall-on-Wall In 5.36, the paneling appears to have been applied onto the surface, in a continuous wood treatment that periodically erupts into a curved fold-out but carries on as a band across the wall (or around the room). Bands formed by the recessed base and cap read as the true wall plane; the paneling emphasizes a new plane in front, an effect that can be heightened by using a material other than wood for the base and cap. Doing so would suggest that the true wall is the material which is mostly concealed by the wood unrolled across it.

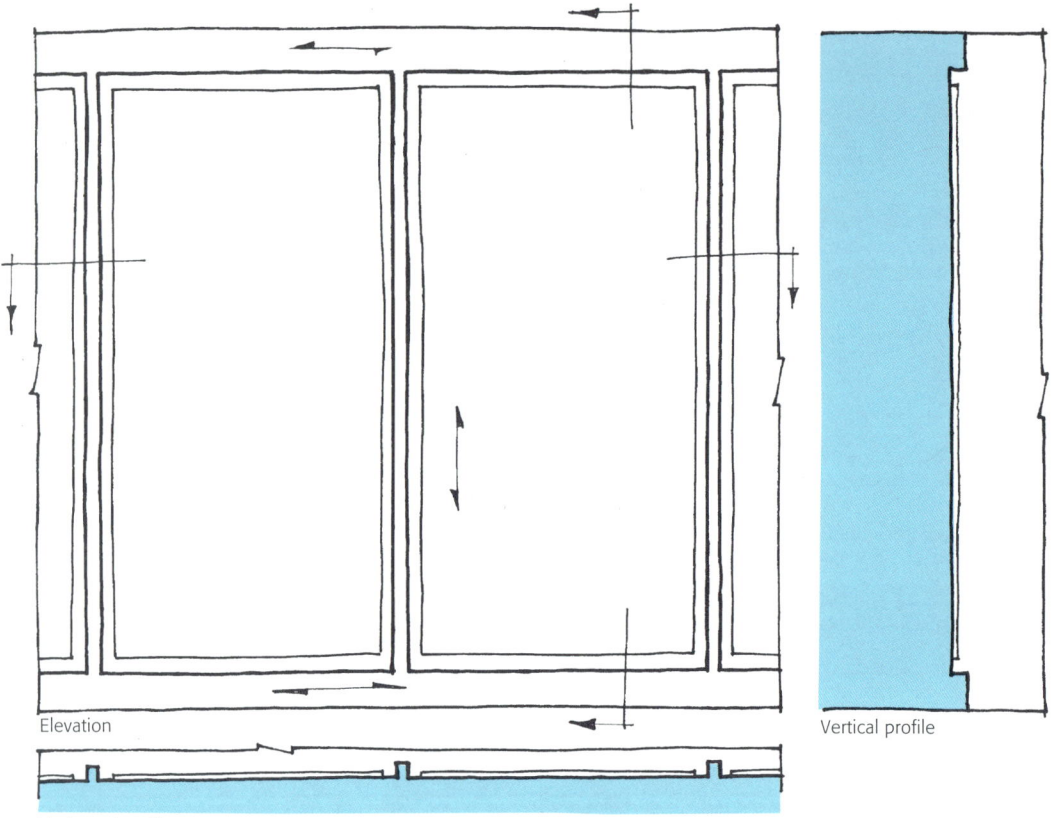

Elevation

Vertical profile

Horizontal profile

5.37 Framed individual panels with reveal detail and recessed base and cap

Framed Paneling In figure 5.37, a wall covered with solidly framed individual panels, vertical detail 5.17 has been matched with base and cap details that are slight variations of 4.12 and 4.31. To heighten the individuality of the panels you could specify center-matched veneers, giving a central axis and completeness to each panel even though each would relate side to side because of the sequence-matching of the sheets of plywood. The effect is a contemporary recall of traditional paneling, often used to indicate that the occupant has the traditions and solidity of the past yet is of the contemporary world.

To further your knowledge of the many options offered by veneer paneling, look at illustrations of wood treatments in the trade magazines. Try to identify the psychological effect that each designer was trying to create, and how this image is communicated to visiting viewers by the occupant of the space.

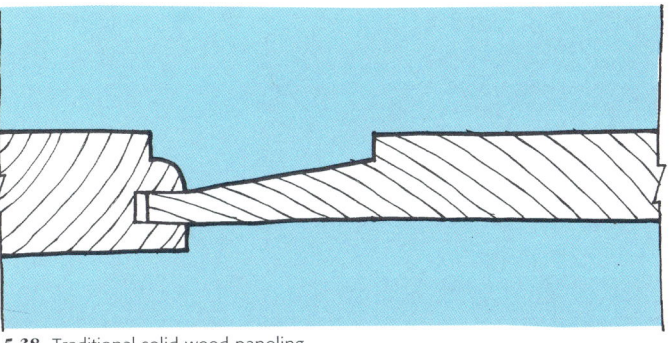

5.38 Traditional solid wood paneling

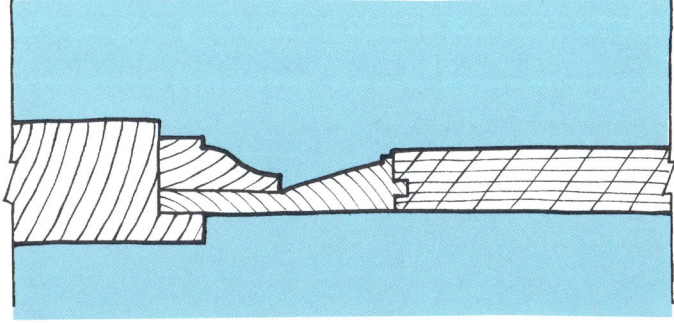

5.39 Beveled solid wood edge, plywood panel

Traditional Paneling

By necessity, traditional paneling was originally made up of small pieces of solid wood. Veneered plywood was as yet unavailable. The wood panel sections were small since solid wood in smaller pieces was less subject to the warping and cracking that normally resulted from changes in humidity. The panel face was usually flat sliced. The grain ran vertically on the panel and the side pieces, called *stiles*, and horizontally on the top, in-between and bottom pieces, called *rails*. The stiles and rails would meet with the effect of a butt joint or a mitered joint, which concealed the actual mortise and tenon or splines in the joint. Today the same system is used except that the panel is more likely to be plywood and therefore can be in larger dimensions.

If you wish to design traditional paneling, study the styles of moldings used in various periods of design. Details 5.38 to 5.41 show a selection of panel/molding profiles. The use of such panel details almost certainly calls for a molded baseboard and a crown molding at the ceiling. It is recommended that you draw a three-dimensional sketch at fairly large scale to weigh the full impact of your design.

Detail 5.38 shows a simple traditional solid wood panel with a beveled edge.

In 5.39, only the beveled panel edge and molding are solid wood while the panel is plywood; this panel could be much larger than the one in detail 5.38.

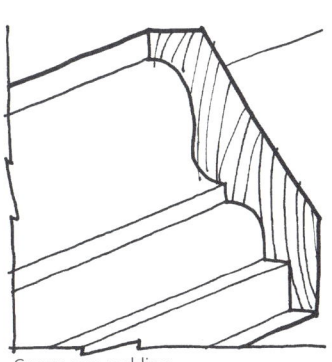

Crown cap molding

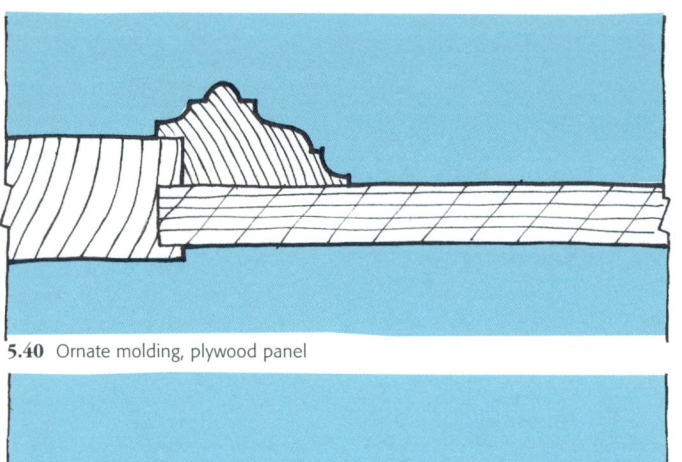

5.40 Ornate molding, plywood panel

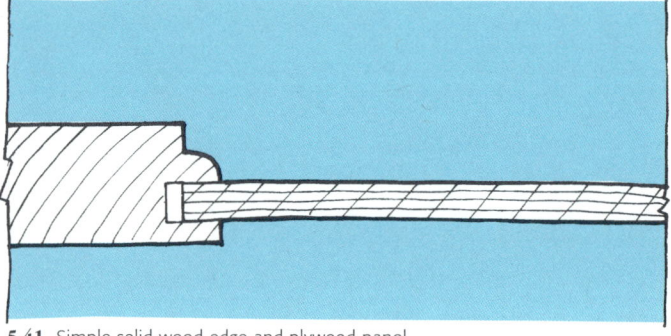

5.41 Simple solid-wood edge and plywood panel

Detail 5.40 is a flat plywood panel with a rather ornately-cut molding. This is a much heavier visual treatment than the relatively low relief of details 5.38 and 5.39.

In contrast, a fairly simple, almost contemporary, panel design is shown in detail 5.41.

Review the section in chapter 2 on special matching of veneers (page 38) and you will see that it is open to your imagination to create wondrous paneling effects with grain patterns, colors, inserts of other materials, and careful attention to detail. The catalyst is your knowledge of how to pull it all together.

The Cabinet-to-Wall Relationship

Now that you have been exposed to the variety and complexity of detailing for wall surfaces, it should be clear that detail choices for a wall relate to and affect the attachment of cabinetry to that wall. Since the overall visual effect will be determined by the relationship of these details, it is important to consider the construction of the wall itself, and how it will affect the methods of attachment. Review hanging of cabinetry in chapter 3 beginning with page 80.

Doors, Door Frames & Glazing

CHAPTER 1 2 3 4 5 6 7

Consider the door, one of the most visible and important features of an interior space. Because it is the means of entering, the door is a major component of the visual introduction to a space, and is usually the first physical contact a visitor will have. The effect a door is intended to communicate—whether inviting or intimidating, passive or secure—must be considered when materials and details are selected.

Basic Doors

Doors are constructed in three basic types: hollow core, solid core/staved wood, and solid core/particle board or mineral foam. In any case the door will have a solid wood edging so that it may be shaped, and have the strength to support itself when screwed to hinges and hung in place.

Standard thickness for a door is 1 3/4" although hollow-core doors are also made in 1 3/8", primarily for residential or low-end commercial use. Width and height in stock sizes may vary as shown in the chart on the following page. The standard door for commercial use is 3'-0" x 7'-0" x 1 3/4" solid core. Check with local suppliers for stock sizes available.

- solid wood edge
- 3-ply plywood facing
- honeycomb support structure
- hollow space

6.1 Hollow-core door

As a designer you should be familiar with the "feel" of a door. Comparing actual showroom samples is recommended; doors are often displayed complete with hardware and hung in door frames. Does the door seem substantial enough to provide the desired feeling of privacy when closed? A hollow-core door is light and has a poor sound rating; a solid door has a weighty feel and provides aural privacy. Even in a residential project your client might want the psychological effect of a barrier with substance.

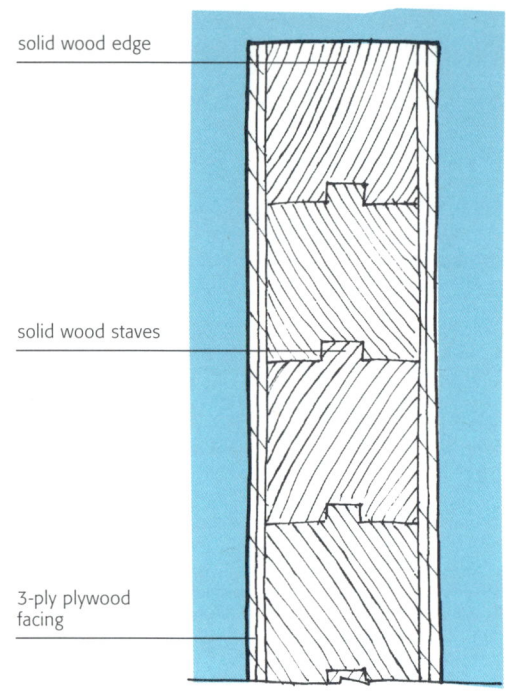

6.2 Solid-core door/staved wood

Standard Door Sizes
Standard thickness is 1 3/4"; hollow core also available in 1 3/8".

	Width	Height
Hollow core	2'-6"	6'-6"
		6'-8"
		6'-10"
	2'-8"	6'-8"
		6'-10"
		7'-0"
Solid core	2'-8"	6'-10"
	3'-0"	7'-0"

Larger sizes available as custom order.

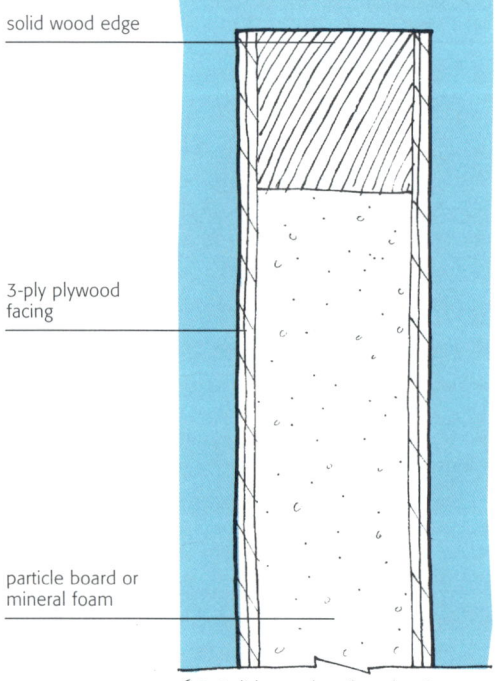

6.3 Solid-core door/board or foam

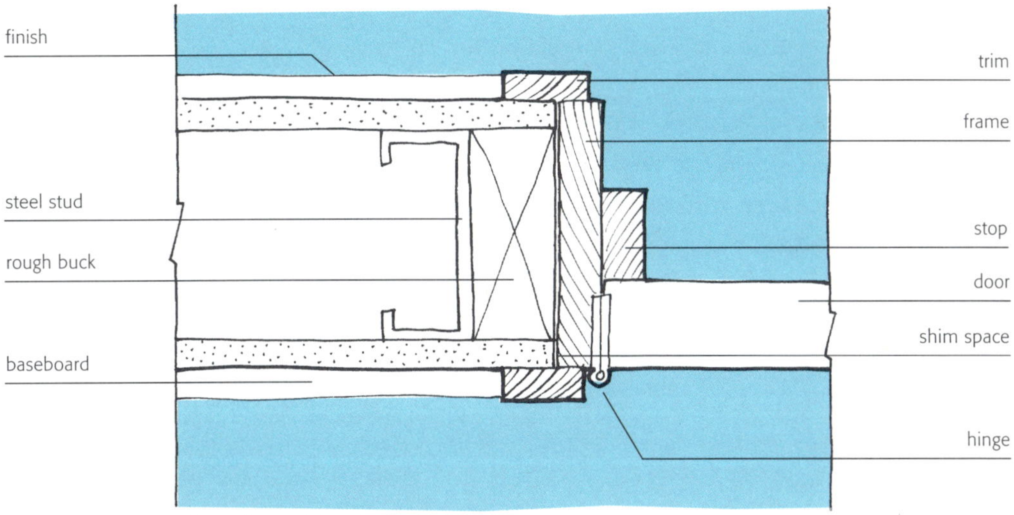

6.4 Basic wood door jamb, plan

6.5 Basic wood door jamb, elevation

Door Frames

A door frame basically has two functions: to hold the door in place, and to cover the exposed, often rough, edges of wall construction and finishes.

In all three basic types of wall construction—wood stud, steel stud, and concrete block—the door frame is fixed to a wood back-up called a *rough buck,* therefore the details relative to wall construction do not vary much. For illustration purposes, a steel stud wall and standard 1 3/4" door will be used. Details will be shown for the hinge side because it is more complex and often presents challenges for the designer. Remember that the various parts of a door jamb such as shown in 6.4—the entire assembly including rough buck, frame, stop and trim—must function as described regardless of the changes you make in the visual appearance of the door frame.

A simple wall construction with a drywall finish and an applied baseboard is shown in detail 6.4 (also see 4.8). The **rough buck** stiffens the flimsy steel stud wall and provides a material to which the **frame** may be nailed or screwed. The wall construction and rough buck are not likely to be true vertical within the close tolerance needed for a well-fitted door, so the shim space is provided to allow for inconsistency in the constructed width of the opening and to allow the frame to be leveled to a true vertical. The

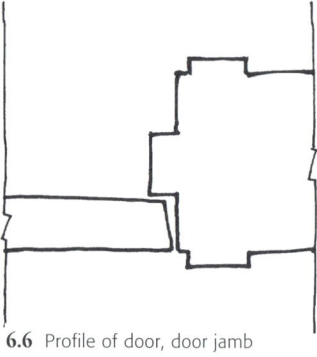

6.6 Profile of door, door jamb

stop prevents the door from swinging too far and putting stress on the hinges. The **trim** covers the rough edges of

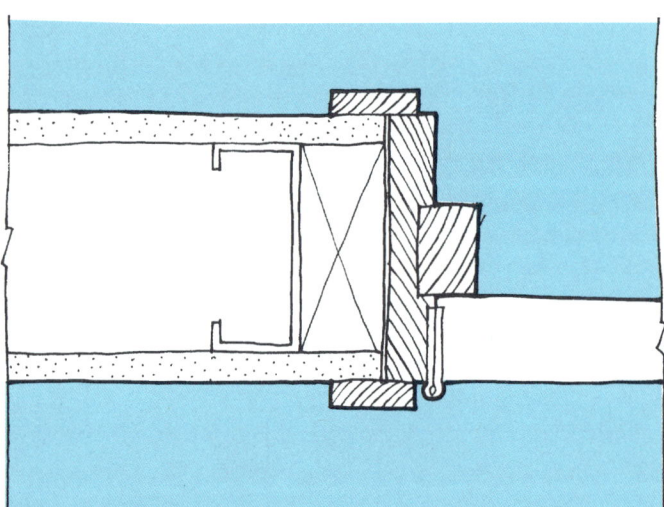

6.7 Jamb with dadoed door stop

the finish and the shim space. Note that the trim is set back from the face of the frame rather than set flush to diminish the surface discrepancy should a gap develop if either or both pieces shrink due to variation in humidity.

Detail 6.6 shows the latch side of the door in profile to draw your attention to the fact that this vertical edge is trimmed back on an angle. This allows the edge of the door to clear the edge of the frame during the arc of the opening/closing swing. A less advisable alternative would be to have the whole door cut well short of the frame, which would leave an undesirable gap.

A door stop which is nailed to the frame is called a **planted stop.** If the stop warps a gap could open between the two pieces; for higher quality work it is preferable to dado the stop into the frame, as shown in 6.7, or rabbet the frame to form an integral stop, as shown in 6.8.

Note that each time there is a plane change another vertical face appears, adding to the "molded" effect of a door frame. In 6.7 both the inside and outside of the frame are identical, while in 6.8 the door side has an additional jog which means the trim pieces do not align on the two sides of the wall, which could be significant if you are dealing with a wall with clear glazing or equal-sized panels on both sides.

A trimmer, more contemporary look may be achieved with a detail like 6.9. Here, the trim and the frame are the same piece, reducing the number of jogs, or *rebates.* This is, however, an expensive detail to produce.

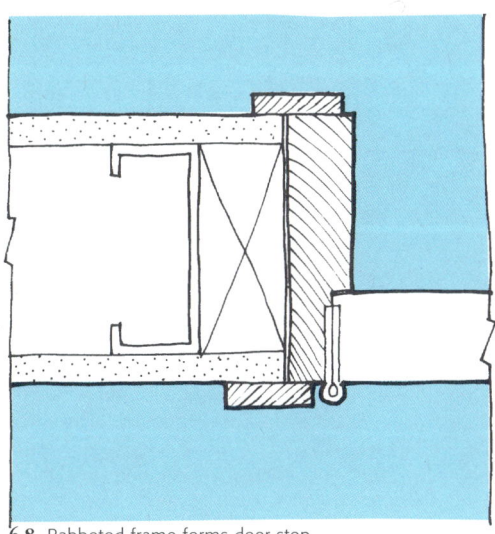

6.8 Rabbeted frame forms door stop

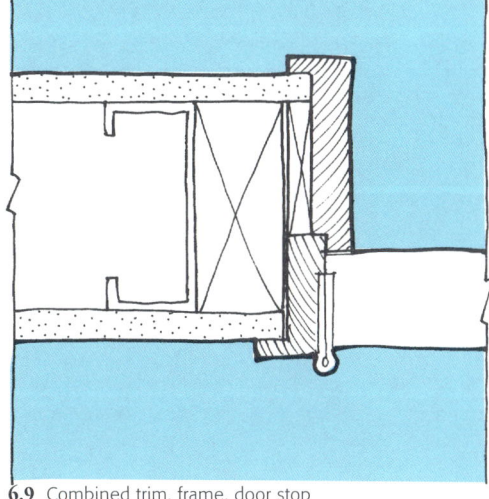

6.9 Combined trim, frame, door stop

151

When relating a door frame and door to a wall with a flush baseboard and reveal (as in 4.11) we need to modify the frame detail to the ones shown in 6.10 or 6.12. Note that in 6.12 the frame edge on the wall outside the door is wider than on the door side. This detail is often considered unacceptable on a project, so use it with caution.

In both situations the baseboard is flush with the faces of the wall and door. Detail 6.11 shows this in elevation; 6.13 shows an optional treatment, however carrying the reveal down to the floor could cause minor problems with flooring installation and maintenance. To surmount this problem, two solutions are described in the details at the lower right.

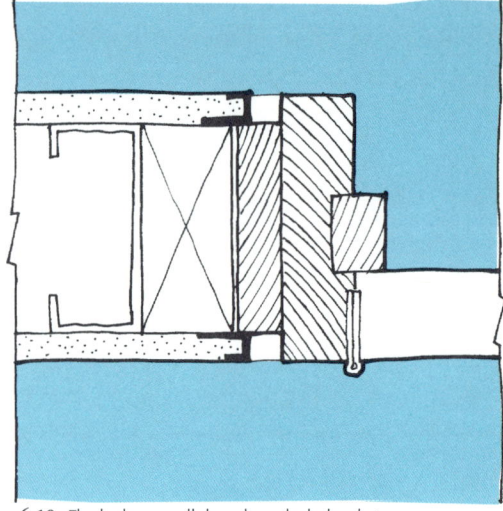

6.10 Flush door, wall, baseboard; dadoed stop

6.11 Elevation of reveal and flush baseboard, frame, door

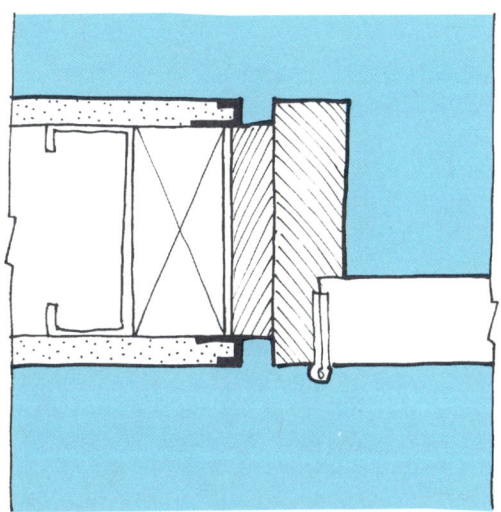

6.12 Flush-set door with rabbeted frame/door stop

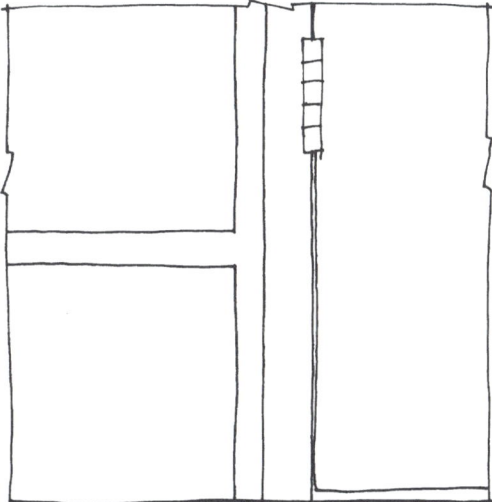

6.13 Elevation showing reveal abutting floor

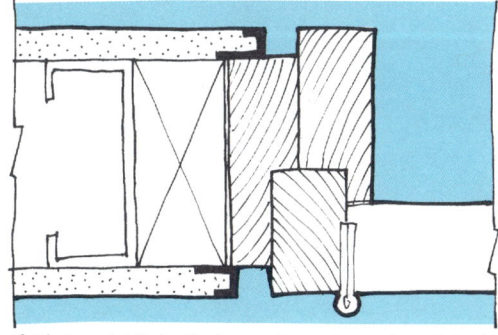 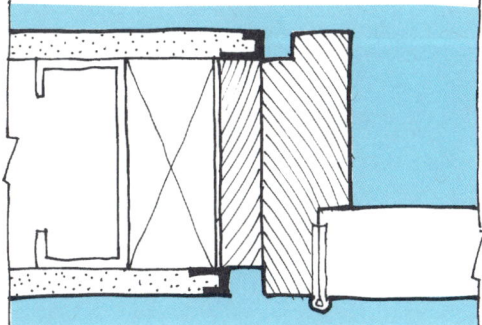

6.14 Two details for flush mounting a door w/equal-sized frame edges

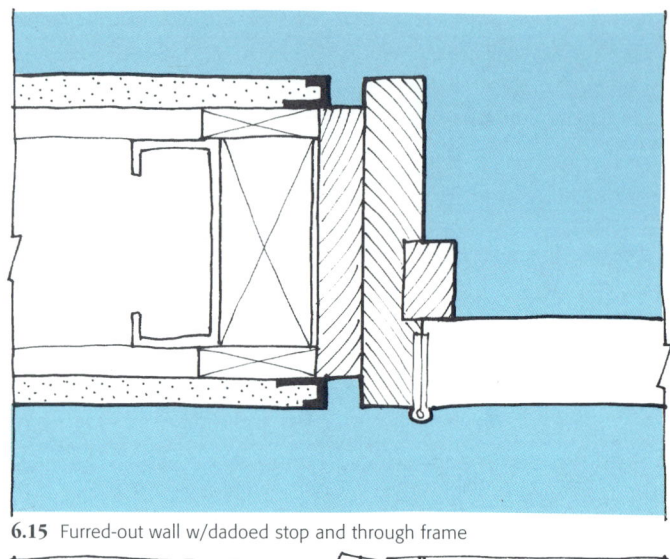

6.15 Furred-out wall w/dadoed stop and through frame

6.16 Elevation showing recessed baseboard

When relating a door frame and door to a recessed baseboard (as in 4.14), the depth of the frame must be increased so that it masters the furring on each side of the wall construction. Details 6.15 and 6.17 each do the job but differently in order to accommodate the door stop variants.

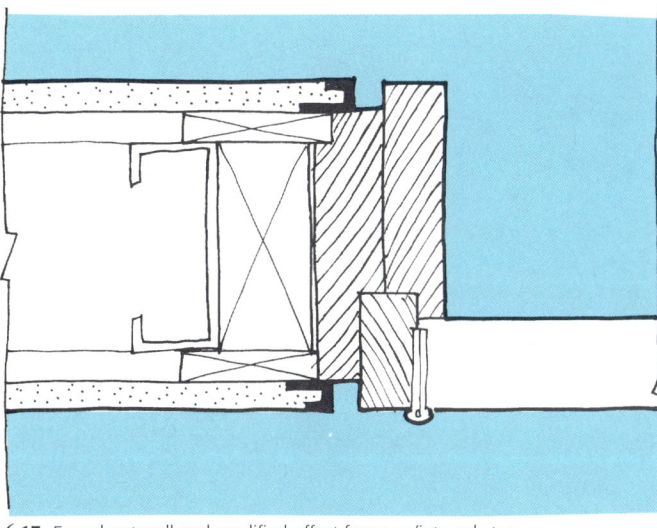

6.17 Furred-out wall and modified offset frame w/integral stop

Door Frames for Paneled Walls

To this point we have dealt with door frames for basic drywall construction. Let us now consider frames relative to wall paneling details, which were described in the previous chapter.

Flat Paneled Walls Detail 5.8 shows butt-jointed paneling which provides a smooth flat wall, not unlike drywall conditions. The details for an adjacent door frame would therefore correspond as shown below.

Detail 6.18 illustrates the standard door jamb treatment with a dadoed stop, but in a paneled wall on strapping rather than a drywall. Detail 6.19 recalls 6.9 with the frame offset for the door stop, except that paneling has been used on one side of the wall and drywall on the other. As you can see, it is a simple variation.

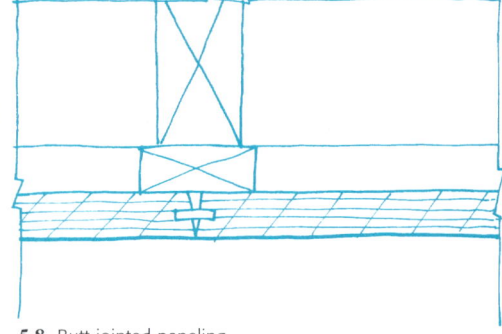

5.8 Butt-jointed paneling

Reveals Separating Panels Details 5.9 to 5.12 dealt with reveals between panels; in 5.13 contrasting material was inserted between the panels. With the substitution of paneling for drywall, 6.15 or 6.17 would be appropriate details for the adjacent door frame.

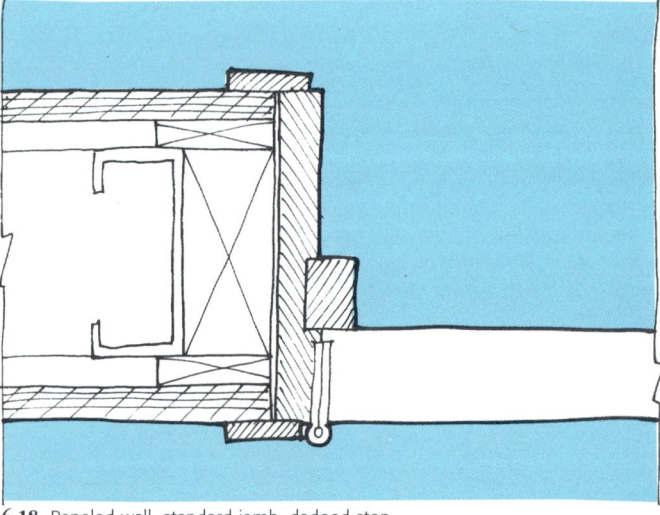

6.18 Paneled wall, standard jamb, dadoed stop

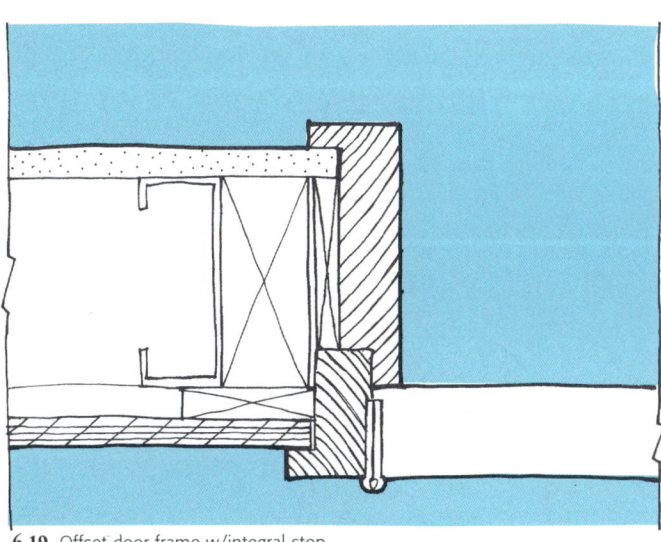

6.19 Offset door frame w/integral stop

Shaped Battens Separating Panels A projecting molding such as shown in 5.14 creates a somewhat different situation in which a transition must occur between the molding and the door frame. This can be solved in several ways; details 6.20 and 6.21 illustrate two solutions. Other variations could be devised dependent on the raised molding that you have applied to the wall (such as 5.15, 5.16, or any other).

Note that in these two examples drywall is shown on one side of the wall. It is unlikely that an elaborate molding treatment would be carried out in two adjacent rooms. This assumption permits us to show two details in each illustration. Remember that for the less elaborate side of the wall you may choose to use a treatment different from the ones shown. While door frame style is usually consistent throughout a project it may vary where special wall treatments have been devised.

In 6.20, the flow of panel-to-molding-to-panel

5.14 Paneled wall w/projecting molding

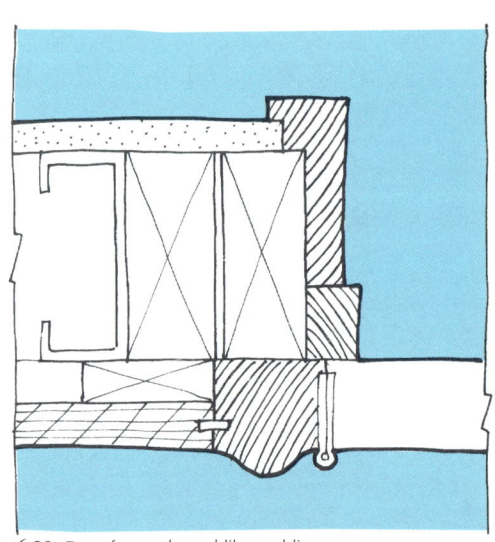

6.20 Door frame shaped like molding

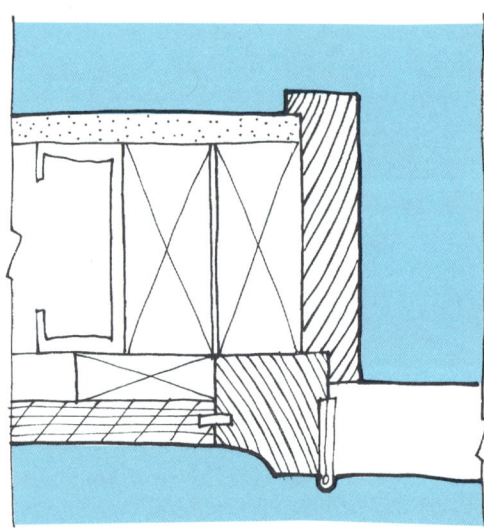

6.21 Door frame curved like molding

has been continued by using the molding shape as the door jamb shape. The continuity would be enhanced if the door veneers were matched to the wall panel veneers.

In 6.21, the panel-molding treatment ends with a curved jamb which sets off the door as a separate entity. In this case the door would probably be finished differently from the wall paneling.

A "framed panel" wall (see 5.17) or a wall with a combination reveal and overlapping batten requires a jamb detail such as 6.22, not unlike that for reveal-style paneling.

Detail 6.23 shows another variant, one way of cleanly separating the panel effect from the door yet having it relate to the door jamb. Make the face dimensions for both the door jamb and the panel trim equal to the reveal dimension.

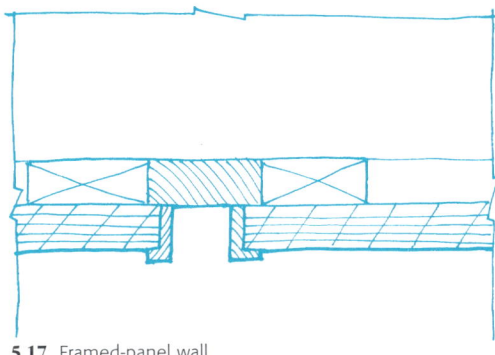

5.17 Framed-panel wall

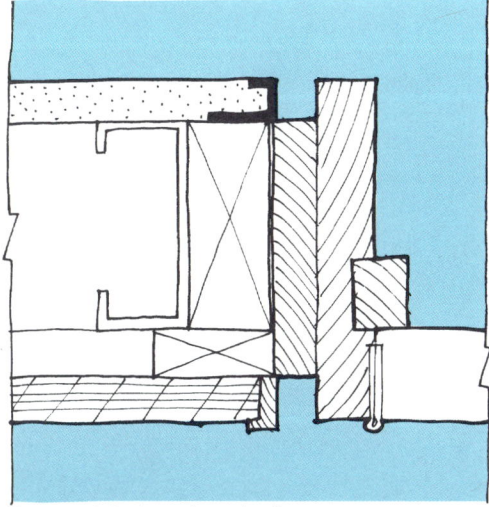

6.22 Jamb for framed-panel wall

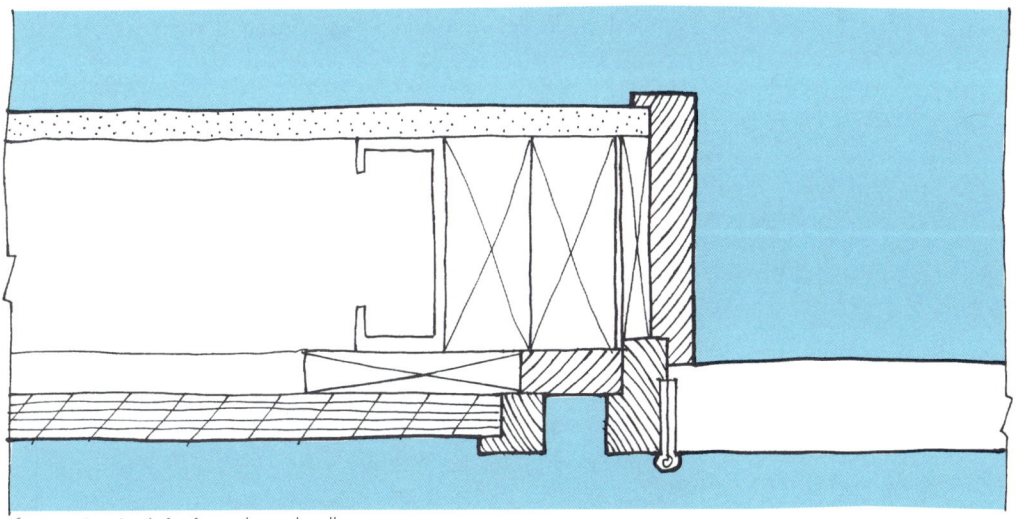

6.23 Variant jamb for framed-panel wall

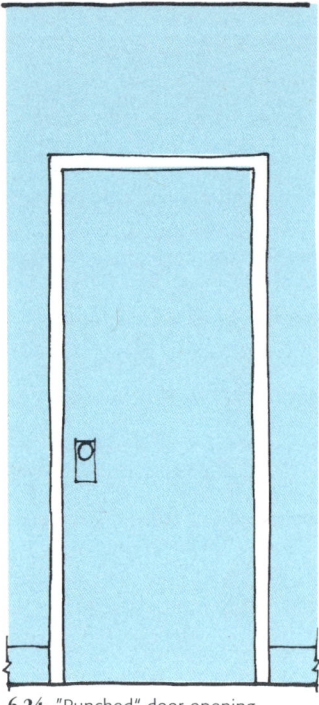

6.24 "Punched" door opening

Door Head Details

You may already have a picture in your mind's eye of how high a door is and what the head detail would look like—probably a detail similar to the jamb but at 7'-0" off the floor. That would be a reasonable and acceptable idea. Detail 6.24 shows this typical "punched" opening in a wall.

A door needn't stop at 7'-0" however, and the head detail needn't be the same as the jamb, although it usually is when the door stops short of the ceiling. If your concept of the space and plane surfaces does not call for punched openings then you may want to carry the expression of the door from floor to ceiling. This can be done in several ways as shown in 6.25 to 6.27.

If paneling has been used, before you complete your design carefully examine door frame details relative to the paneling details. Not all styles are compatible, either from the construction or aesthetic points of view.

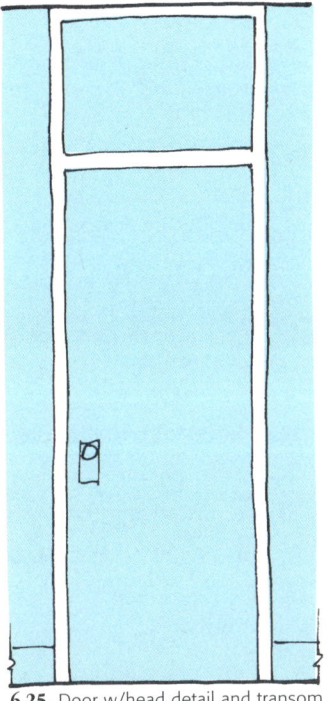
6.25 Door w/head detail and transom

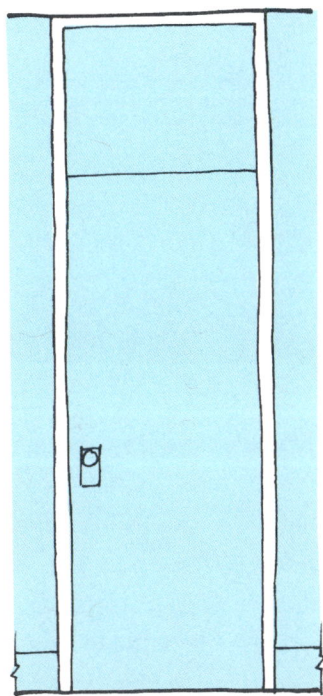
6.26 Door flush with transom panel

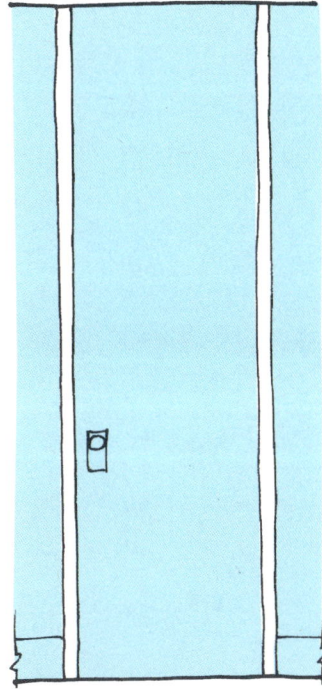
6.27 Full-height door

The door in 6.25 stops at 7'-0" (or whatever height) and a fixed or movable transom panel is installed between a set of head details.

The door in 6.26 has been manufactured full height then cut at the 7'-0" level, with the remainder fixed in place as a transom above and flush with the door. The head detail is above the transom panel. Alternately the door can be left full height and have a head detail.

In 6.27, the door is full room height with no apparent head detail. This configuration calls for a flat frame plate flush with the ceiling, in which case the head detail is just not visible in elevation. Alternately, the ceiling material may carry through the opening; then, except for bracing above the ceiling, there really is no head to the frame.

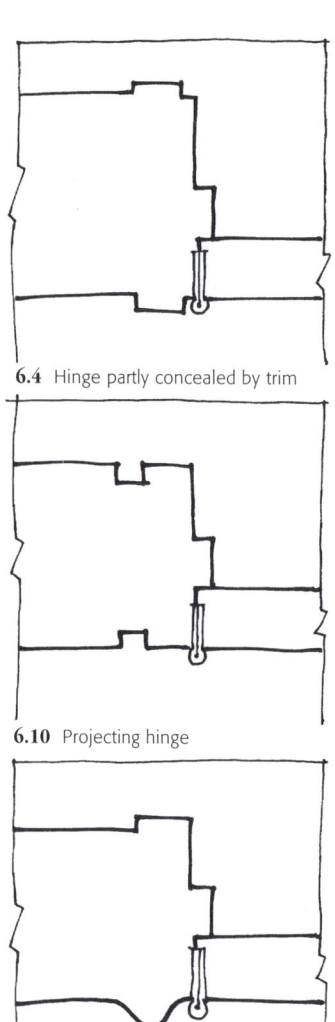

6.4 Hinge partly concealed by trim

6.10 Projecting hinge

6.20 Hinge partly concealed by trim

Hardware for Door Frames

Another point to consider is the location of the various pieces of frame hardware: plain or concealed pivot hinges, door closers, door stays, and so on. For these specialty items you must seek out the manufacturers' or distributors' literature for design possibilities and adaptation requirements. Catalogs and spec sheets will show detail drawings of the modifications necessary for use of various items.

The ordinary **butt hinge** as illustrated in the profiles at left is the subject of this discussion. Note that in profiles 6.4 and 6.20 the door face aligns with the wall plane and the hinge is partly concealed by the projecting trim. In profile 6.10 the door face, wall and trim are all in one plane and the hinge projects.

With the shaped molding of the 6.21a profile the door is brought forward flush with the trim face and well in front of the wall plane; the hinge projects. To diminish the prominence of the hinge, a set-back variation 6.21b has been created in which the door is recessed between prominently projecting trim moldings.

Profile 6.22a shows the door aligned with the trim plane and in front of the framed panel. Shifting the door face to the plane of the wall panel as shown in the variation 6.22b requires an **extended leaf hinge**. In this type of hinge, the leaves are wider so that the door can be recessed but still pivot beyond the trim plane. If an ordinary hinge were used in this situation the door would have to be prevented from opening wider than 90° or it would damage the trim. (You can test this by sketching 6.22b with both hinges and pivoting the lines of each door face.)

For a discussion of pressed metal doors and frames, see page 189 in chapter 7.

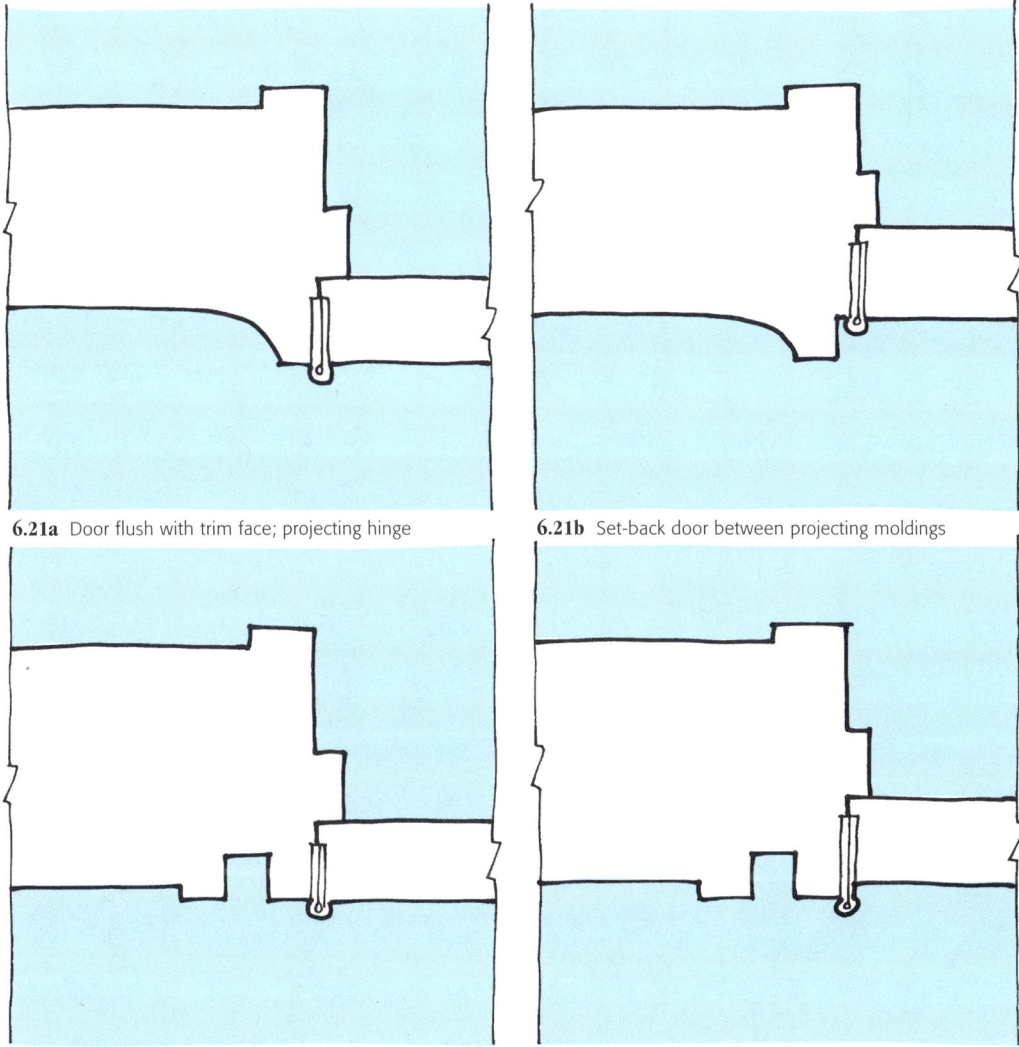

6.21a Door flush with trim face; projecting hinge

6.21b Set-back door between projecting moldings

6.22a Door flush with trim in front of paneling

6.22b Recessed door requires extended leaf hinge

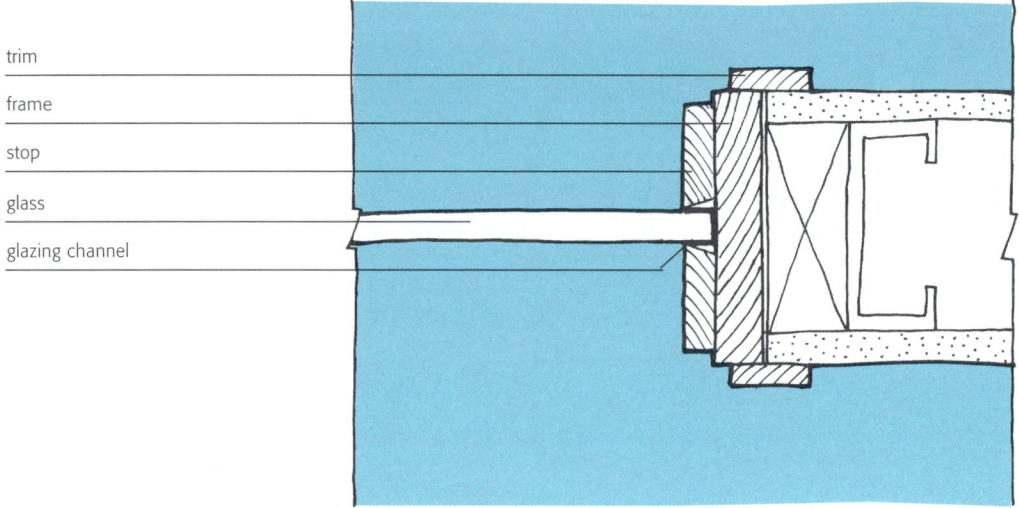

6.28 Standard glazing jamb

Interior Glazing

Glazing on any but exterior walls is the subject of this section of the chapter. Windows on exterior walls have not been included in this description of glazing details since they serve purposes entirely specific to their location as barriers to the environment, and are usually designed by the manufacturers. In exterior glazing the choices are numerous. You must decide on the desired style of window and then search for it in the literature. It is likely that you will find either a style that is compatible with your planned frame/trim details or one that can be modified to suit your purposes.

For a variety of reasons you may decide to have a portion, or perhaps the entirety, of an interior wall in glazing. Let us consider what is involved in designing a wall that is partly glass. (Rigid sheet acrylic may be substituted, and for purposes of this discussion is considered as glazing.) Needed are a frame to conceal the unfinished edges of wall construction and finishes, and something to

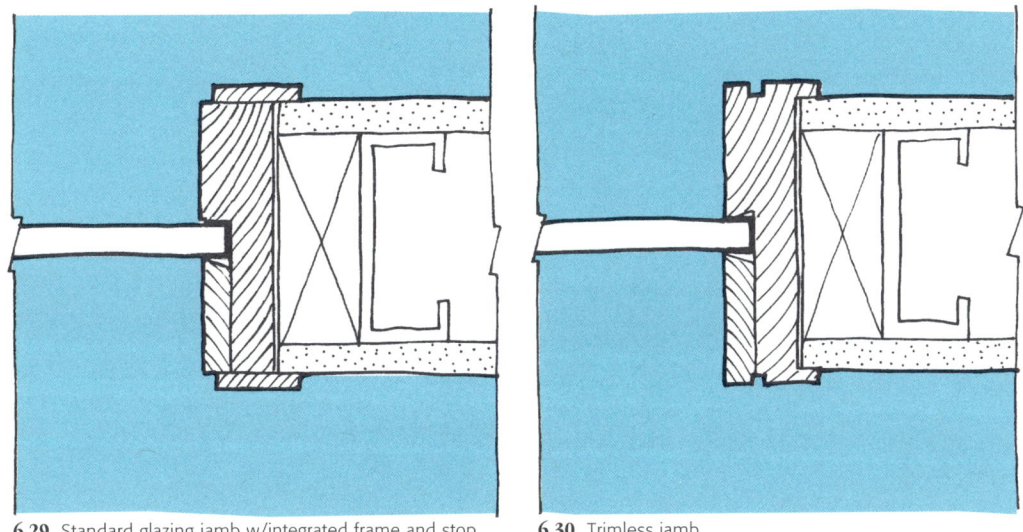

6.29 Standard glazing jamb w/integrated frame and stop   **6.30** Trimless jamb

hold the glass in place. Refer to the sectional plans and details 6.28 to 6.30 above, which illustrate the basic wall-to-glazing configurations.

Plan view 6.28 shows a **standard glazing jamb** with frame, stops, and trim. Check the similarities to the standard door jamb (6.4)—set-backs to disguise gaps at flush meeting points (trim, frame and stops), and trim to cover unfinished wall edges. Stops that enclose glass should be trimmed at a slight angle so that a tight fit is ensured, and at least one stop must be removable to allow the installation of the glass and its replacement if breakage should occur. A glazing channel, which is usually vinyl though felt or leather could be used, is necessary to prevent the glass from rattling in the frame and to cushion it against shocks such as occur when a door is slammed. Variation 6.29 is a similar solution but with an integral frame and stop.

A trimless jamb is shown in detail 6.30; it *looks* simplified but in its simplicity has introduced a problem that must be reconciled. The stop and the frame pieces, should they end flush and butt with each other, would respond to humidity differently, and the joint would probably open up as a gap. Therefore a deliberate gap has been designed in by notching the corner of the frame. If it is important that both sides of the wall be similar then the face of the frame on the other side requires a routed slot—a matching gap.

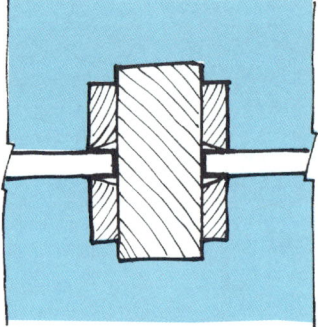

6.31 Mullion w/recessed stop

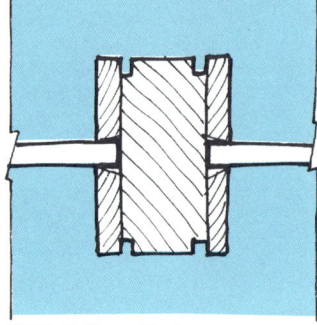

6.32 Mullion w/flush stop

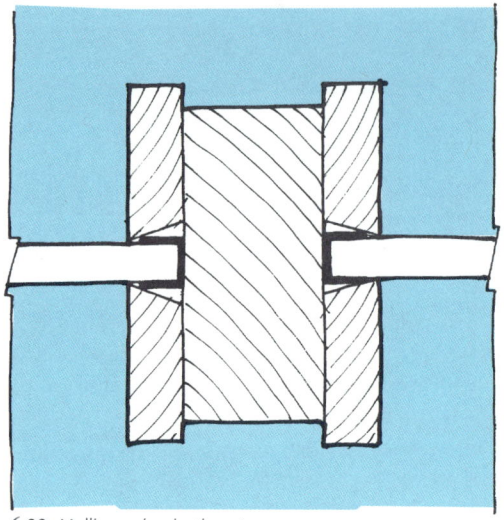

6.33 Mullion w/projecting stop

Mullions Details 6.31, 6.32 and 6.33 illustrate three kinds of intermediate mullions having recessed, flush, and projecting stops. They are interchangable details though sometimes one might be more appropriate than another. Sketch each with matching glazing frames and head and base details to discover their full effects. There could be many other variations; each situation will call for a study of the possibilities. If glazing occurs within a wood paneled wall then a further set of variables would affect the solution. Including door frame details, you now have an interesting list of ingredients for your wall designs.

6.34 Section at ceiling showing a glazed wall hung with no visible framing

- channel wired to underside of slab above
- steel bolts with rubber sleeves and washers
- steel carrying channel
- carrying channel
- acoustic tile or other ceiling material
- trim angles
- non-hardening sealant or removable metal stop
- line of floor surface
- glazing channel

6.35 Floor section showing routed groove

Glazed Walls With No Visible Framing Sometimes you may want to design a glazed wall without visible vertical framing, or with no framing at all—both of which are possible. Vertical connections between sheets of glass can be eliminated as long as the base and top are secured. However, a small gap should be left between the vertical edges so that they cannot rub against each other. If sound or climate control is desirable then a bead of clear silicone sealant can be used to fill the gap.

One way of achieving a glazed wall with no visible frames at the base and top is shown in details 6.34–.35. This method requires a hung ceiling system and a floor into which a groove may be routed for holding the bottom of the glass. If ceiling and floor conditions are known beforehand, you might find other ways to achieve the same effect. However conditions may prevent you from doing exactly what you want. In any case, be flexible; adapt.

If concealment is not possible then a simple frame can be constructed as shown in 6.36; note the routed notch and removable stop. It is also possible to use vertical supports only and dispense with the horizontal. The glass could rest on a rubber or vinyl pad on the floor or a groove in the floor, and stop just short of the ceiling where a sealant could be used if desired.

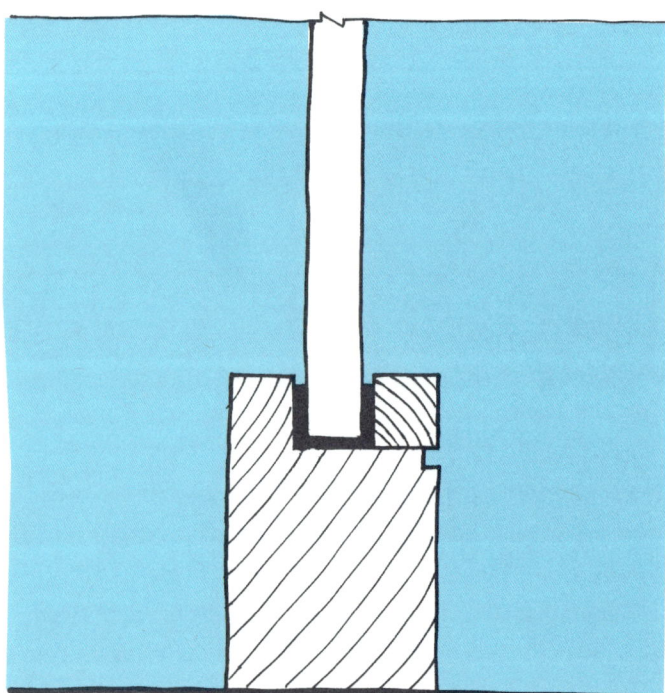

6.36 Simple frame to support glazing

Glass, Plastics & Metals

CHAPTER 1 2 3 4 5 6 ▲7 8

**ndoubtedly there will be occasions other than for doors and glazing when you wish to design with glass**—on top of a surface, in place of another surface material, or perhaps as a featured material in such items as cabinetry, furnishings, showcases and displays. Glass may be obtained in tremendous variety:

> In thicknesses from 3/16" to 1 1/4"
> In a variety of sizes, finishes, colors, textures, structures, and with or without integral wire patterns
> Bent to certain radii depending on the thickness
> "Tempered" to give it added strength or laminated to give it shatter resistance

It is important to contact local distributors to discover what is currently available. Glass is a fascinating material and we explore its use and detailing in this chapter; refer to chapter 6 for specifics on glazing applications. Thorough knowledge of the product may stimulate your thoughts to use its properties in creative ways.

Finishing Typical ways of finishing the cut edge of a piece of glass are:

> **Flat grind**—ground to a relatively smooth, square, and even but unpolished surface
> **Polished**—a smooth, glossy surface; the edges have their sharpness diminished or their shape modified by grinding
> **Arris**—having the square edges removed by grinding them off at an angle
> **Beveled**—having an angle of specified degree ground into the edge, creating a clearly separate, polished surface, or nose. A miter bevel has both sides of the glass edge ground to an angle.

If glass is to be placed on top of another surface, small circles of rubber, vinyl, felt, or leather should be placed under the glass. This prevents the glass from sliding, levels the surfaces, and prevents the dust that gets in between from scratching the surfaces.

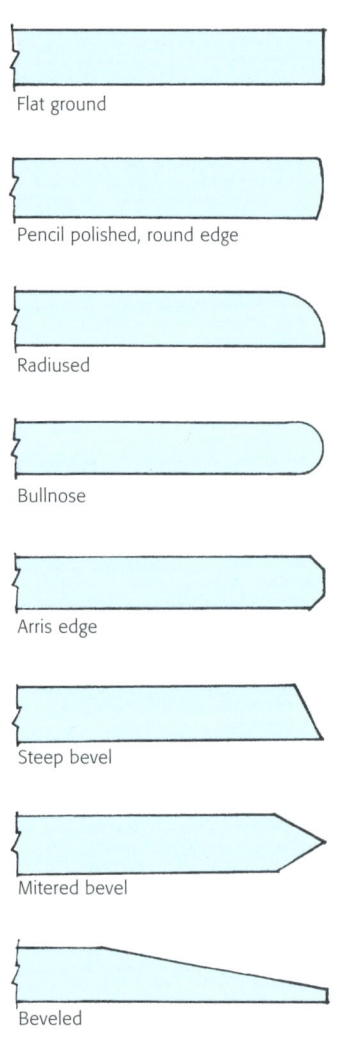

7.1 Typical glass edge treatments

Joining When joining glass to another material, bolts with rubber washers are most commonly used. This ensures a snug fit without breaking the glass. Your selection of a bolt design—and the bolt material itself—become important aspects of the overall design effect. Refer to details 7.2 and 7.3 for examples.

Various angle brackets and clips in plastics or metals such as shown in 7.4 can be used for joining multiple pieces of glass. These can be especially useful for display units. Glass can also be glued to glass, or to a variety of other materials, using single component urethanes, silicones, or foam tapes impregnated with acrylic adhesive.

The standard bolt and nut in plain steel, shown below, looks rugged.

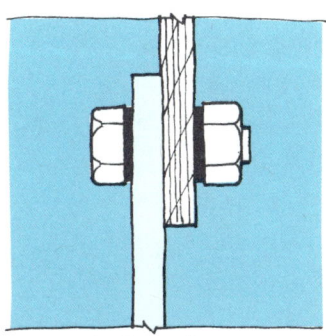

7.2 Standard bolt and nut

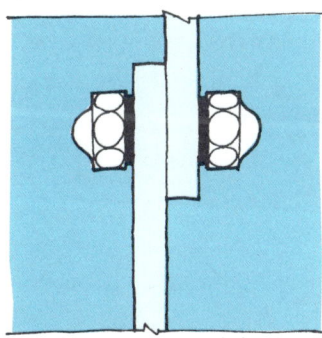

7.3 Cap nut w/matching bolt

A cap nut that matches the bolt head is used to give a finished, polished effect to the detail shown above. Chrome plating would further enhance the intended shiny character.

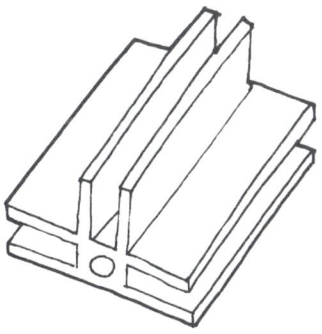

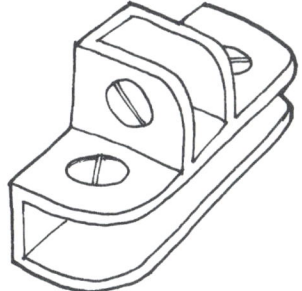

7.4 Assorted glass clips

Figure 7.4 shows some of the assorted lexan and metal clips available for assembling glass units for shelving or displays.

Plastics

Basic plastic materials are divided into two categories, **thermoplastics**—such as rigid sheet acrylic, styrenes, and polycarbonates—and **thermosetting plastics**—such as fiberglass and epoxies. Thermoplastics can be formed and deformed by heat; thermoset plastics entail a catalytic reaction, which transforms the material from a fluid to a solid, and which cannot be reversed. Thus plastics, which in many ways have characteristics comparable to other hard materials, have the unique additional property of being formable and/or moldable.

Particularly if the object that you are designing is to be mass-produced, you might wish to consider a formed or molded shape. Molds for shaping thermoplastics such as acrylic and ABS are relatively inexpensive to make, while molds for thermoset plastics such as fiberglass require a high degree of finishing and are therefore more expensive. So, by amortizing the cost of a mold over a large number of units, forming and molding become cost efficient production techniques.

Rigid Sheet Acrylic

A thermoplastic known by such trade names as Plexiglas, Rohaglas, Lucite, and Perspex, rigid sheet acrylic comes as cast and extruded sheets, rods and tubes. It is stronger and lighter than glass and, in its cast transparent version, it is clearer than glass. However, it attracts dust by static electricity and is softer so it scratches fairly easily. It is available in sheets of less than 1/8" and up to 3/4" in thickness, in round and square rods, and in tubes of various sizes. Other thicknesses and shapes are available on custom order. As with glass, edges may be shaped or polished smooth. And, as with glass, you need to develop a sound knowledge of the product to be able to use it creatively.

Joining While acrylic can be detailed and used in any way that glass can, one of its unique features makes it desirable for many more creative uses; it can be fused together with solvent, or it can be glued. In **solvent welding,** methylene chloride solvent dissolves the acrylic, melting adjacent surfaces and causing them to become one piece when the joint hardens. The solvent dries crystal clear. This type of joint, however, requires absolutely flat contacting surfaces, so it is appropriate for some applications, such as the machined miter of the middle detail at right, and not others.

Glue, on the other hand, is a gap-filling material suitable for the joining of less regular surfaces or edges. One type dries with a slightly yellow tinge. Another, more expensive type is available that dries either clear or opaque white.

Mechanical Attachments Frequently designers choose to emphasize the method of attachment by using metal screws or bolts. Occasionally it is possible to obtain acrylic screws for a more subtle approach to the connection. Sheet acrylic may also be drilled and tapped for coarse-

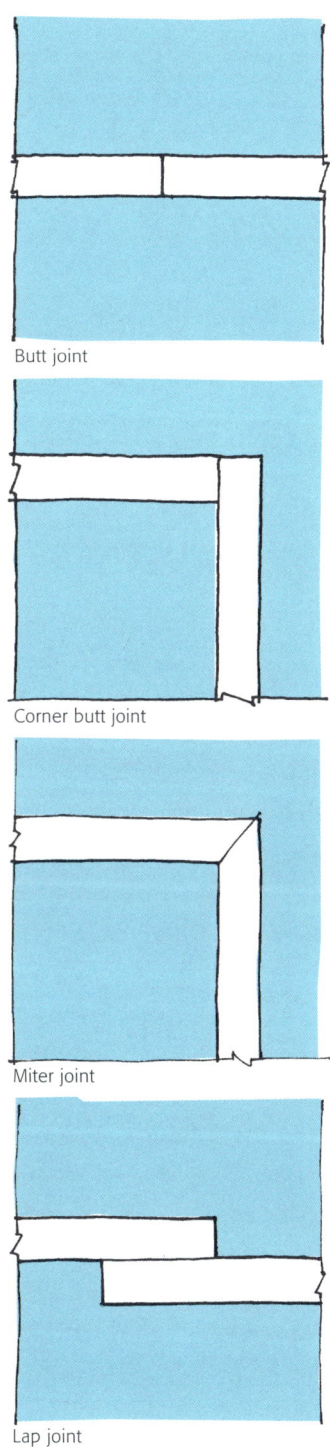

Butt joint

Corner butt joint

Miter joint

Lap joint

7.5 Joining acrylic

Corners can be created using acrylic or metal angles with screws, such as shown below. Alternately, bolts and nuts could be used with the angles.

Bending It is very easy to bend acrylic with the application of heat. The radius of the bend will depend on the thickness of the sheet, that is, the thicker the sheet the larger the radius. For example, one-eighth inch material can be bent to a one-quarter inch radius, as shown in 7.7. A tighter and more controlled radius may be achieved by cutting away material from the inside of the bend with a shallow dado or regular saw blade prior to bending, as in 7.8, though this has the effect of weakening the material at the crease, so is preferable for thicker sheets.

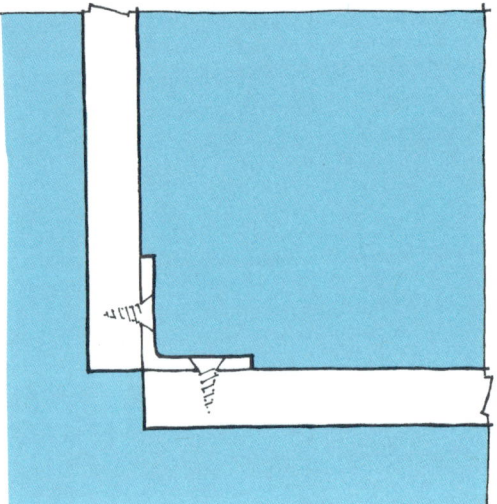

7.6 Acrylic joined w/angles and screws

threaded machine screws when used for non-structural applications. Remember that any drilling of acrylic requires a specially-shaped drill bit, though ordinary tools are suitable for other work with acrylic.

Lighting Another distinctive feature of acrylic is that light shining through it bends and emanates from the edges. If the edges or cuts in the surface are roughened such as with sandblasting, they will glow intensely in lines of light. This characteristic opens up many possibilities for decorative designs; however, it also means that scratches resulting from wear will show more readily than on glass.

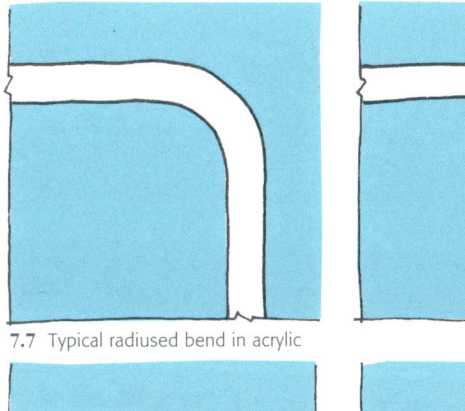
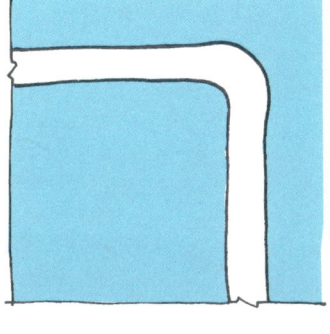

7.7 Typical radiused bend in acrylic

If the radius of the bend is too tight, slight bulging such as shown at left can occur at outer corners. By machining in a dado cut along the inside line of the bend, as shown in 7.8, a much tighter radius results, and the bend edge will be straighter.

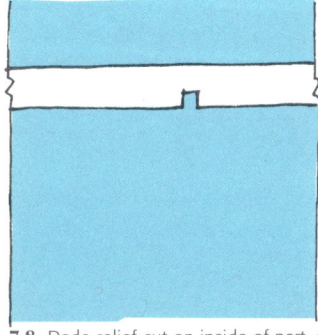

7.8 Dado relief-cut on inside of part, and resulting tight bend

Molding and Forming Some thermoplastics, such as rigid sheet acrylic and styrene, may be formed into various shapes with the use of heat, as in **drape molding,** 7.9 on the following page, or with a combination of heat and pressure, called **vacuum forming,** 7.10. Drape-molded pieces are shaped when the heated sheet goods are draped over or into a simple mold. This is a low-cost method of producing gently curved shapes such as skylights or shallow-dished panels.

In vacuum forming, a hot sheet is forced against the mold face by inducing a vacuum between the sheet

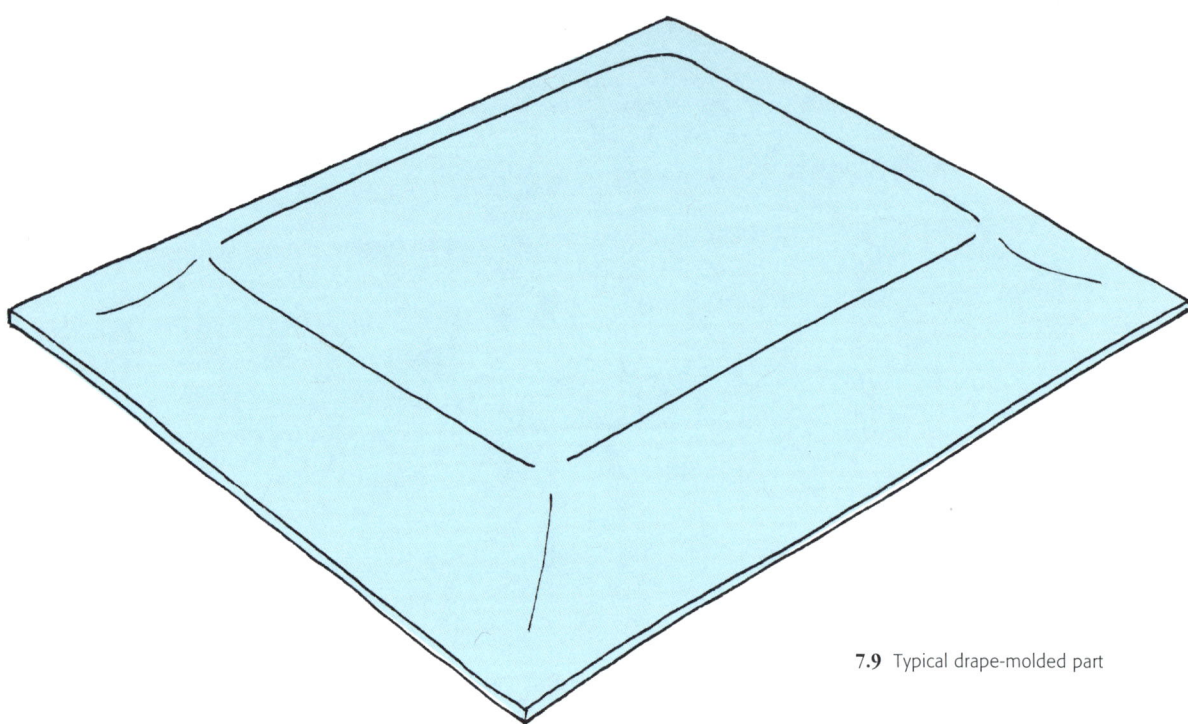

7.9 Typical drape-molded part

Notice that in a drape-molded design, curves have large radiuses and sides are gently sloped. The "draw" is shallow.

and the mold. Deeper parts with more complex surfaces and some undercuts are possible with vacuum forming. Display domes and custom light fixtures are examples of vacuum-formed pieces.

When you design for thermoformed pieces, consider two factors: first, the minimum allowable radius for bends is one-and-a-half times the thickness of the sheet, so a panel 1/4" thick should have bends with a radius of at least 3/8"; and secondly, for a "drawn" part (one designed to be deep), the depth of the draw should be no more than twice the width of the material. So, for a display dome 2' in diameter, the height, or draw, should be no more than 4', depending on the thickness of the sheet.

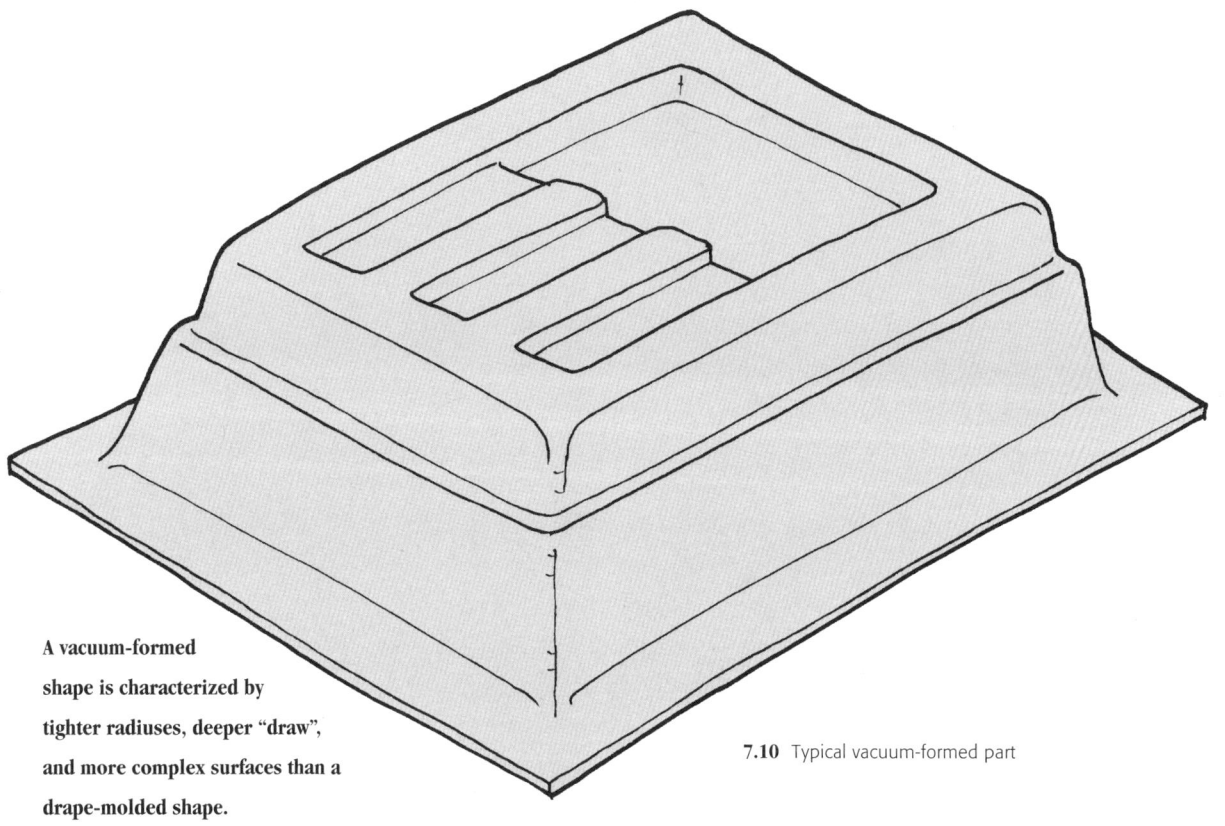

A vacuum-formed shape is characterized by tighter radiuses, deeper "draw", and more complex surfaces than a drape-molded shape.

7.10 Typical vacuum-formed part

Polycarbonate

A unique thermoplastic, polycarbonate is sold under the tradename Lexan. Polycarbonate is much more resistant to extremes of heat and cold than many other plastics, is highly flame retardant, and is especially scratch- and shatter-resistant. It is therefore commonly used as a substitute for glazing in areas subject to heavy wear or vandalism, such as for public shelters and exhibits, and for protection of decorative glass windows. In extra-thick, clear sheets, polycarbonate is even bullet proof, so is used extensively for banks, drive-in teller windows and the like.

As for sheet acrylic, common construction techniques and machine tools, with the exception of drill bits, can be used. Polycarbonate sheets up to 1/4" thick can also be cold-bent in the same way as sheet metal.

Fiberglass

Fiberglass-reinforced polyester (FRP), commonly known as fiberglass, is a thermoset plastic, which means that any discussion of it relates to producing multiples of a design in a mold or molds. It starts as a syrupy fluid which is applied to the mold by spraying, brushing or otherwise coating, is reinforced with glass fibers, and hardens quickly by a catalytic process into an extremely strong, durable material. Fiberglass, which can be formed into very complex shapes if necessary, is normally finished with gel coat, which lends itself to exact color matching. Unlike other plastics, structural or surface damage to fiberglass can be repaired.

Fiberglass has excellent weathering properties; in fact, as temperature drops, fiberglass increases in strength by as much as 40%, and should be considered for low temperature applications. Fiberglass resins approved for contact with food and drinking water or resistant to a variety of chemical agents are also available.

Fiberglass molds are usually highly polished. The mold cost, which can vary from a few hundred dollars to thousands, will be determined by the complexity of your design. This makes FRP particularly appropriate whenever quantities of the same design are required, or when high strength combined with light weight is a necessity. Wall systems, decorative fascia panels and signage, seating units, and planters are often molded in FRP.

Basic considerations for finishing and joining fiberglass are discussed in the following sections. It is recommended that you seek the advice of fiberglass specialists to discover the most appropriate methods for detailing the design and construction of your particular project.

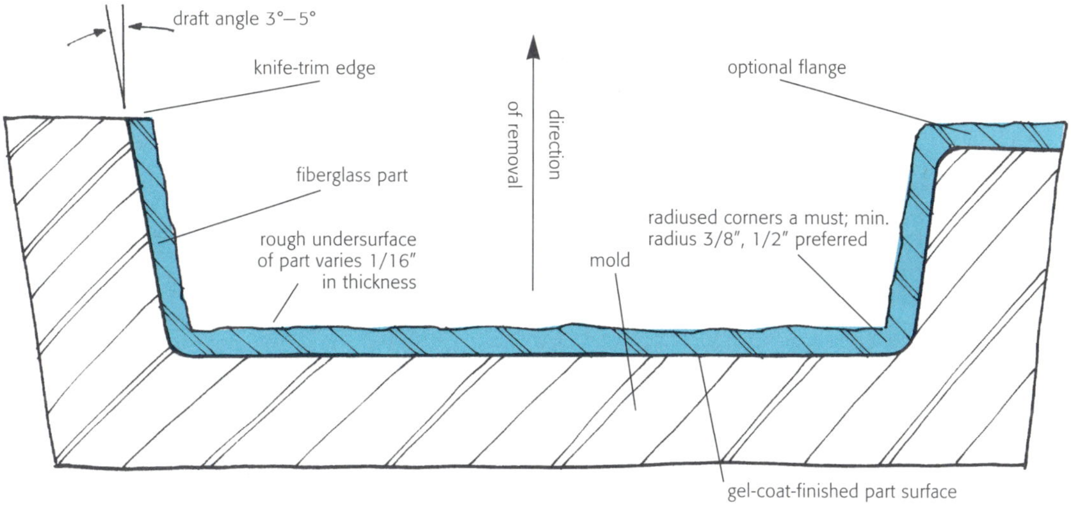

7.11 Typical fiberglass mold and part

Labels on figure: draft angle 3°–5°; knife-trim edge; fiberglass part; rough undersurface of part varies 1/16" in thickness; direction of removal; mold; optional flange; radiused corners a must; min. radius 3/8", 1/2" preferred; gel-coat-finished part surface

Molding A typical fiberglass mold and part is shown above. One of the most important things to remember when designing for any molded plastic part is **draft angle,** which facilitates removal of the part from the mold. Usually, all sides parallel to the direction of removal are angled between 3° and 5°, which reduces or eliminates friction between the part and its mold, and provides clearance when lifting the part away. The draft angle becomes a criti-

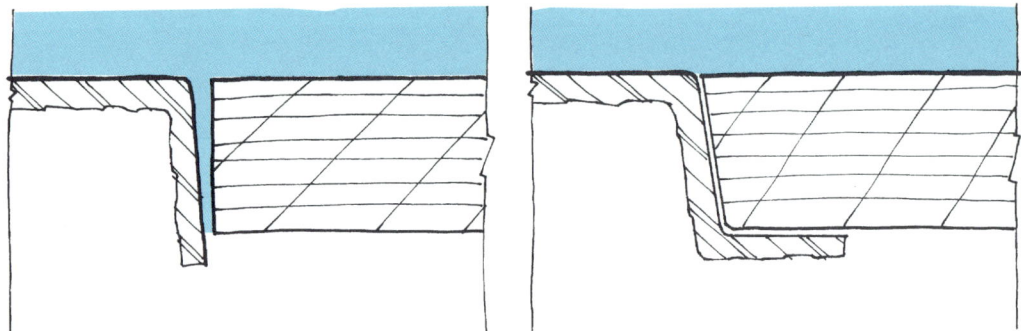

7.12 Compensating for the differences in adjacent plastic and wood parts

Because of the inherent shrinkage of plastic material, dimensional accuracy is impossible to guarantee. Without some sort of compensating detail, surface alignment or butt fit between plastic components and other pieces cannot be achieved. The detail above shows the inherent angular differences of abutting surfaces in plastic and wood.

The detail at upper right features the minimum recommended methods of compensating for the shrinkage and draft angle of a plastic part when it abuts square surfaces. First, flanges should be incorporated into your plastic part design whenever possible; they assist horizontal alignment and provide a surface for attachments. Second, specifying an angle cut in the abutting vertical wood edge will assure a close fit.

cal design factor when molded parts interface with fabricated components—such as when wall panels or bathware adjoin cabinetry. A close and secure butt fit is possible as long as an angle is cut in the wood component to compensate for the draft angle of the plastic part (see 7.12). Economical but nonetheless effective ways of compensating for or disguising the differing adjacent angles—using reveals, offsets, caulks, or moldings—can be incorporated into your design, and offer opportunities to create interest. These are described in the illustrations opposite.

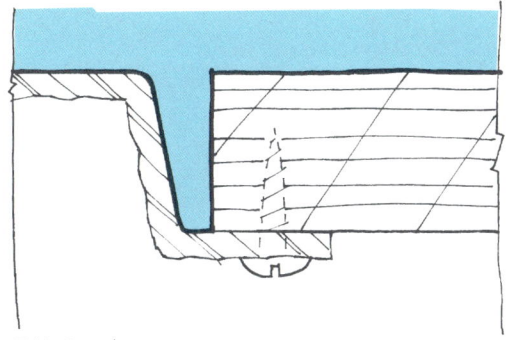

7.13 Reveal

This detail shows a reveal, where the gap has been made an integral part of the design. The transition between dissimilar materials and surfaces is obvious and strong. Note the functional flange on the fiberglass part.

Detail 7.14 is a variant of 7.12, with two significant differences. The parts have been deliberately offset, eliminating any need for leveling; this is another method for handling discrepancies in fit that arise from combined materials. In addition to the angle-cut in the wood edge, a bevel has been cut to accommodate the fillet, or inside radius, of the plastic flange.

    The capped screw is just one of many ways to treat the attachments.

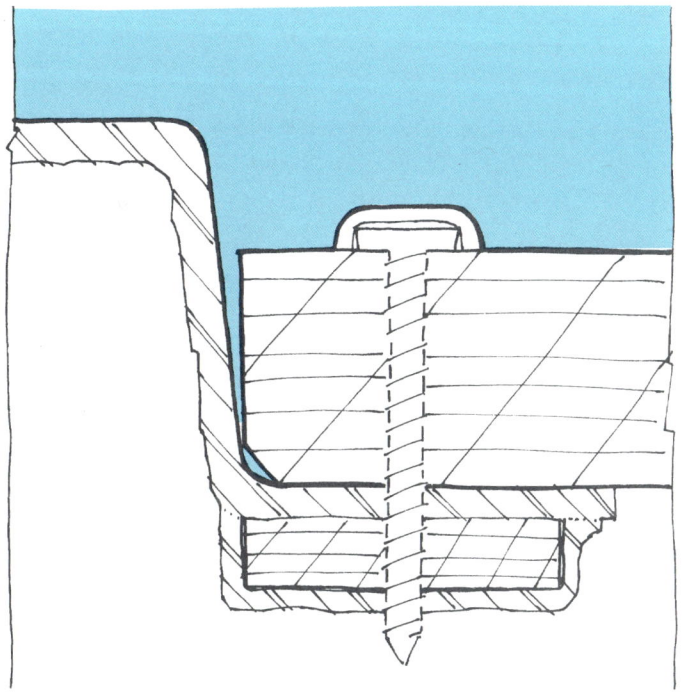

7.14 Butt fit w/offset

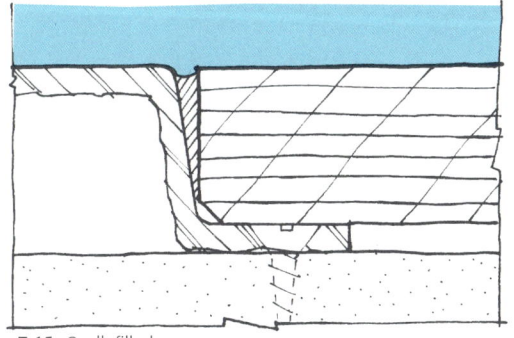

7.15 Caulk-filled gap

Detail 7.15 shows a light-duty horizontal installation. The beveled lower corner on the wood allows a closer fit; when appearance is not important, elastomeric caulk filler can be used to disguise the angular discrepancy in the two edges, and in this case it holds the wood panel in place. Offsetting the two adjacent surfaces is a further recommendation.

Finishing Fiberglass parts are normally finished in the mold with polyester gel coats tinted to the desired finish color, and thus are rarely painted. In special circumstances requiring a lacquer or enamel painted finish, an alternate gel coat—"sanding" gel coat—provides a good base for painting.

The back side of a fiberglass part is normally rough, unsightly, and could pose an abrasion hazard to the unwary; therefore it should be hidden. The trimmed edges of fiberglass parts pose a similar problem, so when exposed are most commonly covered with extruded vinyl, rubber or aluminum trim strips to improve appearance. Where practical, turned-in flanges can be designed for joints to minimize this problem. The gap between the flanged parts that occurs as a result of the draft angle must be accommodated. Batten strips or a glued-in T-molding such as shown in detail 7.16 are often used.

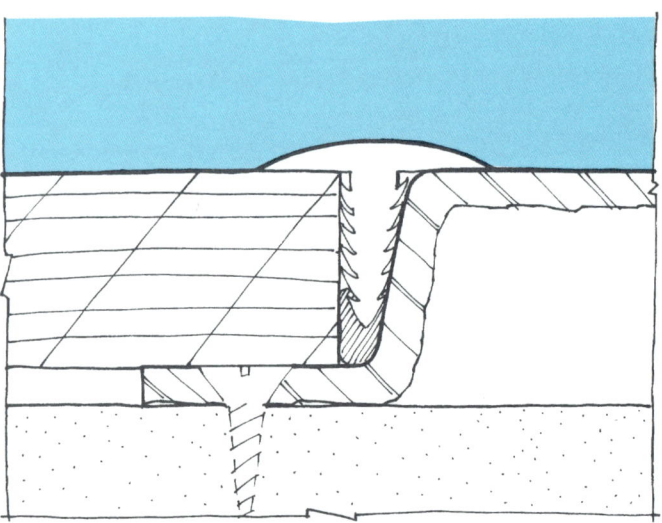

7.16 Gap breached w/extruded molding

Various extruded moldings are available that fill the gaps between dissimilar materials and disguise discrepancies in the surface levels. Glue is a necessary filler to keep the plastic part from shifting once installed.

Joining Fiberglass to Itself and Other Materials   Molded fiberglass panels and parts are most commonly joined together using blind or "pop" rivets with washers, sheet metal screws, and bolts and nuts. Where little tensile strength is required and where the assembly is permanently joined, pan-head sheet metal screws #8 or larger may be used; a pilot hole should always be drilled first to prevent cracking of the material. Bolted assemblies are straightforward unless vibration is a factor, in which case the bolt should be prevented from abrading the surrounding fiberglass by insertion of a rubber grommet.

In some instances, fiberglass panels can also be bonded together. When panels are bonded together, the joint may be filled with a color-matched gel coat, but this is not recommended in locations where the panels are subjected to expansion and contraction or flexing.

Metal components can be fastened to fiberglass using the above methods or by gluing with urethane adhesive. Bonding metals to fiberglass using FRP resin is usually recommended only where extra, structural support is necessary and cannot be achieved by other means. Glass components are typically secured in aluminum extrusions or hinges before attachment to fiberglass. Glass may also be glued to fiberglass using elastomeric adhesives such as urethane.

Plywood, solid wood battens, balsa wood (for contoured surfaces), urethane foam sheet goods (light yet strong), and corrugated cardboard are just a few of the wide variety of materials that can be bonded to the backside of fiberglass to increase stiffness and provide anchor points for cabinets and the like.

Comparing Glass and Plastics
When you are contemplating a choice between glass or plastics consider the various properties, advantages, and disadvantages, then make a reasoned decision. Some of the **selection criteria** are:

- ☐ Strength
- ☐ Weight
- ☐ Durability; resistance to breakage and damaging
- ☐ Scratch-resistance
- ☐ Degree of transparency
- ☐ Availability of colors, patterns, textures
- ☐ Connection methods
- ☐ Shapeability, formability
- ☐ Ease of handling and use
- ☐ Codes and regulations
- ☐ Maintenance requirements
- ☐ Cost

Metals
Iron-based, or ferrous, metals such as wrought iron, steel, and stainless steel, and non-ferrous metals such as aluminum, brass, bronze, copper, zinc, lead, nickel, silver, and gold are all materials with which you may come into contact on various projects. In detailing you are most likely to use steel and stainless steel, aluminum, brass, bronze, and copper. These metals are all available in a wide variety of shapes and sizes—long strips in coils; sheets; bars, tubes and pipes; angles, channels, zees, and tees; wire; cables; and so on. Custom profiles can be designed and extruded for a surprisingly low cost, and are often an economical solution for a challenging commercial design detail. The choice is so broad it is recommended that when you wish to use a product, you verify manufacturers' stock sizes and availability within your project's time frame.

When designing for sheet metal fabrication, keep in mind these two key points: the correlation between sheet metal and paper, and galvanic action.

Sheet metal acts like paper—if you can fold or cut and bend a sheet of semi-stiff paper into the desired shape then you can do it with a sheet of metal. If it cannot be done in paper then it cannot readily be done in sheet metal.

Galvanic Action

When two metals are in contact in the presence of humidity an electric current is set up which corrodes one of the metals; this is called *galvanic action*. The following is a sequential list of metals in which each metal on the list is susceptible to galvanic action by those that follow:

    Aluminum

    Zinc

    Iron or steel

    Stainless steel

    Lead

    Brass

    Copper

    Bronze

    Gold

Remember that if you adjoin two or more bare metals they must be separated with plastic or rubber spacers or finished with some type of coating that prevents them from touching.

Finishing With the exception of stainless steel and fasteners in plain metal, bare metals are seldom used. Around foods or in areas where human contact is a factor, bare metals other than stainless steel should be avoided. Steel is usually plated, porcelain enamelled, powder coated, or painted. Brass, bronze, and copper are usually treated to prevent their surfaces from oxidizing and losing natural color. Of course, if you want an aged, crumbling or deteriorating (but interesting) appearance you can treat copper, brass, and bronze with various acids that accelerate the "antiqued" look.

    Aluminum may be anodized to inhibit corrosion and introduce decorative color to the material itself. Clear anodizing is recommended for aluminum that comes into regular skin contact—such as handrails—to eliminate the dark smudging that results from the chemical interaction between the metal and skin.

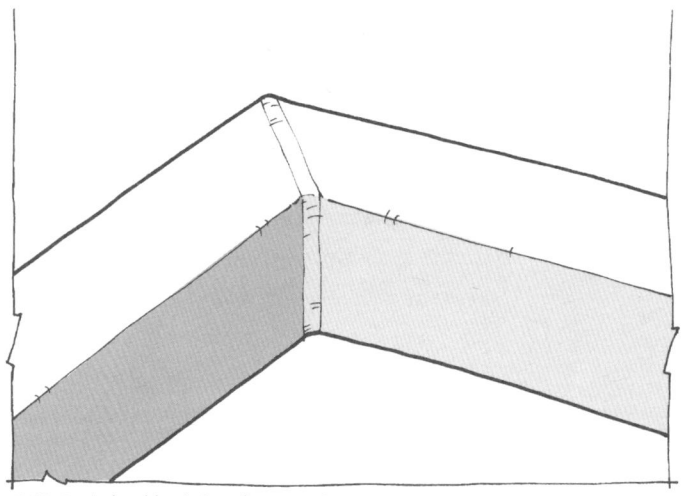

7.17 Typical weld w/mitered square pipe

Joining The principal means of holding metal pieces together are welds, screws, bolts, and rivets, which you can observe by examining typical metal work. High-tech, high-strength adhesives have recently been developed for joining metals, and you will find them particularly useful in decorative situations where hidden joining would be more desirable. Sometimes one method is preferable over another—depending on the visibility of the joint, the strength required, and the shapes involved.

In welding, an electric arc or gas is used to melt a welding rod and fuse it together with the adjacent pieces. This produces a visible bead of metal along the joint (see 7.17). Spot welding, 7.18, usually of a thinner to a thicker metal, produces tiny welded spots that are also visible but less noticeable. It is common to specify that joints are to be ground smooth, though at least one side of either type will likely show evidence of the weld. A field trip to a metalworking shop will heighten your appreciation of this trade.

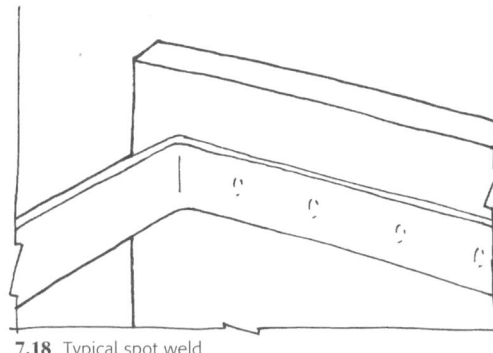

7.18 Typical spot weld

Using screws is a cleaner, crisper way of joining; other mechanical connectors such as rivets or bolts and nuts can become features of the detail design. Adhesives provide an invisible means of joining or layering thin metals in non-structural situations.

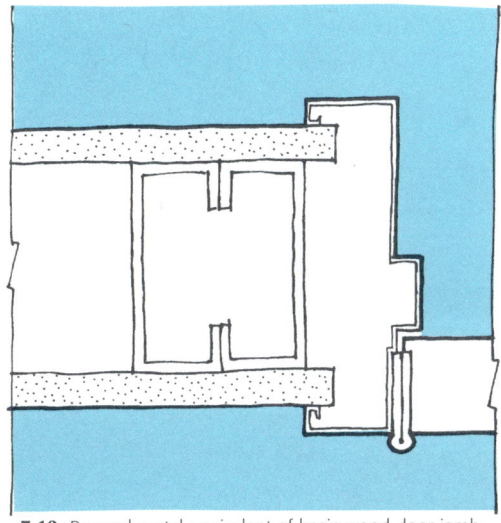
7.19 Pressed metal equivalent of basic wood door jamb

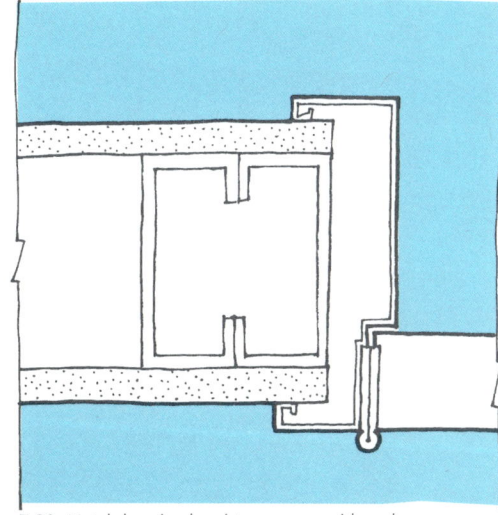
7.20 Metal door jamb w/stop on one side only

Using Metals

In commercial interiors metal is commonly used for hollow core steel doors and pressed metal door frames. Once painted, a hollow core steel door looks like any painted door. The pressed metal door frame however is clearly distinct from a wood door frame. Because it is made from sheet steel that is stamped into shape on a mold, the edges are all slightly rounded and have no joints. Pressed metal frames are usually installed before the wall is built, and various anchoring systems of straps or clips may be used. (Examine details 7.19 and 7.20.) Pressed metal door frames and glazing frames can be designed to mimic most of the variations in wood that have been shown in this book. Although they usually have a painted finish, there is nothing, except possibly cost, preventing their being plated with chrome, brass or copper, giving them a finish distinctly unlike wood.

The three basic types of steel stock are angles, tubes, and solid bars. Solid bars are available in squares and rectangles, and also rounds and half-rounds.

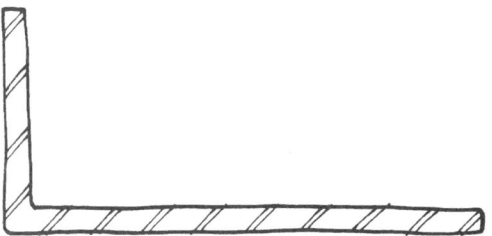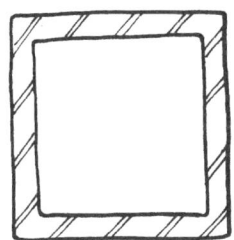

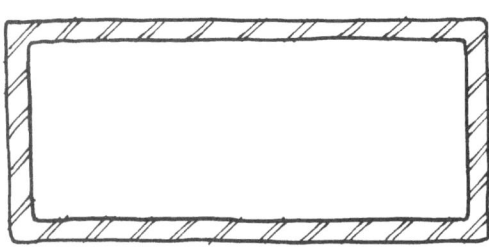

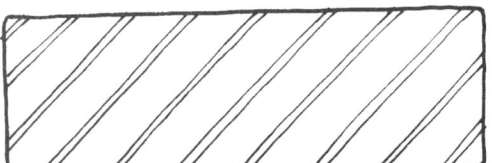

In Case Goods Apart from its use as a decorative element or a finish, metal is frequently used for frames, supports, or connectors in case goods. Solid material, called bar stock, or hollow material, called tube or pipe, and the variously-shaped zees, tees, angles, and channels act in a similar manner to lengths of wood, that is, they are components in the "stick" structure. Because they are much stronger, they can be smaller in cross-section than wood.

However, as with wood, the problem of joining two pieces exists, and using basic wood joints for metal would be exceedingly difficult and expensive. Metal is unique in that pieces may be welded, screwed, or bolted together; lengths of stock

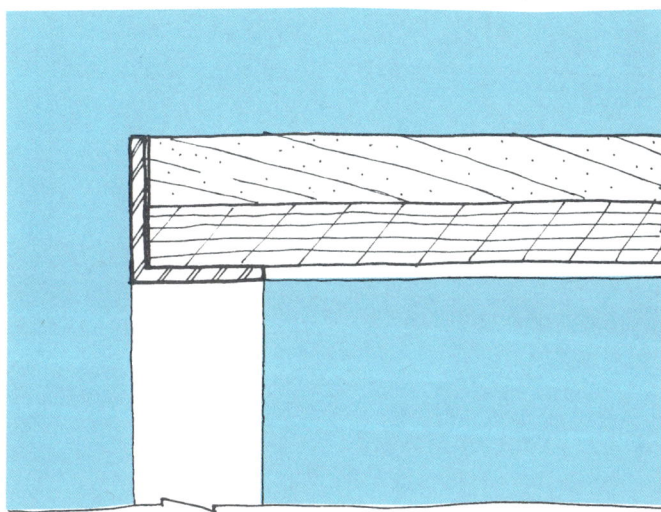

7.21 Section through table top

This is a section detail through the edge of a table top. A frame of steel angles supports the sheet of plywood and granite top. At the corners the angles would probably be mitered, welded and subsequently chrome plated. The legs could be angles, tubes, or solid bar stocks like those shown on the page at left.

can also be bent. For example, a simple butt joint may be either welded or screwed together. Which of the two methods to use is dictated by the nature of the chosen metal and the visibility of the joint. Aluminum is difficult to weld on site, and so screws are the usual connectors. Steel, on the other hand, welds easily but changes color with the heat. If steel parts can be finished after being joined then welding may be the best method to use. However, if the pieces have been plated (chrome or otherwise), the plating would be damaged by the welding process and so screws or bolts should be used. Examine detail 7.21, then sketch several alternative solutions for the legs. Different shapes and sizes of stock such as shown on the facing page may be used. Note how each one changes the visual effect of your design.

Detail 7.22 illustrates a butt joint. The connector is a flat-head, cross slotted screw. The screw is flush with the face in the side view, and on the front becomes an element of visual pattern—clearly but subtly the connection.

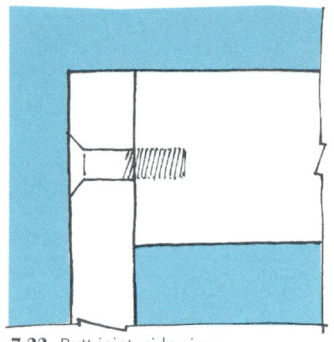 

7.22 Butt joint, side view   Cross-slot screw, front view

Metal connectors such as machine screws or bolts can add another dimension to your design. The shape of the screw- or bolt-head, its individual operational pattern—whether flat-slot, cross slotted, Phillips, Robertson, or Allen—and the profile of it when installed, whether flat, countersunk, or rounded, are important visual considerations. The details on this page will give you a sense of the design possibilities of such elements.

How much emphasis to place on the connections in your design is up to you. Changing the style of connector will alter the design concept; changing its material makes another subtle alteration. Brass cross-slot screws with stainless steel pieces, or copper-plated hex-head bolts with mirror chrome-plated steel are some of the myriad variants. Remember to consider galvanic action when deciding on which metals to mix.

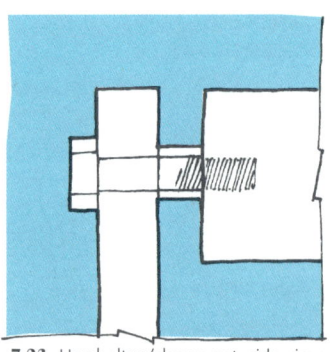 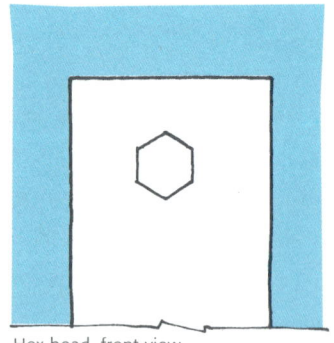

7.23 Hex bolt w/sleeve nut, side view   Hex head, front view

A tube spacer, or sleeve, has been used in 7.23 to separate the two pieces and a hex bolt has been used as the connector. The projecting bolt head is obvious in both side and front views and the spacer draws attention to the fact that two separate pieces are bound together by a third. There is nothing subtle about this connection.

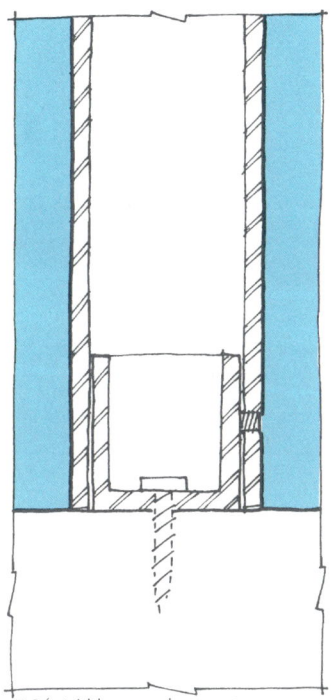

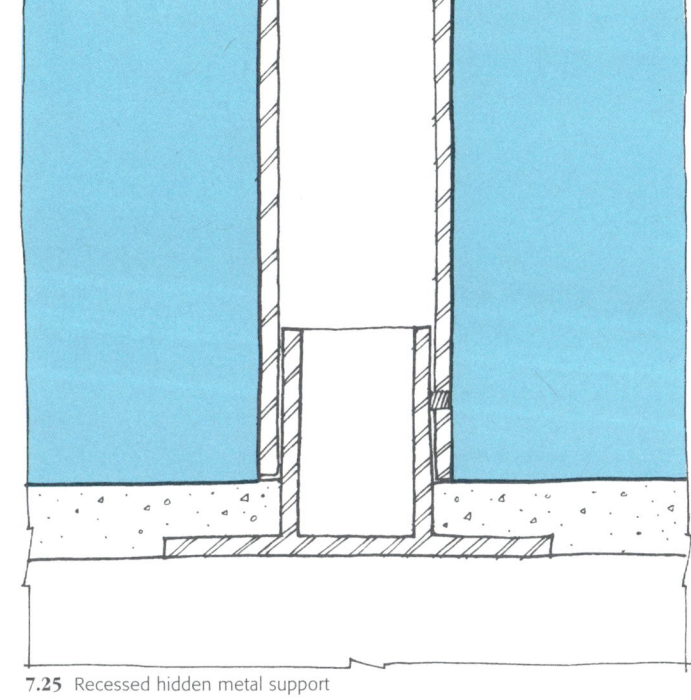

7.24 Hidden metal support

7.25 Recessed hidden metal support

In 7.24, a steel pipe with a capped end is securely fixed to the floor. Slipped over this pipe is the supporting case goods leg which rests on the floor and is held in place by a headless machine screw called a set screw (or "grub" screw).

For installations where heavy wear is expected, a steel mounting pipe is welded to a steel plate which is then grouted (recessed) into the floor. Then, as in 7.24, the support leg is slipped over the mounting pipe and held in place with a set screw.

Metal Supports—Exposed or Concealed? One design concept for structural elements is to expose all of them; another is to conceal them. For example you may want to conceal metal supports that connect case goods to the floor. Details 7.24 and 7.25 describe two methods of concealing this type of connection.

Note that while the word "pipe" is used in reference to lengths of metal stock it should not be taken as meaning round in cross-section. Metal pipe can be square, rectangular, or round. To further clarify, the thickness of the metal is what differentiates a pipe, which is thick-walled, from a tube, which is thin-walled. For some applications manufacturers or distributors have the equipment to bend round and, in some special cases, square tubes to a specific angle or radius. Check your local suppliers for availability of this finishing if it is required.

Metal Laminates

In designing, there will be many times when you need the strength of sheet metal for a surface. On the other hand, if the sheet metal is merely a finish providing color, texture, reflectivity, or whatever, you might want to consider using one of the highly decorative metal/plastic laminates. A laminate consists of a stiffened backing, a thin sheet of pre-finished real metal, and a protective melamine plastic surface layer. Replacing sheet metal with laminates, rather than suggesting design heresy, can be a very practical choice. In many instances plastic laminates are easier to handle in construction and installation, are less expensive, and offer surface characteristics that may make them more desirable for certain projects. Keep them in mind.

Fixed Seating

CHAPTER 1 2 3 4 5 6 7 ▼ 8

Of all the items that you may be called upon to design for an interior, a built-in seating unit, or banquette, is likely to have one of the most convoluted criteria to consider. In addition to the usual functional requirements which lead a designer to select appropriate shapes, materials and methods of construction, seating demands a further consideration—for ergonomics. When the comfort of a specific human activity such as sitting is foremost, the relationship between dimensions, shapes, and materials takes on critical importance. To design a seat that will be truly comfortable requires knowledge of an array of criteria.

Functional Requirements

Just as an office chair must be selected to provide physical support for specific tasks and to function in a specific location, banquette design requires similar considerations. For what purpose is it to be built? In what type of environment? How will it be maintained? These are some of the basic questions to be answered at the outset.

Two of the most common types of projects where banquette seating is used—an eating facility and a drinking facility—are described here briefly, and reference will be made to them throughout the chapter. Each has quite distinct functional and ergonomic requirements, and the amount of time a person will spend in each type of facility is also an important factor. All of these have a direct relationship to the dimensions, materials, and construction details used in a banquette design.

An eating facility can range from being an inexpensive, fast food outlet to being an expensive fine dining experience. Likewise, a drinking facility might have a quick turnover or involve a leisurely stay. Usually the seating in fast food premises is expected to function but not be overly comfortable; the design augments the business strategy, which is to encourage high turnover. For leisurely dining or drinking, comfort usually has higher priority, and the quality of the surroundings, as exemplified in the materials and detailing, can also convey something to the potential visitor about the quality to be expected.

Critical Dimensions

Important dimensional parameters common to all seating should be referred to when developing any banquette seating concept. Certain measurements, proportions, and angles relate directly to the potential comfort of your design.

A - Seat height The distance between the seat surface and the floor varies depending on the hardness of the seat construction. Bare wood or metal at 17" means that the occupant is supported at 17", the standard seat height. Upholstery over a foam cushion means that the occupant will be supported one or more inches beneath the dimensional height depending on the weight of the person and the firmness of the cushion. Therefore, an overall height of 18" is probably more desirable, and would be particularly so if used with a dining-height table, which is taller than a cocktail table.

B - Back height Both comfort and design concept come into play here. Fourteen inches from seat surface to shoulder is acceptable for comfort but you might wish to use a greater dimension for conceptual reasons. As an example, upholstered backs have on occasion been continued all the way to the ceiling.

C - Seat depth While seat depth can be reduced to as little as 15" for short-stay seating, 18"–19" is more comfortable for the average person. Your decision might be

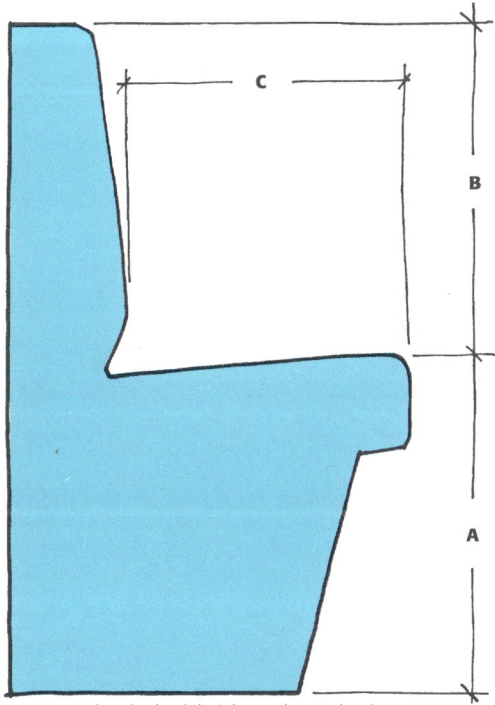

8.1a Seat height, back height, and seat depth

Critical Banquette Dimensions

Seat height	A	17"–18"
Back height	B	14"–18"
Seat depth	C	15"–19"
Back depth	D	5"–6"
Seat slope	E	3°–6°
Back slope	F	2°–5°
Base recess	G	6"–8"

influenced by the amount of total available space and whether the adjacent table is fixed or movable.

D - Back depth This is a less critical dimension. Assuming a fairly thick cushion, 5"–6" could be specified. This dimension can be reduced to as little as 2" depending on the space available, the construction, and the cushion size.

E - Seat slope A surface slope downwards to the back is recommended because sitting on a flat surface is not very comfortable; pressure is placed on bone joints instead of spreading support along the back of the thighs. As well, the shorter the seat depth the steeper the incline should be, which increases comfort. The slope is achieved either by designing an inclined frame support under a flat cushion or by using a slope-shaped cushion on a flat surface.

F - Back slope A 90° vertical back surface does not conform to the shape of a human spine. Examine the profile of an office chair; notice the convex support in the lower lumbar region and the slightly concave form in the upper, shoulder area. This suggests that

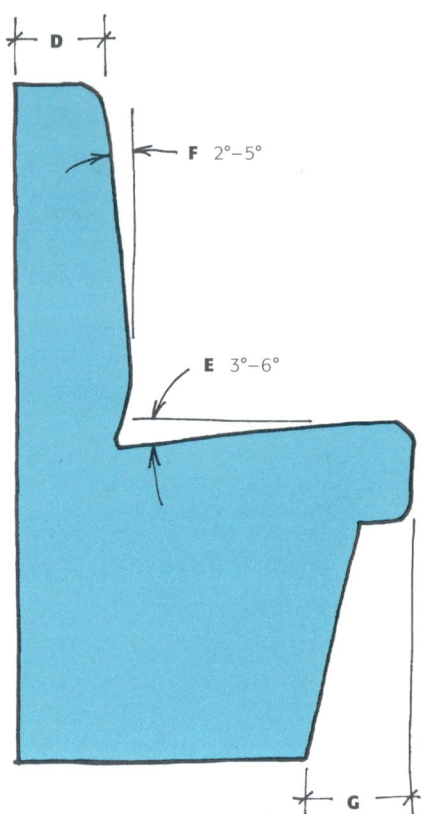

8.1b Back depth, seat and back slope, and base recess

for banquette seating you should design either with a pre-formed cushion, or slope the back to strike a mid-line between the lumbar and shoulder support requirements. While office chairs are precisely designed for people who tend to sit in one position for extended periods, support requirements in banquettes can be modified somewhat. Diners lean forward to eat and sit back to relax, and drinkers tend to move and shift during conversation or socializing. An angle varying from 2°—a fairly upright position—to one of 5° combined with a soft cushion (giving new meaning to the term "laid back") is the usual comfort range for back slope. Consider both the function and the cushion body material when determining the angle.

G - Base recess How does a person get up off a seating unit? Test yourself; watch others. The first movement is likely shifting of the feet back under the center of gravity so that the leg muscles can raise and balance the torso. If the front surface of the banquette runs straight to the floor from the edge of the seat then there is no room to accommodate the backward shift of the feet. Foot space is needed, and the depth of space required is in direct relationship to the depth of the seat, that is, the deeper the seat, the greater the space.

Whether the front surface of the base is sloped back or vertical will depend on your design concept and the construction system that you have chosen to use.

Materials and Construction

Designers have created banquettes in a great variety of styles and configurations; materials are available that are exceptionally well-suited to this type of seating. Study the many examples and sourcebooks before you begin a seating project.

If you are designing seating for a fast food franchise or similar facility, you might use a molded seat/back combination, one either custom designed or purchased from a supplier, and then fit it to an existing or constructed frame. For most other projects, it will be up to you to design a unit which suits the degree of comfort desired.

Some primary considerations for constructing a banquette are:

 Frame: metal or wood
 Base: legs, or box to the floor
 Seat and back:
 –Upholstered:
  Covering: fabric or vinyl
  Cushion density: soft, medium or firm
  Cushion thickness:
   –thin with spring support
   –thick with plywood support
 –Non-upholstered; metal, wood or molded plastic

Practical, functional requirements as well as aesthetic ones will determine your choices in each of these categories, and will have great effect on your design concept. It is recommended that you work out the concept before detailing a specific construction method since there are so many ways to achieve the desired result. Your opportunity to refine the concept will come with the detail work.

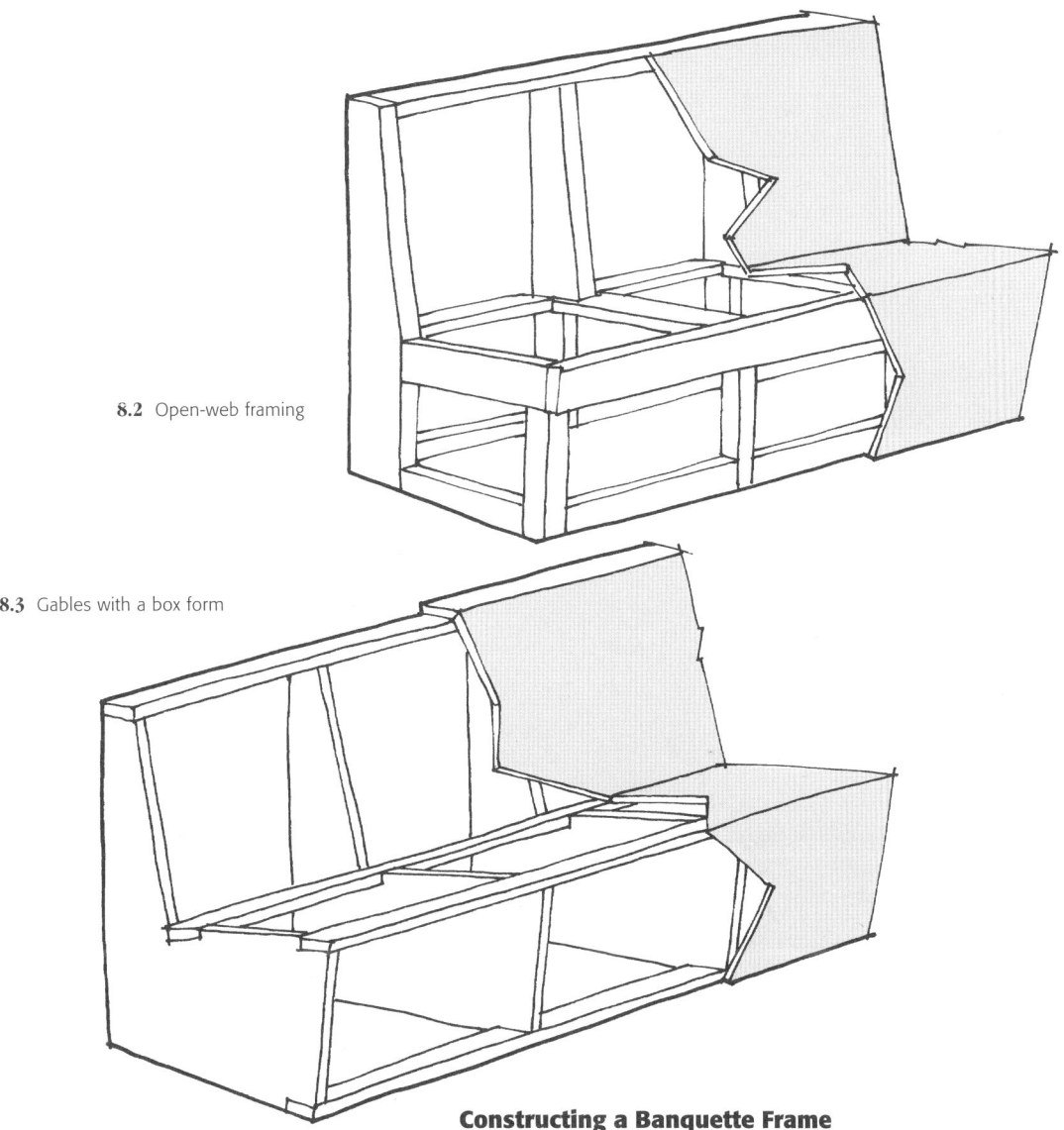

8.2 Open-web framing

8.3 Gables with a box form

Constructing a Banquette Frame

Two usual methods for constructing the basic form of a banquette—open-web framing and gables with a box form—are illustrated here. **Open-web framing,** shown in 8.2, has a system of legs connected with framing members, all of which may or may not be concealed behind plywood facing. **Gables with a box form,** shown in 8.3, are a series of solid plywood gables occurring every two to three feet along the length of the unit joined together with plywood sheets on front and back.

In this type of construction, a thin foam cushion is laid over and secured to a plywood box with no-sag springs across the top. Note that the cushion box has been constructed to the desired slope.

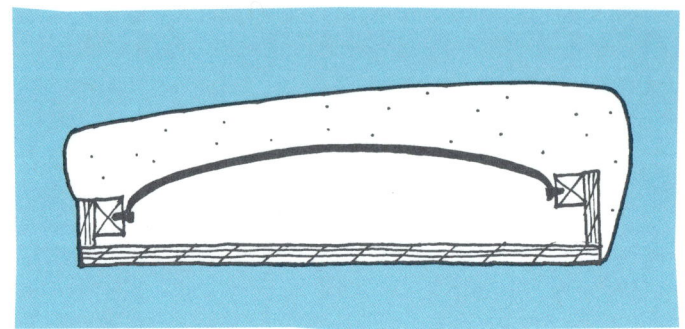

8.4 Cushion box w/no-sag springs

Seat Construction

Two methods are most often used for constructing the seat portion of a banquette, a cushion box with no-sag springs, and a cushion with a plywood base. Foam-on-plywood cushion construction is usually used for upholstered seatbacks as well. In this type of construction, whether for a seat or a back, air holes should be drilled through the plywood support, allowing air to escape when someone sits. Without the holes, air would have to escape through the fabric or the seams, thus putting severe stress on the upholstery.

Cushion Box With No-Sag Springs In figure 8.4 a thin foam cushion of either medium or high density with a thick wrap at the front edge is laid over and secured to an independent plywood box with no-sag springs stretched across its top. The cushion is then upholstered. It is important that the springs be of very good quality; if not they may have a tendency to flex too deeply, and thus lower the desired seating height. The diner's legs in such a situation would be bent rather than relaxed, and the table height would be uncomfortably close to the chin. Note that in the design illustrated the seat box has been constructed to the desired slope.

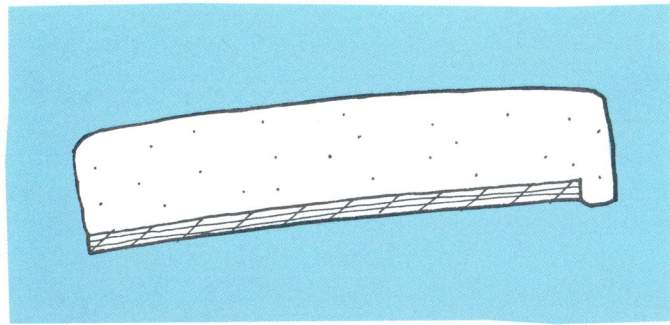

8.5 Cushion unit w/plywood base

This figure shows an easier and cheaper method of cushion construction, but one that can be sufficiently comfortable if the foam is at least 3" thick. Note that with this type of cushion, the frame or gable upon which the cushion rests must be constructed to the desired slope.

Cushion With Plywood Base   Figure 8.5 shows an easier and cheaper method of cushion construction, but one that can be sufficiently comfortable if the foam is at least 3" thick and of medium to high density. A softer, squashier initial effect can be achieved by laminating a 1" layer of medium-density foam onto the top of a high-density piece. With this type of cushion, the frame or gable must be constructed to the angle of the desired slope.

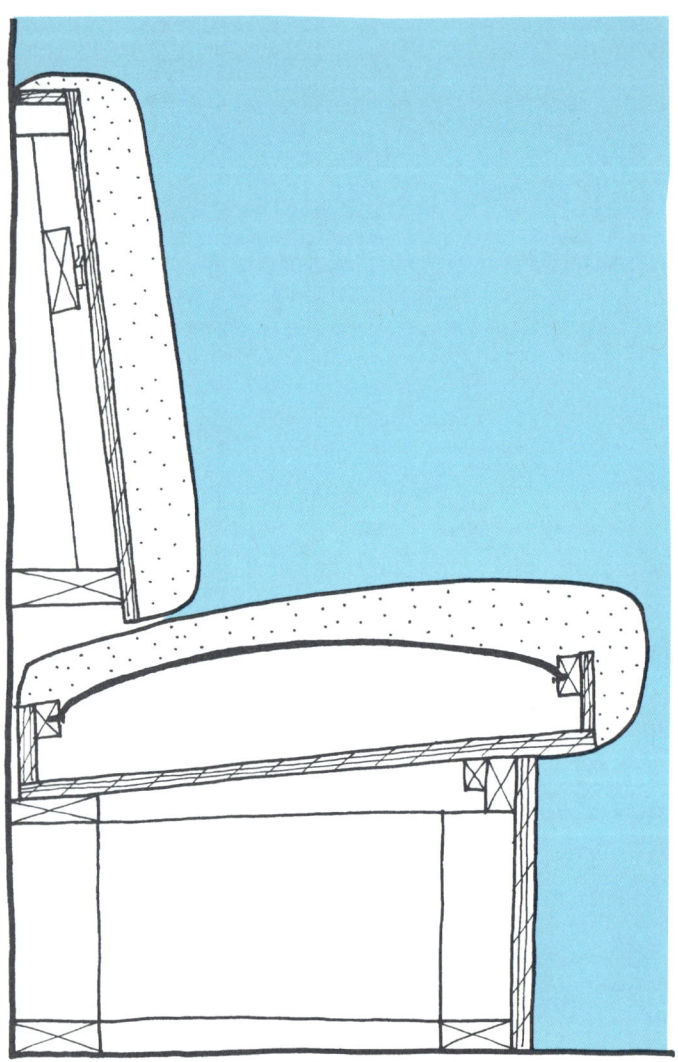

8.6 Upholstery assembly on open-web frame

Banquette Assembly Inevitable wear and vandalism make it important that seats and backs be removable for reupholstering. The illustrations on these pages describe the usual assembly methods, which allow this kind of flexibility. Details within figures 8.6 and 8.7 may be interchanged to suit the design concept or construction requirements.

In figure 8.6, **an open-web frame unit,** the upholstered back is hung with panel clips (see detail, page 85) attached to a crosswise component on the frame back. The upholstered seat box rests on the open-web frame and is held in position by a block

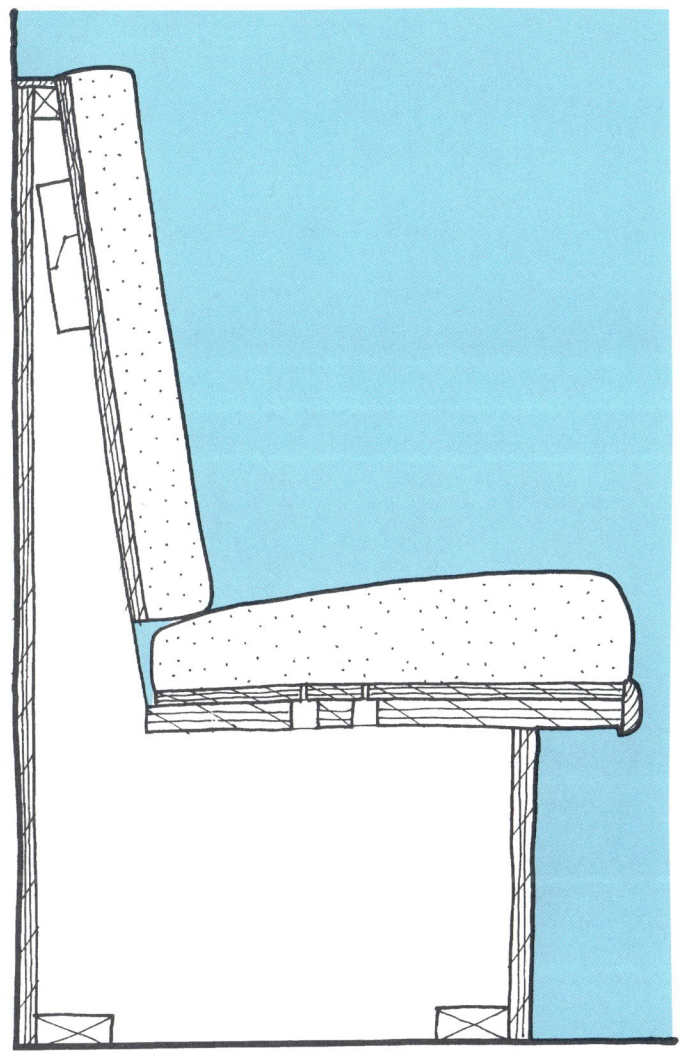

8.7 Upholstery assembly on gables and box

mounted on the box's underside and meeting the front frame. The base frame is usually fixed to the floor to maintain the position of the entire unit.

In figure 8.7, **a gables-and-box unit**, the upholstered back is hung on interlocking wood cleats (shown in detail, page 84); the seat—made up of a thick foam cushion shaped to slope down at the back, set on a piece of plywood and upholstered—rests on a plywood bench top which connects the gables. The seat is prevented from sliding forward by an edge strip of "show" wood across the front. The 2 x 4s on the floor secure the unit in place.

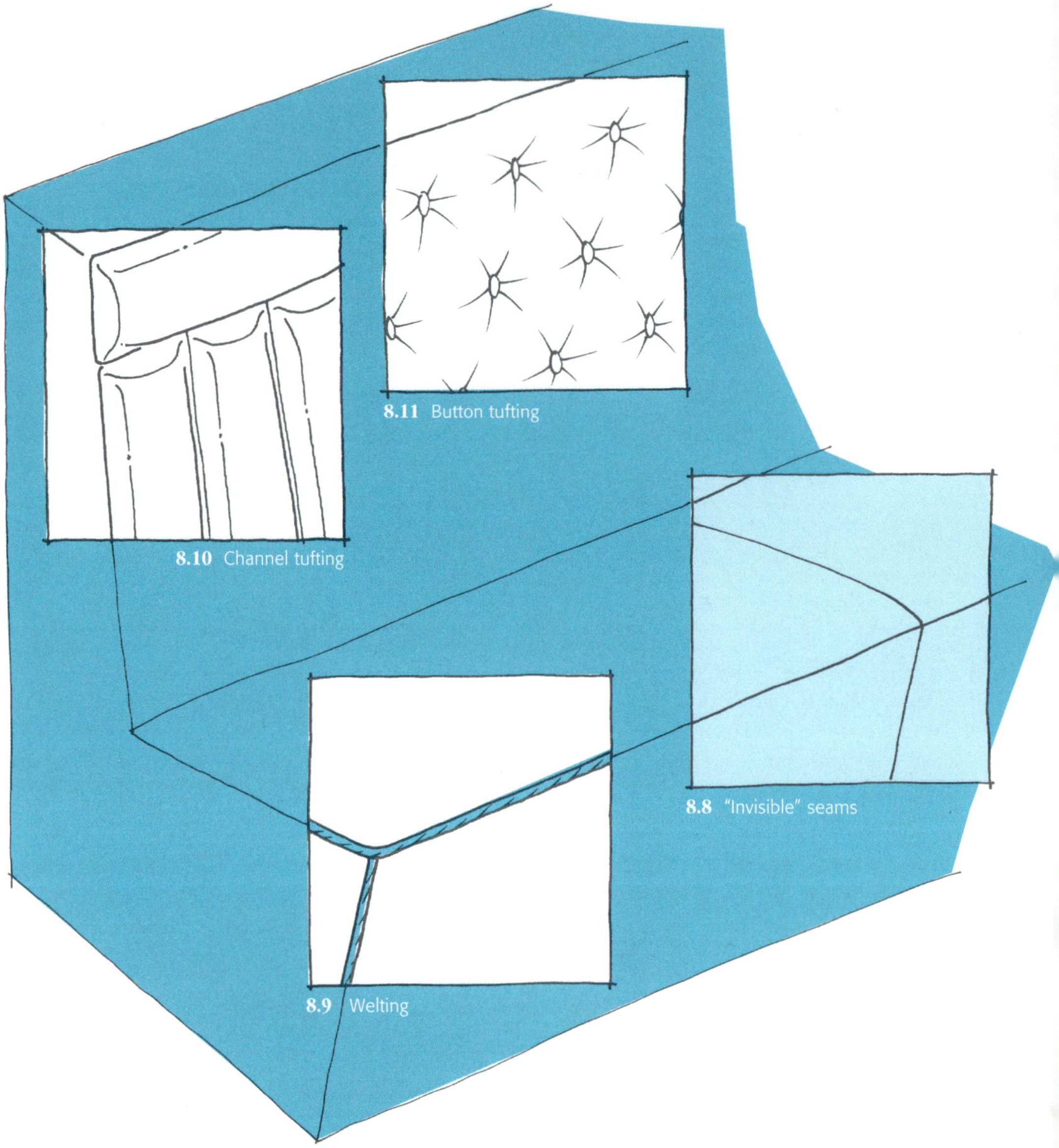

8.11 Button tufting

8.10 Channel tufting

8.8 "Invisible" seams

8.9 Welting

Upholstery

Just as there are several methods for building the banquette and its components, there are several ways of constructing the upholstery. If the project requires that upholstery be a removable covering, it is possible to smooth the fabric out flat and use **"invisible" seams** (see 8.8), or to use **welting** on the edges (see 8.9). In theory, welting protects the edges from wear and can emphasize the lines of the unit. For example, covering the welting in a different color and/or fabric will draw attention to the upholstery edges and thus the banquette's shape. Other, more elaborate upholstery treatments—which are attached to the cushion box and thus require more labor for replacement—include **channel tufting,** 8.10, and **button tufting**, 8.11.

Each style has its advantages and disadvantages: compatibility with construction methods, suitability for certain types of fabrics, and wear and maintenance requirements are some of the considerations. Also, each style creates a different visual effect—from the simple smooth planes of invisible seams to the rich dimensional surface of button tufting. It is important to be familiar with upholstery textiles and their handling properties, and to learn from experienced upholsterers which kinds of fabrics are suitable for the upholstery details that will convey your design concepts.

In the examples throughout this chapter, the dimensions refer to banquettes that are designed for use with dining-height tables. If your project has banquettes in relationship to lounge-height furniture you will need to adjust the dimensions accordingly. In any case it is recommended that you start by carefully checking the dimensions, slope, and configuration of the chairs that you have selected because they are usually manufactured items; the custom-designed banquette can be adjusted accordingly. Also when chairs and banquettes are in conjunction it is preferable that neither type is dominant.

The illustrations and details shown in this chapter are very generic and not meant to emphasize any particular design. As you can see there are many possibilities for the design of banquette seating, once you have grasped the basic requirements. Consider the "why" of each dimension, slope, and component of construction, the comfort factors and visual effect. Then let your mind run free to create the unit that is most suitable for your concept.

Conclusion

**f you are reading the conclusion to this book** I hope it is because you have read all the way through it, and are not one of those people who read the back of the book first because you can't wait to see how it all works out.

If you are the latter type then you are in for a big disappointment since there is no ending. The end of this book is only a beginning—a beginning to many pleasurable hours and days that you will spend in the future working out the details of your designs.

To those of you who have read this book I trust that you now appreciate that the technical aspect of detailing is generic. It is not so much which materials were used to illustrate a point in the book but the "why" of the detail. If you have come to understand the fundamentals discussed and shown here then you will understand that in devising new details, a new combination of materials, or a new configuration, it is this knowledge of the underlying reasons for the details that will light the path to the solution.

Actually, that sentiment is true of all design, wanting to know why is the sign of an inquisitive mind, and knowing why is the key for the designer. I hope that this book will assist you in finding the underlying reasons behind detailing, and open up before you a wonderful world of possibilities, limited only by your imagination.

Bibliography

Architectural Woodwork Quality Standards, 3rd edition. Burlington, VA: Architectural Woodwork Institute, 1984.

Quality Standards for Architectural Woodwork, 8th edition. Burnaby, BC: Architectural Woodwork Manufacturers Association of Canada, 1991.

Other References

Ballast, David Kent. *Interior Construction Detailing.* Monticello, IL: Vance Bibliographies, 1987.

Boyce, Colin, and Lance Wright. *Best of Architects Working Details.* New York: Nichols Publishing, 1982.

Callendar, J. H., ed. *Time-Saver Standards: A Handbook of Architectural Design Data,* 6th edition. New York: McGraw-Hill, 1982.

DeChiara, Joseph, Julius Panero, Martin Zelnik. *Time Saver Standards for Interior Design.* New York: McGraw-Hill, 1991.

Farmer, Gene. *Architectural Detailing for Commercial Construction.* New York: McGraw-Hill, 1991.

Kilmer, Rosemary, and W. Otie Kilmer. *Designing Interiors.* Orlando, FL: Harcourt Brace Jovanovich, 1992.

Ramsay, C. G., and H. R. Sleeper. *Traditional Details for Building Restoration, Renovation and Rehabilitation.* New York: Wiley, 1992.

Ramsay, C. G., and H. R. Sleeper. *Architectural Graphic Standards,* 8th edition. New York: Wiley, 1991.

Reznikoff, S. C. *Interior Graphic and Design Standards.* New York: Whitney Library of Design, 1986.

Riggs, J. Rosemary. *Materials & Components of Interior Design,* 3rd edition. Scarborough, ON: Prentice-Hall, 1992.

Staebler, Wendy W. *Architectural Detailing in Contract Interiors.* New York: Whitney Library of Design, 1988.

Stitt, Fred A. *Architects Detail Library.* New York: Van Nostrand Reinhold, 1990.

Throne, James L. *Thermoforming.* Munich: Carl Hanser Verlag, 1987. New York: Macmillan, 1988.

Whitton, Sherrill. *Interior Design and Decoration,* 4th edition. New York: Harper-Collins, 1974.